AFTER
THE
END

AFTER
THE
END

REPRESENTATIONS OF POST-APOCALYPSE

JAMES BERGER

UNIVERSITY OF MINNESOTA PRESS

MINNEAPOLIS

LONDON

Portions of chapter 2 appeared as "From 'After' to 'Until': Post-Apocalypse, Postmodernity, and Wim Wenders' *Until the End of the World,*" in *Genre* 28 (1995), and as "Trauma and Literary Theory" in *Contemporary Literature* 38, no. 3 (fall 1997). The latter is reprinted by permission of the University of Wisconsin Press; copyright 1997. Portions of chapter 6 appeared as "Cultural Trauma and the 'Timeless Burst': Pynchon's Revision of Nostalgia in *Vineland,*" in *Postmodern Culture* 5, no. 2 (May 1995), and "Ghosts of Liberalism: Toni Morrison's *Beloved* and the Moynihan Report," in *PMLA* 111 (1996). The latter is reprinted by permission of the Modern Language Association.

Published by the University of Minnesota Press
111 Third Avenue South, Suite 290
Minneapolis, MN 55401-2520
http://www.upress.umn.edu

Library of Congress Cataloging-in-Publication Data

Berger, James, 1954–
    After the end : representations of post-apocalypse / James
Berger.
       p.   cm.
    ISBN 0-8166-2932-3 (hc : alk. paper)
    ISBN 0-8166-2933-1 (pb : alk. paper)
    1. United States — Civilization — 1970–   2. Catastrophical, The.
3. Apocalyptic literature. History and criticism.   4. American literature —
20th century — History and criticism.   5. Holocaust, Jewish (1939–1945),
in literature.   6. Apocalypse in motion pictures.   I. Title.
    E169.12.B388   1999
    973.92 — dc21   98-40328

Printed in the United States of America on acid-free paper

The University of Minnesota is an equal-opportunity educator and employer.

10 09 08 07 06 05 04 03 02 01 00 99   10 9 8 7 6 5 4 3 2 1

To my parents and my sisters

Contents

Acknowledgments

It is hard to begin or to finish thanking those who have helped me with this project. I certainly could not have done it without the moral, political, and intellectual orientations that my parents, Arthur Berger and Jean Berger, provided — or without their love, and that of my sisters, Susan and Claudia.

In the book's early stages, as a dissertation at the University of Virginia, Michael Levenson, Jerome McGann, and Pat Gill provided the suggestions and questions that helped me figure out where after the end I wanted to go. I also want to thank my friends at the University of Virginia, whose conversations stimulated my thinking so much and whose comradeship was such a pleasure and necessity: Michael Calabrese, Barbara Judson, Jean Kane, Will Kazmier, James Hurley, Robert Leventhal, Lorna McDaniel, Andrew Shin, Jeff Shors, and Tracy Warren. Particular thanks to Michael Prince and Ken Thompson, whose friendship and advice have become even more valuable since we all have left Virginia.

At George Mason University, thanks to David Kaufmann and John Foster, both for astute comments on several of my chapters and for their help in getting me through two tough years as a visiting assistant professor. And thanks to the students in my Holocaust literature and film class. Their energy and creativity helped me to write chapters 3 and 4.

Thanks to Richard Dellamora, one of the best writers on apocalyptic topics, for his interest in and support of this project.

Special thanks to the Charles Phelps Taft Memorial Fund for allowing me an invaluable year of research and writing at the University of Cincinnati. Thanks to the English Department at Cincinnati, and its chairman, James Hall, for their support and hospitality. Thanks especially to Tom LeClair for his wisdom and humor about literature and basketball, to Beth Ash for her friendship and thoughtful reading of several chapters of this book, and to Josip Novakovich for good conversations and for making me feel better about my tennis game.

Thanks to my new friends and colleagues in the English Department at Hofstra University for their support and encouragement in finishing this book.

Finally, thanks to Jennifer Klein, who teaches me how to read history, and whose love, courage, and brilliance inspire me.

"Young man, I was with Mr. Kane before the beginning. And now, here I am — after the end."

BERNSTEIN, THE ACCOUNTANT, IN *CITIZEN KANE*

What does this mean, this oxymoron "after the end"? Before the beginning and after the end, there can only be nothing. At the beginning, something begins; and at the ending, it ends. Of course, we know these are figures of speech. Bernstein had a life before he met Charles Foster Kane, and he is alive as he speaks and remembers. But Bernstein only recognizes significance in that intermission, between that beginning and that end. The story — the set of linked, cohering, shaped events — transpires within those boundaries, and outside them, before and after, is chaos and insignificance. Everything after the end, in order to gain, or borrow, meaning, must point back, lead back to that time; and everything before that beginning (seen as the "beginning of the end") reconfigures itself into prologue and premonition. Kane's life and career become a fulcrum or prism that repositions, refocuses all that preceded or follows. The departed Kane still occupies the center of every consciousness in the film. As Donald Barthelme wrote in *The Dead Father,* "Dead, but still with us, still with us, but dead" (3), so Kane and his catastrophe (that hulking collapse from his colossal striding across the center of American mass culture into humiliation and doddering irrelevance) continue to haunt and scar all the stories that try to describe him.

And Kane's catastrophe is not just his own. Through the process of piecing together Kane's story, Orson Welles uncovers the underlying catastrophe of American culture: the end of the possibility of social reform, its dissolution into greed, egotism, vested interests, celebrity culture — and the confusions of representation, whether journalistic, cinematic, or (transferring "representation" to its other realm) political. Kane tells his reporters in Cuba, "Gentlemen, sup-

ply me with the pictures, and I'll supply the war." Kane's rise towed with it
the full barge of American optimism, idealism, and the progressive faith in rationality before the First World War. It contained also the naïveté and megalo-
mania that led to Kane's personal downfall. In Welles's portrayal, all crash together, leaving a world of damaged survivors with damaged memories, living
in the artificial harmony of a culture now dominated by the mass media Kane
helped to found.

When *Citizen Kane* begins, the end has already happened. What is gone is
now irretrievable and incomprehensible, and to live after is to inhabit a world
of shifting memories and of objects broken off and hurled away from the cataclysm. "Rosebud," Kane's last word, which begins the movie and the reporter's
search for the word's meaning, is simultaneously a false lead and an empty symbol, and a clue stuffed so full that it cannot contain all its meanings. It pushes
the catastrophe back even further, to the end, the loss, of childhood, suggesting that merely the entry into adulthood is an apocalypse — an event that forms
and reveals but leaves nothing but ruin. One can always go further back. In
some gnostic traditions, the Fall came at the moment of Creation, when God
became separated from Him/Her Self. And there is a long tradition of retrospective prophecy, correctly predicting events that have already occurred, thus
authenticating prophecies for the apocalypse to come. The signs will have been
already in place, already identified as signs.

This book is not about apocalypse or apocalyptic thinking or millennialism.
It is about aftermaths and remainders, about how to imagine what happens after an event conceived of as final. It is more concerned with history than with
prophecy. But historical events are often portrayed apocalyptically — as absolute breaks with the past, as catastrophes bearing some enormous or ultimate
meaning: the Holocaust, for example, or Hiroshima, or American slavery, the
American Civil War, the French Revolution, the war in Vietnam and the social
conflicts of the 1960s. This book seeks to understand the apocalyptic representations of historical catastrophes, how writing about history constructs scenarios "after the end," in which the ending, paradoxically, both does and does
not take place.

Therefore, I will not be writing about recent millennialist phenomena —
the events at Waco in 1993, the Heaven's Gate cult, the poison gas attacks in
Tokyo — although I will show how apocalyptic thinking is almost always, at

the same time, post-apocalyptic. My focus, rather, will be on what I consider a pervasive post-apocalyptic sensibility in recent American culture. It seems significant that in the late twentieth century we have had the opportunity, previously enjoyed only by means of theology and fiction, to see after the end of our civilization—to see in a strange prospective retrospect what the end would actually look like: it would look like a Nazi death camp, or an atomic explosion, or an ecological or urban wasteland. We have been able to see these things because they actually occurred. The most dystopic visions of science fiction can do no more than replicate the actual historical catastrophes of the twentieth century. Modernity is often said to be preoccupied by a sense of crisis, viewing as imminent, perhaps even longing for, some conclusive catastrophe. This sense of crisis has not disappeared, but in the late twentieth century it exists together with another sense, that the conclusive catastrophe has already occurred, the crisis is over (perhaps we were not aware of exactly when it transpired), and the ceaseless activity of our time—the news with its procession of almost indistinguishable disasters—is only a complex form of stasis. The visions of the End that Frank Kermode analyzed in terms of a sense of an ending have increasingly given way to visions of after the end, and the apocalyptic sensibilities both of religion and of modernism have shifted toward a sense of post-apocalypse.

I began to imagine this project from several directions. First, I was fascinated by 1980s action movies, in which depictions of catastrophes seemed to be growing more explosive, conclusive, and repetitive. Why, I wondered, was there such an urgent need to see violent culminations over and over in these endless successions of *Terminator*s, *Die Hard*s, and *Rambo*s? Why, it seemed, did nearly every popular film have to contain some mini-apocalypse, some payoff of absolute destruction—of cars, airplanes, helicopters, buildings, cities, along with their flimsy human occupants? I was disgusted, yet, at the same time, I felt the appeal. I loved seeing civilization as we know it burst open in flaming centrifugal ecstasy. And I loved seeing those stories of aftermaths, the post-apocalypses in the *Blade Runner* mode, in which every gesture seemed pure, somber, and meaningful when performed in a garish wasteland.

I also spent the 1980s trying to understand and endure the Reagan presidency. In its effort to portray a nostalgic vision of American perfection, Reaganism erected gorgeous mechanisms of amnesia. There was so much not to think about. It occurred to me that the most ideologically approved posture was not to think at all. Just do it, says Nike. Just buy. Perhaps "thinking" was a function of a historical epoch that was now ending, and I imagined writing a parody of Martin Heidegger's essay "The End of Philosophy and the Task of Thinking" to be titled "The End of Thinking and the Task of Marketing." I never wrote the essay; I think the joke was funny only to me. Instead, I began trying to figure out what it was that Reaganist amnesia was trying to forget. Most immediately, it was trying to forget the 1960s or, rather, to reinvent the 1960s movements for social justice and peace as destructive and infantile—to forget their content and the serious problems they addressed. More broadly, I began to conceive of Reaganist ideology as a method of forgetting and denying historical traumas altogether—the social conflicts of the 1960s, American racism, even (as in Reagan's performance at Bitburg in 1985) the Holocaust. It was not that traumatic events did not happen, but Reaganist ideology denied that they had any lasting consequences. I began to think then about issues of historical transmission—of events, aftermaths, symptoms, representations that in various ways conveyed, transformed, and suppressed historical events; how certain events, it seemed, could not be said, and others must not be said. The Holocaust became a case in point, the apocalypse in history that we are living after and that symptomatically permeates our culture.

I felt, though, that I also needed to consider my own position in these formulations of post-apocalypse. I was spectator and consumer, someone detached though intermittently consumed. I was also an academic, intellectual analyst of these cultural phenomena—a theorist, a more extreme detachment. I set up a vantage point from which I would have a cognitive advantage over any mere participants. But out of these relationships with the material, I would not have written this book. I would have written some other book, which retained more confidence in its theoretical vantage. For I realized, if I spoke of a post-apocalyptic, post-Holocaust world as traumatized, a world of symptoms, then I too must be traumatized, and my language must also be symptomatic. I have not abandoned faith in analysis and narrative, and I share the psychoanalytic idea of "working through" the symptomatic impasses generated by traumas. Nevertheless, I remain inside the subject matter, and I have tried to show in the book my position inside. To be inside is to be without theory, without advantage.

The tools of theory—in this case, psychoanalysis, poststructuralist approaches, and old-fashioned close readings intersecting with historical research—help pull me to the boundary of the material and help me distinguish where that boundary might be. But then, these theoretical languages themselves (as I show at various points in the book) often reveal thoroughly post-apocalyptic orientations. In addition to this epistemological quandary, I have also my personal history, and I have chosen to put some of this history into the book. My character, including my identity as a scholar, has been shaped by particular traumas and aftermaths. In the end—or rather, at the beginning—it was not my aesthetic and political frustrations during the 1980s but rather my personal understandings of catastrophe that date from much earlier that most of all motivated me to write this book. Therefore, some autobiography is essential—which may be true of every scholarly or literary project but is especially true here.

After the End is organized into three parts. In the first, "Thinking the Post-Apocalypse," I describe the problematics of representation after an actual or imagined catastrophe. The first chapter, "Post-Apocalyptic Rhetorics: How to Speak after the End of Language," explores the paradoxical, oxymoronic character of post-apocalyptic discourse and draws on autobiographical material, the Book of Revelation, science fiction, and some recent theorizations of "otherness." This chapter also describes the representation of apocalyptic cataclysm as a means of banishing, symbolically obliterating, whatever the apocalyptic writer deems unacceptable, evil, or alien. The second chapter, "Trauma and the End of the World," links these apocalyptic obliterations to psychoanalytic concepts of trauma, repression and denial, and symptom formation. Broadened to include social and historical events, the idea of trauma provides the best description of how events have influence long after they occur. The study of a post-apocalyptic world is a study of symptoms and of representations that partly work through and partly act out the past that haunts them. In this regard, largely through an analysis of Wim Wenders's film *Until the End of the World,* I examine the languages of postmodernism in Jean-François Lyotard, Fredric Jameson, and Jean Baudrillard, and argue that their formulations of a postmodernity based on technological or theoretical or economic determinants should be revised to incorporate a clearer sense of historical trauma, especially the continuing reverberations of the Holocaust. Their terminologies of fragmentation, schizophrenia, and ecstasy—all thoroughly apocalyptic—strongly suggest an interpretation centered on trauma. I end the chapter with a discussion of ghosts and angels in contemporary American culture as post-traumatic, post-apocalyptic symptoms.

The book's second part, "Aftermaths of the Holocaust," concerns recent representations of the Holocaust in fiction (chapter 3) and literary theory (chapter 4). While the Holocaust remains a central and defining trauma—an apocalyptic event—in Western culture, its modes of transmission are changing as it recedes farther into the past. The privileged position of eyewitness and testimony in Holocaust representation has necessarily been put in question as the last survivors of that generation grow old and die. As the last witnesses disappear, a plethora of forms of Holocaust representation have emerged. Many of these have been criticized as morally offensive appropriations of horrific events, and yet these troubling forms are symptomatic of the Holocaust's continuing traumatic and revelatory impact—and to a pressing cultural need for that vision of extreme cultural trauma, for a touchstone, a limit, a paradigmatic instance. In what might be called the "third generation" of Holocaust fiction, the Holocaust has become open for universal appropriation. Departing from the forms of actual and fictional testimony that characterize the work of Primo Levi and Elie Wiesel, the Holocaust in "third-generation" fiction enters the autobiographies and bildungsromans of people who were never themselves in the camps; it enters comic books, pornography, movies about Vietnam, avant-garde experimentation, and postmodern parody. Chapter 3 examines the new problematics of "third-generation" Holocaust representation in Emily Prager's *Eve's Tattoo,* D. M. Thomas's *The White Hotel,* and Cynthia Ozick's *The Messiah of Stockholm,* showing the tensions between an ethics and epistemology of Holocaust testimony and the pressures of the passing of time and of geographical relocation, and of personal concerns, consumer culture, and the fragmenting, antitestimonial impetus of poststructuralist literary theory. These changes are not necessarily to be condemned or lamented, as, for instance, Saul Friedlander and Alvin Rosenfeld have done. Rather, this proliferation of Holocaust fiction "after the end" of testimony is, in effect, a new form of testimony, marked by a trauma that is already textualized and incorporated into myriad forms of mass culture.

The appropriation of the Holocaust thematized in third-generation Holocaust fiction has since the 1980s also become a topic for the poststructuralist theorists Jacques Derrida, Jean-François Lyotard, and Hayden White. But while the fictions of Ozick, Thomas, Prager, and others have problematized testimony, historical narrative, and literary genre — the apocalyptic impact of the Holocaust having disrupted these forms of transmission — the Holocaust's effect on recent poststructuralist theory has been to problematize the possibility of dispensing with notions of historical reference and narrative. This theoretical turn toward the Holocaust has taken place, of course, in the wake of the disclosures concerning Paul de Man's collaborationist writings and the additions to our knowledge about Heidegger's Nazi sympathies. (It has occurred also in the context of the more general move toward historicism in literary theory, although, interestingly, the Foucauldian analyses of the New Historicism have not yet made the Holocaust a topic for analysis.) The return of the Holocaust as a matter of interest to literary theorists is a response both to the recent politics of literary history and to a crucial gap in poststructuralist thinking itself. Lyotard (in his discussions of the *differend*), White (in his essay on the "middle voice"), and Derrida (in his writings on the cinder and the shibboleth) have addressed the Holocaust in the terms set out by their own problematizations of reference and narrative — as that event that most resists and yet most requires representation, a historical irreducible that tests and disrupts their previous theorizing. The explicit and belated entry of this century's central historical catastrophe into a philosophical discourse characterized by powerful but unspecified imagery of rupture, disintegration, and erasures of history should help us rethink poststructuralism as a post-apocalyptic genre that has begun to remember its catastrophe only in the wake of its fall from grace in the academy.

Part III, "American Post-Apocalypses," discusses post-apocalyptic phenomena in recent American culture. Chapter 5, " 'Achieved Utopias': The Reaganist Post-Apocalypse," describes Reaganism as a complex, often paradoxical, post-apocalyptic form that combines optimism with paranoia, nostalgia with millennialist fantasy, and fundamentalist religion with consumerism in ways that consistently refer to past traumatic/apocalyptic events while at the same time denying any lasting traumatic impact from those events. Reaganism follows in a long tradition of American millennialism but occupies a unique place in trying to reconcile its vision of America as an "achieved utopia" (to use Baudrillard's loaded term) with destabilizing events and ideas — particularly those of the 1960s — that called this vision into question. This chapter is organized in three sections. The first discusses Reaganism as a view of history. I outline the political coalition of neoconservatives, middle- and working-class whites, and fundamentalist Christians that formed the movement, describe Reaganism's relation to previous American millenarian impulses (the Puritans' City on a Hill, the ideologies and mythologies of the American West), and show the interplay in Reaganism between Cold War anticommunism and the violent reaction against the social changes of the 1960s. The Reaganist tendencies toward denial of trauma and millenarian nostalgia are best exemplified — again, the Holocaust provides the limit case — in Reagan's performances at Bitburg and Bergen-Belsen in 1985, in which he invoked the Holocaust only to disavow its traumatic impact and then affirm the Western, and Christian, alliance with West Germany against the Soviet Union. Second, I describe forms of "Reaganist advertising" in which the triumph of consumerism and corporate values in the 1980s is explicitly linked to Reaganist post-apocalyptic nostalgia. Finally, this chapter analyzes one of the most striking and characteristic popular culture forms of the 1980s, the TV talk show, which I describe as a distorted form of personal and social healing. While it takes the form of therapeutic confession, the talk show's fascination is found in its never-ending panorama of traumatic reenactments, not with their cure or closure. The talk show shares the postmodern, post-apocalyptic sense that a definitive catastrophe has already occurred and combines this sense with the 1980s worship of celebrity and Reaganist nostalgia for the family. The talk show is a ghostly, uncanny cultural form whose participants have survived trauma to become momentary celebrities. It is a kind of mediated afterlife.

In the final chapter, I discuss important alternatives to Reaganist post-apocalypticism found in two historical novels from the 1980s. I interpret Toni Morrison's *Beloved* and Thomas Pynchon's *Vineland* as post-apocalyptic novels that explore the processes of historical transmission, demonstrating how apocalyptic-traumatic moments — of slavery, family violence, political and sexual betrayals — are repressed and transformed, and subsequently proliferate as cultural symptoms. Both novels, I argue, intervene in specific political and historical debates of the 1980s regarding the interpretation, first, of the social crises of the 1960s and, more broadly, of American history as a whole. *Vineland* confronts Reaganist polemics by proposing a revaluation of nostalgia in which memories of unfulfilled utopian possibilities from the 1960s enter the 1980s entwined with the traumatic-apocalyptic memories of violent failure and betrayal. Further, Pynchon shows how this transmission necessarily takes the forms made available to it in the highly mediated, consumerist culture of the 1980s. *Beloved*, I argue, intervenes in the 1980s debates concerning the African American family and the "underclass." In presenting a traumatically broken family just after slavery, and in stressing both institutional racism and Black self-destruction, Morrison implicitly invokes the controversies surrounding the Moynihan Report of 1965—controversies that continued to structure discourse on race twenty years later.

Continuing the discussion of ghosts from chapter 2, this chapter describes how Pynchon and Morrison use embodied ghosts as figures of historical transmission. The Thanatoids in *Vineland* and Beloved in *Beloved* show that history is both incarnated and social. The past—and not only but markedly the traumatic past—lives among us, apparently ordinary, almost indistinguishable, entirely alive: not a narrative but a living organism. At the same time, discursive mechanisms are always already in operation to assimilate the traumatic historical symptom into a social and symbolic order. *Vineland* and *Beloved* describe the textual and media processes of transmitting, distorting, and forgetting cultural memory. These novels also, however, describe necessary but uncertain methods of constructive "re-memory" (to use Morrison's term in *Beloved*) and "karmic adjustment" (Pynchon's parodic term in *Vineland*)—attempts to work through and genuinely come to terms with historical trauma—enabling the novels to serve, in a sense, as practical first steps toward articulating what a post-apocalyptic world has forgotten.

Very few scholars have approached what seems to me the pervasive post-apocalyptic sensibility of recent American culture. Jean Baudrillard and his adherents have portrayed the world "after the orgy," after the permanent dissociation of sign from referent. But Baudrillard's work, and that of Arthur and Marilouise Kroker and the contributors to Dietmar Kamper and Christoph Wulf's volume *Looking Back on the End of the World,* seems to me too ecstatically immersed in the catastrophe. Some such immersion, I believe, is inevitable, and I try in this book to indicate my own, but it is not the whole story. Analysis and narrative remain possible and necessary, and while I enjoy reading Baudrillard's satires (for I believe that truly is the genre of his descriptions of contemporary life), the spirit of my work is not Baudrillardian. Likewise, much of the work of postmodern and poststructuralist theorists (as I discuss in chapters 2 and 4) is implicitly concerned with questions of post-apocalyptic representation but does not address crucial issues of historical trauma and its aftermaths. The only scholar I am aware of who works explicitly on post-apocalyptic topics is Josef Pesch, a German scholar based in Freiburg. Pesch is working on a book I hope to see completed soon that brings together literary and architectural analyses, discussing post-apocalyptic literary texts with reference to the rebuilding of the devastated cities of Europe and Japan after the Second World War and to the contemporary designs of the American architect Frank Gehry.[1] Yet, while there has been little work done that explicitly addresses post-apocalyptic culture, I have been greatly assisted by the enormous scholarship on religious and secular apocalypticism, for the emotional responses of fear, desire, relief, fascination, horror, contempt, agony, and nostalgia inspired by imagining some definitive End are similar whether this end is imagined as yet to come or as already occurred.[2]

The language of post-apocalypse demands a "saying the unsayable," providing an account of an unimaginable aftermath. And yet, these aftermaths, however unimaginable, have actually happened, and languages for them exist. Since the Second World War, a variety of "unspeakables" have seldom been silent, although their utterances have often been disguised or symptomatic. I try to show in this book how recognizing and understanding post-apocalyptic representations is crucial in evaluating recent American history, and how analysis of post-apocalyptic culture can help reshape important questions regarding historical transmission, historical trauma, and the representation of all events and objects that in some sense "resist" representation. Finally, in an age that has been indelibly marked and formed by events so overwhelming as to appear apocalyptic, I hope that *After the End* will contribute to what Saul Friedlander has called "a rhetoric appropriate to modern catastrophe."[3] I hope, that is, not only to describe the overwhelming, often denied traumatic presences of the past that characterize our post-apocalyptic/"postmodern" present but also to suggest ways for "coming to terms" with the past, for moving toward a future with moderate hopefulness, yet without amnesia.

PART I: THINKING THE POST-APOCALYPSE

1. Post-Apocalyptic Rhetorics
How to Speak after the End of Language

My two younger sisters, my only siblings, are mentally retarded. Susan and Claudia cannot talk. They can think in certain ways. They laugh and cry. They can understand a lot of things, down-to-earth, concrete things, about food, getting dressed, going to the bathroom, helping with things. They can make many of their wishes known. Claudia, the younger sister, has learned some sign language, about thirty words, and she can even form a few two- and three-word sentences. But they cannot live independently, and they cannot talk. Something went wrong; no one is quite sure exactly what.

And so I came into consciousness with a certain knowledge about catastrophe. I knew that it was possible and that it existed. I knew that catastrophe could even be indistinguishable from a secure and happy life. My sisters were my sisters. Other people had sisters, and so did I. And my sisters were damaged. I came out of infancy, into consciousness, in the wake of an originary catastrophe. I learned to speak in the presence of my sisters' speechlessness. I stress language. My sisters' fates — or is it better just to say their lives — are somehow unspeakable. They cannot speak them. And I can only speak around them, defining their outlines with a surface of words. My method resembles Kierkegaard's technique of "circumnavigation," in which he maps an unknown territory by circling around it:

> If I imagined two kingdoms adjoining one another, with one
> of which I was fairly well acquainted, and altogether unfa-
> miliar with the other, and I was not allowed to enter the un-
> known realm . . . I should still be able to form some concep-
> tion of its nature. I could go to the limits of the kingdom . . .

and follow its boundaries, and as I did so, I should in this way describe the boundaries of the unknown country. (*Either/Or,* 1: 52–53)

The unknown country, for Kierkegaard and for me, is also the *unknowable.* The circum-narrative is an approximation; the interior remains blank.

In another sense though, I can only speak my sisters' lives. They inform my whole language, and I cannot not speak them. There was never another world, and my catastrophe was not a Fall from innocence. Though I have trace memories from before my sisters were born and began to develop, my thinking and language began in their presence. My discourse, my text, my attempts at coherence, the forms of my incoherence issue from that wake, and are those of a boy growing and seeing what he loves most thwarted and misformed.

My father is an optimist who remembers a depression followed by prosperity, a war followed by victory and peace, atrocities, the Holocaust, to be remembered and reflected on — but buried, parts of a cycle or continuum. Others preceded, others will follow. I remember my father looking into his father's grave, and I thought, as I will one day look into his, and as, I hope, a child will look into mine. That is optimism — that things continue and are at least no worse. When his daughters were born, my father was already formed. He lived before the catastrophe, and the catastrophe did not form him or break him.

And certainly there has been no cause for my father or mother to be broken by their daughters' lives. Susan and Claudia are wonderful, affectionate, quirky, humorous, and even, in odd ways, clever people. Nor am I broken by my sisters' lives. Quite the reverse, as I have been saying, I am formed by them. They came to me at the beginning, like a revelation of a world blighted at its creation.

And so I see in my experience a parallel with the contemporary world. My father is premodern. His favorite authors are Thackeray, Dickens, and Tolstoy, for he finds in them ways to understand society as complex but whole, human nature as deep but fathomable. But I prefer Dostoyevsky, his accounts of pointless crimes, pointless suffering. In Dickens and Tolstoy one finds every cruelty and catastrophe but finds them contained in a world that heals its own ravages and digests its crises. But then, not really every cruelty, not those that cannot be contained, perhaps not even represented. The originary revelations of the contemporary world are Auschwitz and Hiroshima. What we see there and try to say, and cannot, or must not, say forms our discourse — as my damaged sisters form mine. And my mother, I should add, prefers mystery novels (whodunits, not thrillers), the genre at whose beginning and center always stands a silent witness — that is, the body, the corpse. The mystery is a narrative of ingenuity, of finding a solution. And yet the purpose of the ingenious solution is not to make the silent witness speak but precisely to maintain its silence, to prevent the corpse from leaving its proper boundaries. The whodunit mystery is a genre of circumscription; its moral posture is one of innocence.

This book explores the idea of post-apocalypse, of modes of expression made in the wake of catastrophes so overwhelming that they seem to negate the possibility of expression at the same time that they compel expression. I intend the term *apocalypse* in three senses. First, it is the *eschaton,* the actual imagined end of the world, as presented in the New Testament Apocalypse of John and other Jewish and early Christian apocalypses, or as imagined by medieval millenarian movements, or today in visions of nuclear Armageddon or ecological suicide. Second, apocalypse refers to catastrophes that resemble the imagined final ending, that can be interpreted as eschaton, as an end of something, a way of life or thinking. The destruction of the temple in 70 C.E. and the expulsion from Spain in 1492 worked in that way for Jews. And in our age the Holocaust and the use of atomic weapons against Japan have assumed apocalyptic significance. They function as definitive historical divides, as ruptures, pivots, fulcrums separating what came before from what came after. All preceding history seems to lead up to and set the stage for such events, and all that follows emerges out of that central cataclysm. Previous historical narratives are shattered; new understandings of the world are generated. Apocalypse thus, finally, has an interpretive, explanatory function, which is, of course, its etymological sense: as revelation, unveiling, uncovering. The apocalyptic event, in order to be properly apocalyptic, must in its destructive moment clarify and illuminate the true nature of what has been brought to an end.

The apocalypse, then, is The End, or resembles the end, or explains the end. But nearly every apocalyptic text presents the same paradox. The end is never the end. The apocalyptic text announces and describes the end of the world, but then the text does not end, nor does the world represented in the text, and neither does the world itself. In nearly every apocalyptic presentation, something remains *after the end.* In the New Testament Revelation, the new heaven and earth and New Jerusalem descend. In modern science fiction accounts, a world as urban dystopia or desert wasteland survives. Very seldom — as in Mary Shelley's *The Last Man* or Gore Vidal's *Kalki*—does the end of the narrative coincide with the end of the world. Something is left over, and that world after the world, the *post-apocalypse,* is usually the true object of the apocalyptic writer's concern. The end itself, the moment of cataclysm, is only part of the point of apocalyptic writing. The apocalypse as eschaton is just as importantly the vehicle for clearing away the world as it is and making possible the post-apocalyptic paradise or wasteland.

Temporal sequence becomes confused. Apocalyptic writing takes us after the end, shows the signs prefiguring the end, the moment of obliteration, and the aftermath. The writer and reader must be both places at once, imagining the post-apocalyptic world and then paradoxically "remembering" the world as it was, as it is. The "time loop," as in the *Terminator* movies, is a perfect apocalyptic/post-apocalyptic plot line. Every action before the apocalypse is simultaneously an action after the apocalypse, and the event itself exists as a monstrous possibility made more or less likely by actions that, if it occurs, will never happen. The "signs of the times" are replayed as post-apocalyptic messages sent back to anticipate the apocalypse. Thus, John Connor's father returns from after the end both to save the world and to propagate his own impossibility. And in an episode of *Star Trek: The Next Generation,* the *Enterprise* is saved from a catastrophic time loop by a post-apocalyptic Commander Data's encrypting a message to be received by himself before the next repetition of the catastrophe. The narrative logic of apocalyptic writing insists that the post-apocalypse precede the apocalypse. This is also the logic of prophecy. The events envisioned have already occurred, have as good as occurred. Once the prophecy is uttered, all the rest is post-apocalypse. The mind of the writer, and of the believer, is already there, after the end. In *Terminator II: Judgment Day,* Linda Hamilton shouts at her psychiatrist-jailer, "You're dead, don't you understand that? You're already dead."

And yet the world, impossibly, continues, and the apocalyptic writer continues to write. It is a common pattern. A disaster occurs of overwhelming, disorienting magnitude, and yet the world continues. And so writers imagine another catastrophe that is absolutely conclusive, that will end this world. The initial disaster, which distorts and disorients — which, in a sense, is not an apocalypse in that it does not reveal — requires imagining a second disaster that *is* an apocalypse and thereby gives the first disaster retrospective apocalyptic status. The second temple was destroyed, and the world continued. Jesus was crucified, and the world continued. John, on Patmos, imagined the definitive ending that would redeem both these catastrophes. Similarly, the science fiction apocalypses of the 1950s came in the wake of the atomic detonations in Japan. T. S. Eliot wrote *The Wasteland* in the wake of the First World War. The apocalyptic writings of American Christians in the 1970s followed from Cold War anxieties and perceptions of domestic social breakdown in the 1960s. Apocalyptic writing itself is a remainder, a symptom, an aftermath of some disorienting catastrophe.

Apocalyptic and post-apocalyptic representations serve varied psychological and political purposes. Most prevalently, they put forward a total critique of any existing social order. From the Book of Revelation's condemnation of Babylon, through the millenarian movements of the Middle Ages, to more recent apocalyptic thinking — both religious and secular — visions of the end and its aftermath emphasize that no social reform can cure the world's diseases. Every structure of the old world is infected, and only an absolute, purifying cataclysm can make possible an utterly new, perfected world. The desire to see the old order disintegrate links such religiously and politically disparate apocalypticists as the romantic anarchist Henry Miller,[1] the poststructuralist theorist Michel Foucault,[2] 1970s Punks, more recent cyberpunk science fiction writers, and Christian New Right theologians like Hal Lindsay.[3] For all of these, the world is poised to end and is so suffused with moral rottenness and technological, political, and economic chaos and/or regimentation that it should end and must end, and it must end because in some crucial sense it *has* ended. This weird blend of disgust, moral fervor, and cynicism helps explain the enormous, ecstatic, fascinated pleasure many people in late-twentieth-century America feel in *seeing* significant parts of their world destroyed — over and over in all the *Die Hard*s, *Terminator*s, *Twister*s, *Dante's Peak*s, *Asteroid*s, and *Independence Day*s.

Apocalypse is a semantic alchemical process; it burns and distills signs and referents into new precipitates. The study of post-apocalypse is a study of what disappears and what remains, and of how the remainder has been transformed.

It is a study of the ideological and psychological forces that direct the apocalyptic fissions and fusions. The apocalypse would be the *definitive* catastrophe — not only final and complete but absolutely clarifying. It would unmistakably separate good from evil, true from false. The apocalypse would replace the moral and epistemological murkiness of life as it is with a post-apocalyptic world in which all identities and values are clear. This scenario of moral unveiling has been portrayed in texts from Revelation to Stephen King's *The Stand*. The post-apocalypse in fiction provides an occasion to go "back to basics" and to reveal what the writer considers to be truly of value. In Walter Miller's novel of nuclear post-apocalypse, *A Canticle for Leibowitz,* the catastrophe is referred to, centuries later, as "the simplification"; after the technological civilization is reduced to ruins, the remaining intellectuals and technicians are massacred. Miller presents these murders unsympathetically, but the novel seems to agree with the murderers' judgment that knowledge and technology lead inevitably toward mass destruction. The apocalypse reveals technology in its true nature. In Larry Niven and Jerry Pournelle's *Lucifer's Hammer,* a comet hits the earth, and the resulting social chaos causes a reversion to a kind of natural aristocracy, in which such decadent luxuries as feminism, democracy, and social justice must be jettisoned in favor of more natural values more suited to survival.

This is the traditional post-apocalyptic scenario. But sometimes, especially in the past century or so, there have been complications. It may be that when the seals are broken and absolute evil is identified and isolated, the Blessed will look across the abyss and see themselves. Herman Melville's Indian Hater story (in *The Confidence Man*), Joseph Conrad's "Heart of Darkness," and Max Horkheimer and Theodor Adorno's *Dialectic of Enlightenment* provide revelations of this sort — "We had to destroy the village in order to save it" — enlightenment is indistinguishable from barbarism. Moral distinctions themselves compose the surface that is shattered, and under that surface is a universal murderous chaos. This shift in apocalyptic sensibilities exemplifies the cataclysmic transition into modernity — the sense, in Marx's phrase, that "all that is solid melts into air."[4]

If the post-apocalypse of the *doppelgänger* is characteristic of modernity, the post-apocalypse of the postmodern is Baudrillardian simulation. In Baudrillard, the catastrophe is the end of the whole apocalyptic hermeneutic itself.

There can be no unveiling because there is nothing under the surface: there is only surface; the map has replaced the terrain. Commodification is universal, and no longer even under the interpretive control of notions of the "fetish." What, after all, would there be for the commodity to disguise? Not only "God" but also "labor relations" or "material conditions" would have no revelatory value. The Baudrillardian, postmodern post-apocalypse is also the site of "post-history" as envisioned by Francis Fukuyama and others. And here the idea of post-apocalyptic representations as part of a social critique becomes more difficult. Lee Quinby has described the Baudrillardian vision as an "ironic" apocalypse and considers it to be a support of the corporate-political status quo.[5] Her condemnation of a postmodern political quietism resembles Jürgen Habermas's attack on Lyotard and other poststructuralists. The totalizing critiques advanced by poststructuralists that depict systems of domination that co-opt all opposition are wrong, Habermas argues, and even contribute to the persistence of domination by seeming to preclude any alternatives. Habermas would see a logical, inevitable link between leftist poststructuralists like Baudrillard, Lyotard, and Foucault and post-historical neoconservatives like Fukuyama. A more sympathetic and, I think, also a more compelling appraisal comes from Bernard Yack, who argues that radically antihumanist apocalyptic rhetoric often masks a radical but frustrated humanism. Nietzsche, Rousseau, and Marx (and by extension poststructuralists from the 1960s through the 1980s) saw their contemporary societies as inherently dehumanizing, and regarded bourgeois, industrialized mass culture as inimical to genuine human development. The only form of society that could nurture or create a properly human species must necessarily be radically other than the existing forms. The humanist nihilism of these thinkers, however, as Yack argues, is hemmed in by a paradox of its own making—which is precisely the post-apocalyptic paradox: their critiques of the dehumanizing tendencies of bourgeois society are so total that they inadvertently place themselves in the position of trying to imagine a humanity that has no social basis at all. They demand a complete destruction of existing practices and institutions and then, not surprisingly, are unable to imagine what would come after that ending.

Most frequently, representations of post-apocalypse, sometimes intentionally, sometimes inadvertently, blur these distinctions and categories. Even the Book of Revelation, in its overwhelming hatred for the world, uncovers in its double-edged "lament" for Babylon a moment of nostalgia for what will be lost: "No more shall the sound of harpers and minstrels, of flute-players and trumpeters, be heard in [Babylon]; no more shall craftsmen of any trade be found in you; no more shall the light of the lamp be seen in you; no more shall the voice of the bride and bridegroom be heard in you!" (18: 22–23 New English Bible). And the attitude toward what remains, in the ruins, is often more complex than it appears. In many science fiction post-apocalypses, what survives is some version of humanity in the midst of the inhuman. Humanity in its essence — such is their claim — is what these apocalypses unveil. In the film *Road Warrior,* for instance, Max, who lives alone, somewhere between the values of the human remnant and of the "punk" barbarians, is forced to choose whether or not to remember how to be part of a human community. The deck is stacked, of course. It is a cowboys-and-Indians scenario: the gallant, embattled humans versus the garishly repellent and sadistic wastelanders.

There is another odd touch, however, in the *Road Warrior*'s wasteland vision. In the film's precursor, *Mad Max,* Max's wife is murdered, and Max has no subsequent erotic attachments. In *Road Warrior,* the human community appears rigorously chaste. There are men, women, and also children; all are clean and physically attractive. But something in their blondness (even their clothes are blond) or in their relentless altruism seems to preclude sexuality. When Max arrives, there appears the possibility of a connection between him and the sexy woman warrior with the wispy hair. She initially dislikes him, as per standard romantic formula, and then they gradually grow to respect each other's martial virtues. But the romantic or erotic link never develops. The society of the barbarian horde, on the contrary, is highly eroticized. Not only could their clothing be parodies of sadomasochistic sexual costumes, but it is their society that contains the film's only clearly defined romantic relationship, that between the ferocious, mohawked biker and his young boyfriend.

After this ending of civilization, the human community seals itself off from — at times it appears primarily from — sexuality. The apocalypse in this case has split sexuality in two. The first part entails an almost complete repression, an end of sex and, by extension, of all duality. The second lives as continual transgression, a polymorphous release of sexual and violent energies onto diverse forbidden objects — objects that are in fact religiously forbidden, taboo, sacred: human life, which must not be taken, and the male anus, which must not be penetrated.[6]

In the context of the film, of course, the Punks resemble fascists while the human remnant upholds democratic values. But if we take these representations as caricatures, or as propaganda for the "Human," then, the sexual repression implicit in the film's vision of humanist virtue looms large, and we must ask the question, what are these people trying to protect? The answer, I believe, is their integrity; that is, their wholeness, inviolability, and sense of a self identical to itself. They want not to be killed, and not to be fucked. Their postures of defense of their bodies as objects of violence and as objects of sexual desire resemble each other so closely that their two fears — of biological death and of sexual contact — merge with each other and become indistinguishable. Their enclave itself embodies a sexual defense, with only one entrance, in the front and always sealed and guarded; and at the center are an oil well and refinery, emblems of industrial fertility. The Punks, on the other hand, have no buildings, no outer protection. They have only weapons, cars, projectiles. And while the Punks pour out of their clothing, most of their bodies open to contact, the Humans live in their soft, blond, enveloping leather garments as in a second, more durable skin; they are never undressed.

Anxieties over nuclear catastrophe in *Road Warrior* become strangely merged with anxieties over sexual relations. The problematic position of sex, and particularly of women's sexuality, is an enduring feature of apocalyptic discourse. From the Whore of Babylon in Revelation to the young woman in the film *A Boy and His Dog* (in which Don Johnson and his talking dog eat the woman who might have been Johnson's sexual and romantic partner) to the gleeful end of feminism of *Lucifer's Hammer* and the antifeminist energies of recent Christian apocalypticism, there is an important strand of apocalyptic imagining that seeks to destroy the world expressly in order to eliminate female sexuality.[7]

In the post-apocalypse, desire and fear find their true objects; we see what we most want and most abhor. And these objects frequently are the same object — some instrument of universal annihilation. Terry Gilliam's film *12 Monkeys* provides an extraordinary portrayal and critique of post-apocalyptic sensibility. It shows first that the apocalypse is a product of imagination and the post-apocalypse a site of fear and desire. The film is full of clues that, as the psychiatrist (Madeleine Stowe) tells her patient and possible visitor from a post-apocalyptic future (Bruce Willis), "you made all this up out of your head, out of bits and pieces." The messages that come through to the investigators after the end—the clues, signs, and symptoms revealing the nature of the catastrophe—turn out to be invented and sent by Stowe, and not by the Army of the 12 Monkeys. The apocalyptic plot is self-referential. The plot's construction seems to stem from the visitor's personal catastrophes, which he figures, psychotically, as apocalyptic. The plot focuses, ultimately, in the repeated, traumatic, primal scene at the airport, which turns out to be his witnessing his own death. The apocalyptic plot is vertiginous, it falls into itself, a quality that explains the film's numerous references to Alfred Hitchcock's *Vertigo* and that film's obsession with the construction of an object of fantasy. In *12 Monkeys,* the imagination of the end of the world is . . . the imagination of the end of the world. The post-apocalyptic narrative is tautologous. What it cannot contain, what it circles around and can only exclude is, precisely, the apocalypse, the revelation that would explain the catastrophe.

And yet, the film also makes clear that just because the post-apocalypse is a self-referential construction and the apocalypse an excluded external referent does not mean that the end of the world cannot happen. In the film, it does. But it does not happen as part of the plot. The actual agent of apocalypse, in a sense, does not signify—he flies under the apocalyptic radar. He provokes no signs, leaves no traces or symptoms. He is a blank—the actor looks blank. The test tubes he carries appear empty. The end of the world can happen. But the event will be purely destructive, obliterating. It will not be hermeneutic, not a question of signs. It will just happen, and suddenly everything will have changed, changed utterly. Insofar as we represent it at all, we are not representing it.

There is a crucial moment in the Book of Revelation just after the New Jerusalem descends when an angel *measures* the heavenly city (21:15–17). That is, in effect, he measures the incommensurable, and he does so, the text states, with human measurements. This seems surprising, this explicit description of the Other in terms of the same. The terms of measure adequate for Babylon should not apply to the New Jerusalem. Seen, however, from the privileged perspective of the prophetic writer, it is not heaven that is Other but, rather, Babylon and the world; it is *only* heaven that can be measured, that exists in accordance with divine measure. It is, rather, Babylon that cannot be measured. Earlier in the text, before the final cataclysm, the writer is instructed to measure the temple but is told not to measure the outer court or the city (11:1–2). In the New Jerusalem, on the other hand, there is no temple structure, for God himself is the temple (21:22) who, presumably, now permeates everything. There is, indeed, no sun or moon to illuminate the new heaven and earth; they are lit directly by the glory of God. Thus, in measuring the New Jerusalem, the angel measures everything that is. *Measure,* in this text, is always true measure. Babylon, the site of economic exchange and shifting values, is the incommensurable Other of the divine that the apocalypse annihilates.

What could constitute a discourse entirely (of the) other? For this is the fundamental semantic and formal question apocalyptic writing addresses. As the Book of Revelation suggests, it is impossible to write absolute alterity. The other can only be inscribed in an already existing discourse. With regard to the "other" of gender or to the subaltern, post-colonial "other," we should rather say that the jagged discursive relations are conflicts, struggles, and mis-understandings — not that they are instances of incommensurability. As Donald Davidson points out in "On the Very Idea of a Conceptual Scheme," a discourse that is genuinely, radically "other" could not be recognized as such, for we would lack the means to distinguish such a form as discursive in the first place. "Different points of view make sense," Davidson writes, "but only if there is a common co-ordinate system on which to plot them; yet the existence of a common system belies the claim of dramatic incomparability" (184). Thus, Thomas Kuhn, in Davidson's example, in describing the new and mutually in-commensurable "worlds" produced by shifts in paradigm "is brilliant at saying what things were like before the revolution using — what else? — our post-revolutionary idiom" (184). Or, as Wittgenstein wrote in the introduction to the *Tractatus,* "in order to draw a limit to thinking we should have to be able to think both sides of this limit (we should therefore have to be able to think what cannot be thought)" (27).[8]

Such is the post-apocalyptic representational impasse. If apocalypse in its most radical form were to actually occur, we would have no way even to recognize it, much less to record it. The Polish science fiction writer Stanislaw Lem illustrates some of the consequences of this paradox in his novel *His Master's Voice,* in which a group of scientists attempt to decipher what appears to be an organized transmission from another solar system. The scientists' disagreements, however, are not so much over what the transmission says but over whether it constitutes a "message" at all, for it is untranslatable in a far more radical way than is evidenced in the incongruities among human languages. And yet, the transmission's alterity becomes apocalyptic — both catastrophic and revelatory — when a tiny piece of it is "translated" into a mathematical formula that spells out implications for a new technology of destructive potential far beyond that of nuclear weapons. This translation would seem to represent an apocalyptic wish for the end of the world. In deciphering apocalyptic messages, the reader generally finds what he is looking for. The destructive technology turns out, fortunately, to be inoperable, and the transmission never is deciphered. So, the apocalyptic word is received but cannot take effect, as it is "written in a language that does not belong to the category of the language we are now using" (143).

Post-apocalyptic discourses try to say what *cannot* be said (in a strict epistemological sense) and what *must not* be said (what is interdicted by ethical, religious, or other social sanctions). Nuclear war, for instance, has been considered "unthinkable" in both these senses. Kant wrote of the Biblical injunction against representations of God (what must not be portrayed) as an exemplary instance of the sublime (what is beyond representation). Post-apocalyptic representation, like Kant's sublime, often takes place at a site of conjunction between this "cannot" and "must not" — a site where language stops, both for reasons of internal logic and of social prohibition. Sex, death, and waste thus become emblematic in post-apocalyptic representations.

Sex itself is apocalyptic. We saw in *Road Warrior* how apocalypse could reveal the traumatic fissure of sexual difference. But merely the self-shattering experience of orgasm is apocalyptic, and, as *jouissance*, it has assumed an important role in critical terminology as a trope of radical inexpressibility. Each orgasm is a closure, however temporary, of desire, the "little death," foreshadowing Yeats's "Black out; Heaven blazing into the head." When we come, our personalities disperse, our autobiographies are suspended, we are over, are coming, have come. What is revealed or unveiled in orgasm? Exactly what is revealed in any apocalypse: nothing, or nothing that can be said. That bodies are bodies, or that God is God. Tautologies. That bodies are God, or that God is a body, speaking flesh, dying speech. Nonsense.

The orgasm, and our sexuality as a whole (orgasm being its most focused moment), is unspeakable, our entry into a paradise of nonexistence, of sensation beyond speech. Sexuality is always in excess of any symbolic system, and so must be regulated, submitted to rule, measured. To speak about sex is to assume the role of the angel measuring the New Jerusalem, measuring the incommensurable, and this is the function of the term *jouissance* ("bliss," "joy," "orgasm") as theorized by Roland Barthes in *The Pleasure of the Text.* Barthes wrote, "*Jouissance* is unspeakable, inter-dicted," and, quoting Jacques Lacan, that *jouissance* "is forbidden to the speaker, as such," and "cannot be spoken except between the lines," and, quoting Serge Leclaire, that "whoever speaks, by speaking denies *jouissance,* or correlatively, whoever experiences *jouissance* causes the letter—and all possible speech—to collapse in the absolute degree of annihilation he is celebrating" (21). Three things stand out in these passages. First, *jouissance* is unspeakable; that is, it *cannot* be put into language, is epistemologically incommensurable with language. Second, *jouissance* is "inter-dicted," forbidden to enter language by whatever moral or political imperative informs language. Third, *jouissance* is apocalyptic, in that it annihilates language, replacing it with what previously we were both unable and forbidden to conceptualize.

Poststructuralist feminists in the 1970s adopted *jouissance* and its apocalyptic connotations in their efforts to imagine feminine discourses outside the political and grammatical reaches of male domination. Alice Jardine argued for the liberating potential of the "unrepresentable" because in its namings as "nature, Other, matter, unconscious, madness, hyle, force" it has "throughout the tenure of Western philosophy carried feminine connotations" (88). Specifically, it was feminine *jouissance,* located "in the space of the Other," that constituted an "ultimate limit to any discourse articulated by Man" (167) Woman and women's sexuality, for Jardine, were both unable and forbidden to be spoken. What was legally repressed was also rendered literally ineffable, and the unimaginable post-apocalypse was nothing other than a fully sexual woman—a return of that repressed, and the reinvention of a banished nonlanguage.[9]

Certain Jewish Kabbalist traditions bear an interesting relation to *jouissance* in representing a violent tension between an incommensurable sexuality, its links to divinity and death, and a regulatory symbolic system. According to these traditions, as Elliot Wolfson relates, circumcision is really the symbolic inscription of the Tetragrammaton (JHWH: the four-letter name of God that Jews are forbidden to pronounce) onto the penis. Furthermore, this inscription is shown, like a passport, after death to allow the (male) Jew entrance into paradise. The ceremony of circumcision is clearly an act of submission of human sexuality to God—and, particularly in the case of Judaism, to God's law, to a symbolic order. But the signature inscribed during circumcision is itself ineffable, exceeding the legal-symbolic system that it authorizes. And so the excessive, incommensurable fact of sexuality is written by means of a term that also resists articulation. Finally, this link through which the body and its desires—which cannot adequately be represented—submit to the transcendent—which cannot, indeed must not, be named—brings the body through death and into paradise.

In contemporary American culture, another interdicted and apocalyptic sexual discourse has been that of homosexuality. Especially in the wake of the AIDS epidemic, gay writers have figured their individual and collective histories in apocalyptic terms.[10] In *Angels in America,* Tony Kushner presents AIDS as a catastrophe in itself, but also as a revelation uncovering the catastrophic breakdowns in every area of American politics and culture. The American cultural immune system was already diseased, the plays suggest, and those who are physically sick are not the symptoms of that larger disorder. The country is sick—with its sexual and racial repressions, conservative brutalities and liberal hypocrisies, its Roy Cohns and Louis Ironsons—and AIDS is gratuitous, a superfluous apocalypse that nevertheless has happened. The angels? They are forces of stasis and death that render earthly life insignificant in a great cosmic perspective. In fact, the principal angel, who appears to Prior, represents and brings with him a variety of *jouissance,* a blissful and terrifying combination of agony, death, and sexual release. The angels must be rejected. *Angels in America,* while constantly invoking the apocalypse, finally is about removing the apocalypse from historical catastrophe, about opposing apocalypse with politics.[11]

Sex, *jouissance,* the impossible and forbidden discourses of sexuality, can figure apocalypse, the place beyond the limits of language. So can waste, refuse, excrement: the ultimate, most worthless remainders. What is there left after the end? Paradise or shit. Or some condition in which these two opposites have become indistinguishable. This is the paradox identified by Freud and elaborated by Georges Bataille and Norman O. Brown.[12] The most valuable and most worthless, most precious and most despised, take the same sign; both are "priceless," beyond the possibility of measurement or evaluation. In post-apocalyptic representation, dirt, excrement, the wound, the corpse all can be symptoms of catastrophe and instruments of revelation. In a crucial scene early in Thomas Pynchon's *Gravity's Rainbow,* Slothrop goes fantastically down and through a toilet — in fact, he has been pushed down by Malcolm Little (Malcolm X before his conversion) — and there, amid "shit nothing can flush away," Slothrop discovers "patterns thick with meaning" (65). He goes further, through "a tidal wave, a jam-packed wavefront of shit," until he reaches what seems to be another world, "a place of sheltering from disaster." And yet, this protected world, on the other side of the flood of excrement, is also damaged. "Something else has been terribly *at* this country, something poor soggy Slothrop cannot see or hear... as if there is a Pearl Harbor every morning, smashing invisibly from the sky" (67). And then occurs a bizarre mythic clarification, in which the American western conquest is reenacted by Crutchfield, "the westwardman. Not 'archetypal' westwardman, but *the only.* Understand, there was only one. There was only one Indian who ever fought him. Only one fight, one victory, one loss" (67). Through the apocalyptic shit, the American apocalypse of racial oppression and resentment (precipitated in this instance by Malcolm X), comes the mythic clarity, which is also apocalyptic, the single combat to the death. And this myth itself, as Pynchon presents it, is regulated by the mysterious political-corporate powers that animate the entire novel. Excrement is the apocalyptic medium, but the clarity on the other, post-apocalyptic side is illusory. The shit has no boundary.[13]

After *jouissance,* orgasm, the "little death," we exist blessedly and uncomprehendingly inhabiting our bodies. Why can we not do the same after death? — jerk back into life and finally put into words everything we hope and fear. Apocalyptic writing is prophecy, and the prophet is a reanimated corpse. Every prophet dies — that is, before his prophecy. Jonah is swallowed by the whale, Daniel enters the furnace, Isaiah goes to heaven and tastes the burning coal; in Elie Wiesel's *Night* the old beadle returns as if from the dead to tell his village of the coming genocide, and Wiesel's novel ends with the autobiographical protagonist looking into a mirror and seeing the face of a corpse.

The apocalyptic writer writes as his own ghost. If Hamlet had, in fact, been mad and had hallucinated the ghost of his father and thereby heard the ghost reveal exactly what he most feared and hoped ("Oh, my prophetic soul!"), he would have stood in the position of the apocalyptic/post-apocalyptic writer. His father has been murdered, his uncle is a usurper, his mother is adulterous and incestuous, and he must act now to set the times right. Hamlet's situation is analogous to that of the author of the Book of Revelation, to whom the dead Christ (the Father and the Son in one person) appears to reveal the murderous alliance of the usurper Satan and the Whore of Babylon. And Hamlet's vision, although he does not realize it, is also eschatological. As the ghost, in purgatory, waits for salvation, the play also is in a state of waiting for the end. Hamlet knows all he needs to know — the revelation is complete — in the first act. His subsequent actions all are trial runs at accomplishing the apocalypse: that is, his feigned madness, the rewriting of his father's murder, substituting the deaths of Rosencrantz and Guildenstern for his own, killing Polonius, effecting Ophelia's suicide, jumping into Ophelia's grave. Through these partial catastrophes Hamlet prefigures and at the same time puts off bringing about the thorough and final purgation of all the rottenness of Denmark. They are like the explosive repetitions of a stutterer.[14] Hamlet cannot get the words out. His problem is not only that he cannot act. In fact, he also cannot speak, although he is always talking. That is, he cannot speak effectively; his words have no effect. He is not, until the end, like Christ in the Book of Revelation who speaks with a sword extending from his mouth. He is, rather, like Claudius — or a reversal of Claudius: "My thoughts fly up, my words remain below." For what Hamlet wants to do, there is no accurate language. It is not "revenge." *Hamlet* is not *The Spanish Tragedy*. It is the complete transformation of everything human — the melting of the solid, or sullied, flesh; the end of seeming; the end of the cycle of dying fathers; the end of procreation and incest barriers; even, or particularly, the end of language, which has been corrupted by Claudius's duplicity, by Rosencrantz and Guildenstern's sycophancy, by Polonius's obtuseness, by Ophelia's madness, and is unable to be redeemed by Hamlet's subtlety. The world, in the form of Denmark's court, ends, and "the rest is silence" — or would be, except that Fortinbras enters, clears the stage, and forms a new government whose principal and impossible goal undoubtedly will be to disavow all connection with the preceding catastrophe.

2. Trauma and the End of the World

In the first chapter, I discussed post-apocalyptic representation as a paradoxical, oxymoronic discourse that measures the incommensurable and speaks the unspeakable; a discourse that impossibly straddles the boundary between before and after some event that has obliterated what went before yet defines what will come after. Even in that discussion of representational limits and possibilities, political and historical factors were crucial, for the unspeakable and incommensurable are not eternal constants. What can or cannot be represented, what survives and what is obliterated in a post-apocalyptic imagining are affected by particular historical contingencies. I suggested that post-apocalyptic representations often respond to historical catastrophes and that, either explicitly or obliquely, the apocalypses of post-apocalyptic representations are historical events. This chapter pursues the relation between post-apocalypse and history, and examines in more detail how historical catastrophes come to be rendered in apocalyptic terms, how apocalypse, the incommensurable shattering event, enters history. Further, I link the idea of apocalypse with the psychoanalytic concept of trauma. Apocalypse and trauma are congruent ideas, for both refer to shatterings of existing structures of identity and language, and both effect their own erasures from memory and must be reconstructed by means of their traces, remains, survivors, and ghosts: their symptoms. Post-apocalyptic representations are simultaneously symptoms of historical traumas and attempts to work through them.

In post-apocalyptic representations, we face the question, did it happen? Did anything happen? At a recent American studies conference at the University of Freiburg, I spoke with a German scholar, a man in his early sixties, who contested the whole notion of "post-apocalypses." *The* apocalypse can only be singular; it is by definition the unique event. Moreover, he continued, the apocalypse has not happened yet, so there can be no discussion of any "post-." But, I countered, is the world not full of evidence, of symptomatic marks of definitive catastrophes that continue to shape the world? No, he replied, I do not see that. And I see nothing else, I told him. A panel was resuming, so our conversation broke off. But I wanted to insist on my point and to remind him of the significance of our speaking in Freiburg, a city whose current architecture proved my assertion. The center of Freiburg was bombed to the ground during the war. The cathedral was the only building that remained nearly intact. Today, however, the city looks almost precisely as it did before the war: a beautiful medieval town with buildings dating back to the thirteenth century. It was rebuilt according to photographs, paintings, and surviving architectural plans to be exactly as it was in every detail. No historical plaques mention the reconstruction; guidebooks overlook it. Only a few details give it away. The gutters below the roofs of the reconstructed buildings are too even, all at the same level. Only when you encounter a block where the gutters are all at different heights do you see actual medieval buildings that the bombs missed. Freiburg, and other charming medieval German cities (notably Munich), are post-apocalyptic simulacra, products of a purposeful historical amnesia, rebuilt so as to deny that the years from 1933 to 1945 ever really took place.[1]

Trauma, the Psychoanalytic Term for Apocalypse

Events took place, catastrophic and defining in political, physical, and moral senses — but they will not be or cannot be remembered or represented. Events occurred and seem to leave no trace — and yet the entire landscape is an immaculate tombstone bearing a misleading epitaph. The landscape must be read. It is a sign, or rather a symptom. Trauma is the psychoanalytic form of apocalypse, its temporal inversion. Trauma produces symptoms in its wake, after the event, and we reconstruct trauma by interpreting its symptoms, reading back in time. Apocalypse, on the other hand, is preceded by signs and portents whose interpretation defines the event in the future. The apocalyptic sign is the mirror image of the traumatic symptom. In both cases, the event itself is so overwhelming as to be fundamentally unreadable; it can only be understood through the portents and symptoms that precede and follow it. Both apocalypse and trauma present the most difficult questions of what happened "before," and what is the situation "after." The apocalyptic-historical-traumatic event becomes a crux or pivot that forces a retelling and revaluing of all events that lead up to it and all that follow.

Michael André Bernstein, with reference to the Shoah, argues against any such "apocalypticizing" of history. He criticizes what he calls "foreshadowing," or retrospectively assuming an inevitable sequence of events leading up to and determining the catastrophe. Quite correctly, Bernstein points out that no event or sequence of events is inevitable, that no event can be understood on the basis of prophetic signs and portents, and that history moves on the basis of contingencies, choices, accidents, and possibilities. Opposing foreshadowing, Bernstein recommends "sideshadowing" as a better means of historical understanding, that is, the description of historical alternatives, the other things that could have happened but did not, and an empirical—not a retrospectively prophetic—analysis of why the catastrophe occurred. The Holocaust did not *have* to happen: it was not the inevitable result of Western technology, or German anti-Semitism, or (as in some Zionist histories) the inevitable result of diaspora and assimilation. Bernstein is right, and contemporary historians, including historians of the Shoah, understand this point quite well. But despite the need, and the ongoing practice (which Bernstein largely ignores) of history writing that contests notions of inevitability, an overwhelmingly catastrophic event like the Holocaust does occupy a central position, dividing history into a "before" and an "after," and radically restructuring our understandings of all events on either side. It is not *inevitability* that gives a historical event an apocalyptic character. It is its ability to obliterate existing narratives, to initiate a new history that takes the form of an ominous and symptomatic aftermath.

Another problem in describing history as traumatic and apocalyptic is the temptation to regard catastrophe as universal, as in Walt Whitman's lines from "This Compost":

> Something startles me where I thought I was safest...
> O Earth!
> O how can the ground of you not sicken?
> How can you be alive, you growths of spring?
> How can you furnish health, you blood of herbs, roots,
>   orchards, grain?
> Are they not continually putting distempered corpses in
>   you?
> Is not every continent worked over and over with sour
>   dead? (208)

Whitman's poem suggests that trauma or apocalypse — some form of utterly destabilizing disaster — is a universal condition of life and symbolization. Society, in this view, would be organized around some ongoing process of trauma and symptom formation, quasi-apocalyptic destruction and post-apocalyptic regeneration in which the *particular* catastrophe is not important as such — a view of apocalypse and trauma as structural rather than historical.

These tensions have been at the core of trauma theory since Freud, who made three principal forays toward a theory of trauma. His earliest idea, in *Studies on Hysteria,* concerned the dynamics of trauma, repression, and symptom formation. Freud described how an overpowering event, unacceptable to consciousness, can be forgotten and yet return in the form of somatic symptoms or compulsive, repetitive behaviors. This initial theory of trauma and symptom became problematic for Freud when he concluded that neurotic symptoms were more often the results of repressed drives and desires than of traumatic events. Freud returned to the theory of trauma in *Beyond the Pleasure Principle,* a work that originated in Freud's treatment of First World War combat veterans who suffered from repeated nightmares and other symptoms of their wartime experiences. Here, the traumatic event and its aftermath again became central to psychoanalysis, but again Freud shifted his emphasis from the event to what he considered a more comprehensive frame, in this case a biological urge toward equilibrium that Freud then theorized as the "death drive." Finally, in *Moses and Monotheism,* Freud attempted a theory of trauma that would account for the historical development of entire cultures. Especially valuable in this work is Freud's elaboration of the concept of "latency," of how memory of a traumatic event can be lost over time but then regained in some symptomatic form when triggered by some similar event. In this way, each national catastrophe invokes and transforms memories of other catastrophes, so that history becomes a complex entanglement of crimes inflicted and suffered, with each catastrophe understood—that is, misunderstood—in the context of repressed memories of previous ones. A major problem with *Moses and Monotheism* is its overreliance on the mythical, Oedipal anthropology of Freud's *Totem and Taboo*. All *historical* traumas are seen ultimately as repetitions of a "phylogenetic" ur-trauma, the murder of the primal father—an interpretation that, in addition to being fanciful, once again discredits the event, whether in a personal or a social history, in favor of some all-encompassing instinctual-biological determination.

All Freud's thinking on trauma manifests this ambivalence regarding the significance of the historical event. Reading Freud, we are tempted to ask, are there events, are there traumas at all? That is, do events in history have consequences—as Freud urges in the first movements of each of his theoretical ventures—or, as he concludes in each of his second movements, are events secondary to desire, instinct, or a form of genetic history? It is difficult, perhaps impossible, to reconcile these opposing movements. In Freud's own writings, the second—the biological or cosmic—consistently won out over historical and traumatic factors in explaining the etiology of symptoms. Furthermore, to devalue the event means simultaneously to reduce (to the individual) and to inflate (to the universal) all interpretations of symptoms. Thus, all individuals repress the same desires, and all cultures repress memories of the same primal crimes. Such an approach can say very little about specific personal or cultural responses to particular events, however catastrophic.

A better approach would be to reject Freud's final claims and return to his ambivalence—to recall the importance of sexual abuse, war traumas, and particular historical events in Freud's successive theories of symptom formation. Psychoanalysis is most valuable as a means of confronting events, histories, and consequences and individuals' and cultures' relations to their histories, which include relations based on fantasy. Seen in this way, we will put the apocalypse back into psychoanalysis, which means to put back catastrophe and history, to reemphasize the event that reverberates beyond itself. We might study in this regard a late text (written, like all Freud's later work, at a time of alarming political crisis) in which the ambivalence over trauma and history appears especially acute. In *Analysis Terminable and Interminable* Freud subordinates trauma, and especially any social or historical trauma, to constitutive or biological factors. Freud argues that the accidental or contingent quality of trauma makes its analysis amenable to closure, while the "biological bedrock" of instinctual life is the final cause of most neurosis and will forever elude analytic treatment. Indeed, the struggle of conflicting instincts is figured as a grappling of cosmic forces, as the principles of Eros and Death compete for world mastery.[2]

Yet, persistently, almost like a symptom, trauma returns to the text of *Analysis Terminable and Interminable,* as Freud cannot escape his own observations that people have histories and that personal histories take place within social histories that are themselves traumatic. We see this unintended entrance of historical trauma most clearly when Freud recalls the case of the Wolf Man, describing how he helped bring an end to the patient's resistances and subsequently his symptoms by threatening to stop the analysis at the end of a year. "When he left me in the midsummer of 1914, with as little suspicion as the rest of us of what lay so shortly ahead, I believed that his cure was radical and permanent" (217). What follows, of course, is the First World War. Yet when the patient returns to Vienna after the war, like so many others "a refugee and destitute," and with his neurotic symptoms also having returned, Freud draws back from pursuing the possibility of the war's having had traumatic consequences, noting only that he "had to help him master a part of the transference that had not been resolved" and that "this was accomplished in a few months." Freud then quotes the extraordinary conclusion to his 1923 footnote to the case: " 'since then the patient has felt normal and has behaved unexceptionably, in spite of the war having robbed him of his home, his possessions, and all his family relationships' " (218). It is difficult to imagine what such a normal and unexceptionable life might consist of, but surely these losses must entail exceptional consequences that Freud does not mention. When the patient continues to require psychotherapy (he is treated by another analyst), Freud describes his problems as "offshoots of his perennial neurosis" (218). In this way, Freud acknowledges a historical trauma that enters the text in the form of a world war and ruins a patient's life, but then dismisses the trauma as entirely subsidiary to preexisting childhood neuroses and constitutional factors.

This puzzling situation in which traumatic events are acknowledged and denied in the same text recurs in recent psychoanalytic writings. The most compelling contemporary thinking on trauma is that of Slavoj Zizek. In Zizek's analysis, following Jacques Lacan, trauma is the destabilizing intrusion of the Real into a symbolic order. The Real, for Zizek, is the inevitable lack or incompleteness that ruptures the symbolic. All societies' representational systems seek a wholeness, a seamlessness, a sense that the important questions have been answered, that social harmony, if not entirely achieved, is at least well understood and close at hand. But this wholeness always breaks down, for no symbolic order is coherent. A gap, a rip, appears, which cannot be accounted for. This gap, wound, incoherence is, for Zizek, *both* a particular traumatic event or condition *and* a structural inevitability. Trauma, as the continuing effects of a historical catastrophe or an intractable economic or social contradiction (e.g., class or racial conflicts), shows the inadequacy of a society's stories about itself. Enormous ideological energy then will be used to stitch this tear in the symbolic fabric back together.

Zizek cites "the two great traumatic events of the holocaust and the gulag [as] exemplary cases of the return of the dead in the twentieth century. The shadows of their victims will continue to chase us as 'living dead' until we give them a decent burial, until we integrate the trauma of their death into our historical memory." Having acknowledged the symptomatic aftermaths of historical traumas, however, Zizek continues immediately that "the same may be said of the 'primordial crime' that founded history itself, the murder of the 'primal father' (re)constructed by Freud in *Totem and Taboo*" (*Looking Awry,* 23). And earlier, in *The Sublime Object of Ideology,* Zizek wrote of concentration camps ("the 'perverse' obverse of twentieth-century civilization"):

> All attempts to attach this phenomenon to a concrete image ("Holocaust," "Gulag" . . .), to reduce it to a product of a concrete social order (Fascism, Stalinism . . .) — what are they if not so many attempts to elude the fact that we are dealing here with the "real" of our civilization which returns as the same traumatic kernel in all social systems? (50)

For Zizek in this passage, all traumas are the same trauma — Auschwitz is the "same" as the Second World War internment camps for Japanese Americans. Thus, it seems right to ask, as Judith Butler does, whether "Zizekian psychoanalysis can respond to the pressure to theorize the historical specificity of trauma, to provide the texture for the specific exclusions, annihilations, and unthinkable losses that structure . . . social phenomena?" (202). As Zizek makes clear (and as Gilda Radner used to say), "There's always *something*," that is, there will always be a disruptive force of some kind that will force a symbolic order into some ideological adjustment. But at the same time, traumatic disruptions are of very different types and magnitudes. Butler is right that we cannot simply cry "Trauma" to explain every cultural phenomenon, for that will explain nothing. We must, rather, examine specific cultural wounds, the continually reopened wounds that seem to structure a culture's symbolic systems, and try to trace their representations back toward some earlier rupture in the social fabric. Zizek provides what we might call a poetics of trauma, a sense of how traumatic symptoms remain alive and active in the present, forcing language and ideology to change according to their dictates and contours.

A post-apocalyptic theory of trauma discovers that events happen and, to borrow Yeats's apocalyptic rhetoric, "things fall apart" and "change utterly" — but that remainders and reminders, signs and symptoms survive. For trauma is not simply another word for disaster. The idea of catastrophe as trauma provides a method of interpretation and posits that the effects of an event may be dispersed and manifested in many forms not obviously associated with the event. Moreover, this dispersal occurs across time, so that an event experienced as shattering may actually produce its full impact only years later. In its emphasis on the retrospective reconstruction of the traumatic event (for the event cannot be comprehended when it occurs), an analysis of trauma is both constructivist and empirical. It pays the closest attention to the representational means through which an event is remembered, and yet retains the importance of the event itself, the thing that did happen. Most important, the idea of trauma allows for an interpretation of cultural symptoms — of the growths, wounds, scars on a social body, and its compulsive, repeated actions.

But how are these signs and symptoms recognized and interpreted? How does the trauma present itself in the present and become represented? After it occurs, after it has disrupted memory and become subject to unconscious and conscious repressions, how does the trauma — the apocalypse in history — intersect with symbols and become readable? And how can we read what we take to be a traumatic-apocalyptic inscription considering that we, the interpreters, live in the same landscape and suffer the symptoms we would interpret?

Freud set the terms for these questions with misleading simplicity. He distinguished broadly between the physical repetition, or acting out, that characterized the symptom and the narrative, therapeutic working through the symptom toward a renewed memory of the trauma. Repression, or obliteration, of memory brought on by a traumatic event results in forms of symbolic repetition. This symptomatic acting out may be (as in the "fort-da" game) an attempt to master the trauma or work through it at an unconscious level. Or it may indicate a more complete immersion in the trauma's repressed force. In either case, healing cannot take place until the trauma is brought to consciousness through narrative. Freud's discussion of mourning presents another version of these processes. Mourning is a form of working through the traumatic fact of a loved one's death, including the working through of unresolved conflict, hostility, or guilt that may have existed in the relationship between the mourner and the deceased. An extended period of melancholy or depression from which the mourner cannot escape represents an unconscious, guilt-ridden self-punishment brought on by the repression of the memories of such conflicts. Again, memory, in language, is the key to releasing the sufferer from symptomatic actions or feelings.[3]

Later, Freud began to recognize that it might be possible for someone to remember but not remember, to tell the story of a traumatic event and yet fail to acknowledge its effects. Something happened, yes, but it is over now and I am all better. This is the response Freud calls denial, or negation, "a kind of intellectual acceptance of what is repressed, though in all essentials the repression persists" ("Negation," 236). Freud also describes the process of fetishizing, in which an act of denial is played out in relation to a physical object. The object represents the event that did, and did not, take place.[4]

Denial and fetishism blur the distinctions between acting out and working through, and make possible more insightful analyses of symptoms of social traumas. Symptoms in this view are not entirely unconscious and not entirely physical; they are also discursive and are not wholly repressed. This is a direction that recent theorists have taken up quite effectively. Eric Santner has described how narrative itself, the tool of working through, can itself function as a fetish object "consciously or unconsciously designed to expunge the traces of the trauma or loss that called that narrative into being in the first place" (144). Discussing the work of nationalist German historians of the "historians' conflict" of the early 1980s (and referring also to Ronald Reagan's speech at Bitburg, which I will discuss in chapter 5), Santner describes a refusal or inability to mourn that does not involve repression of traumatic memory but is rather "a strategy of undoing, in fantasy, the need for mourning by simulating a condition of intactness . . . by situating the site and origin of loss elsewhere" (144). Telling the story of trauma in this case is not a method of working through but is itself a traumatic symptom.

Dominick LaCapra also recognizes that working through and acting out cannot always be distinguished, and he adds that in many cases it is important that they exist together in the same text. He argues that a discourse utterly without symptomatic traces is not possible, that such a cleansed text could only be a pure fetish, a narrative of fake redemption. But LaCapra also criticizes texts that, in his view, do nothing but act out responses to trauma — in particular citing theories of postmodernity and the sublime that are "obsessively preoccupied with loss, aporia, dispossession, and deferred meaning" (xi). To work through historical symptoms, LaCapra argues, one must first recognize the symptomatic status of one's own discourse and one's historical and personal relation to the traumatic event. In representing a traumatic event, a writer should not assume that a narrative working through is impossible, but neither should he believe that *his* representation will do the job and put the past to rest.

Cultural artifacts can be forms of acting out (or fetishes) or — or even simultaneously — forms of working through. Yet they also seem to be indexical impressions of the traumatic wound. The landscape of symptoms is a landscape of scars that point back toward the event that initiated their production. That is, the event did not exactly, directly produce them. There are gaps in the causal chain, and the symptoms point back across those gaps. Zizek discusses the traumatic Real as "the rock on which every formalization stumbles" (*Sublime Object,* 172), a "hard, impenetrable kernel resisting symbolization" that is nevertheless "produced by the symbolization itself" (169) — that is, which cannot be apprehended until it is put into symbolic form. Symbols refill the gap that trauma has crashed through; thus, symbols must take the shape of the breakage created by the trauma. The relation between trauma and representation is both entirely direct and entirely oblique.[5]

Analyses of post-apocalyptic and traumatic representations also must address the emotional and libidinal investments in cultural symptoms (the in-

vestments of those who create and consume the artifacts and of those who analyze them). For Freud, the sexual fetish was a disavowal of trauma and also
an object of desire. The same can be said of Santner's narrative fetish. The
forms of representation that both activate and keep alive yet at the same time
neutralize and assimilate a culture's central traumatic concerns will become
objects of the most intense feeling. Zizek invokes the term *jouissance* to describe the emotional and libidinal connection of a traumatized culture to its
symbolized symptoms that give the culture back its completeness and coherence. *Jouissance,* for Zizek, is an ecstatic identification with the trauma, its
symptoms, and their symbolizations and with the imagined, ideological wholeness that results from the symbolic healing of the traumatic wound. Without
the symptom, there is nothing — "Pure autism, psychic suicide" — but the symptom is "a signifying formation penetrated by enjoyment," that is, *jouissance*
(*Sublime Object,* 75).

Zizek presents a situation of traumatization and ideology from which it seems
impossible to escape. Every healing narrative will only, ultimately, serve as
another layer of symptom covering the open wound. I do not think we need to
go this far. Historical traumas take longer to heal than most political institutions
are willing to accept, and we should take seriously Zizek's warning against
the "over-rapid historicization" of trauma (*Sublime Object,* 50). Most of this
book analyzes forms of denial and symptomatic acting out. But I still believe
that narrative and representation can have therapeutic effects, that things can
get better, that societies do not need to be caught in endless cycles of horror,
jouissance, and ideological fetishizing. Trauma has the effects that it has, is as
painful and apocalyptic as it is, because it really happens. It is not just a structural void in the symbolic order — though it creates such voids, and it is not
the result of fantasy, though it structures fantasies. But also because trauma
really happens, It can eventually be addressed, remembered, retold, and different futures can be imagined and lived.

WHERE WAS I WHEN THE WORLD ENDED?

In this book, I describe contemporary American culture as traumatized, and as
permeated with symptoms transmitted through a variety of cultural forms. These
symptomatic forms at the same time are engaged in overriding efforts to deny,

disavow, and fetishize the social-historical traumas that have informed them. In the United States, over the past fifteen years, Reaganism provided (and in its offshoots continues to provide) the most striking and effective forms of denial. The compulsive repetitions — and denials — of racial antagonisms, and the refighting of the Vietnam War in various political, military, and aesthetic sites have been two of the principal Reaganist symptoms of American historical traumas. But Reaganism has not been the only symptomatic response to traumatic history. A horrified, but not entirely unpleasant, fascination with images and narratives of cataclysmic endings intensified in the late 1970s through the 1980s, and these endings became more and more gripping both in their verisimilitude and in their sense of necessity. These things *will* end because they *must* end, and this feeling of imminent and necessary breakdown emerged in the midst of the Reaganist denial that anything at all was amiss.

In the 1981 film *Escape from New York,* the entire island of Manhattan is turned into the ultimate maximum-security prison. Walled in, sealed off, no one who goes in ever leaves; New York at last is turned over entirely to the criminals! But this disciplinary prophylaxis does not render the rest of America wholesome and safe. The country is ruled by a phony democracy and a fascistic national police force, and threatened by uncontrollable terrorist groups and international nuclear flash points. At the end, it is a humorous and light-hearted moment when "Snake" Pliskin substitutes the cab driver's Glenn Miller cassette tape for the president's top-secret taped plan to preserve world peace — thus ensuring nuclear war. Or consider the triumph of Batman in the 1989 Tim Burton film. The Joker — that crystalline, unyielding concentrate of homicidal madness — is destroyed, but what is improved? Gotham City, the town that, as the Joker accurately describes it, "needs an enema," is exactly the same as it was before. And the Joker, the insane killer, was also the film's only figure of enjoyment and represented the only possibility for change. Gotham City was already dead. It took the Joker, himself symbolically dead, to begin to realize the anarchic polymorphous and polysemous pleasures and horrors available to the living dead. Batman, also dead, seeks to resist the ecstatic decomposition offered by the Joker, to shut the lid of the tomb and embalm the inhabitants (he himself, of course, is mummified in his body armor). Burton's *Batman,* as much as any *Night of the Living Dead,* is a post-apocalyptic vision of America as necropolis.

Batman, Escape from New York, and other aesthetic and mass cultural products are representations of a world "after the end" — a world that must be interpreted as *our* world. But they are also themselves post-apocalyptic symptoms informed by the continually repeated catastrophes and disintegrations of this century. Late-twentieth-century American culture is not monolithic, and for that reason it is all the more striking to see the conclusive social cataclysm repeated in so many related forms, and with so much pleasure. It requires a concerted effort for a fiction *not* to portray the end of the world. In Leslie Marmon Silko's novel *Ceremony,* a wise character warns the Native American protagonist about how European-American stories end:

> They want it to end here, the way all their stories end, encircling slowly to choke the life away. The violence of the struggle excites them, and the killing soothes them. . . . And they would end this story right here, with you fighting to your death alone in these hills. . . . [I]f you don't go with them, they'll hunt you down, and take you any way they can. Because this is the only ending they understand. (232–33)

Tayo, Silko's protagonist, manages to resist the apocalyptic ending. And yet, the novel itself, as anti-apocalyptic as it is in its argument, is entirely a post-apocalyptic product. For American Indians, the worst catastrophe imaginable has already happened. And Silko's novel is part of, emerges in response to, the shattered world it depicts.

We see this multiple status — as representation, as critique, and as symptom of a post-apocalyptic/post-traumatic scene — also played out in the field of literary and cultural theory, which consistently uses imagery of rupture, disintegration, and catastrophe to distinguish itself and its objects from theories and objects of previous periods. The enormously influential theories of the modern by Foucault and of the postmodern by Lyotard, Baudrillard, and Jameson all take as their starting point some cataclysmic and irrevocable shattering or flattening or decentering that infiltrates and rearticulates all areas of culture. The theories of the postmodern initiated by these thinkers diagnose a post-apocalyptic condition. At the same time, insofar as these theories tend to focus on developments in epistemology or economics and lose sight of more concrete social and political disasters, they are themselves symptomatic of the traumas they fail to mention.[6]

And where does my own discourse stand in relation to this post-apocalyptic scene it intends to name, analyze, diagnose, critique? Very much like these other postmodern products: horrified and fascinated, resisting and complicit. To think that everything really is over would be a great relief, and a positive satisfaction. So many self-righteous and complacent individuals and institutions would get their comeuppance in a hurry. Except that it has already happened. What will happen *has* happened, is happening. But the world is still here, exactly as it was: that is what is intolerable. And therein lies the pleasure in imagining its destruction, and the horror and confusion in reflecting that such enormous, such definitive catastrophes have actually and in the flesh taken place. I sense a continuing, slow-working cognitive, emotional, moral, and political disaster taking place around us and within us, in the context of an economy that can still — just barely — make a claim to prosperity. Beavis and Butthead are Beckett characters about to enter the service economy.[7]

Therefore, I take great pleasure in recent secular apocalyptics. In Baudrillard: "The explosion has already occurred; the bomb is only a metaphor now." "We have missed a certain point for turning back, a certain point of the contradiction in things, and have entered a universe of noncontradiction alive, of blind rapture, of ecstasy, of amazement about the irreversible processes that nevertheless have no direction at all" ("The Anorexic Ruins," 34, 32).

In DeLillo: "Come on, hurry up, plane crash footage." "Every disaster made us wish for more, for something bigger, grander, more sweeping." "What a surprise it was to ... discover that my own son was at the center of things, speaking in his new-found voice, his tone of enthusiasm for runaway calamity. He was talking about the airborne toxic event in a technical way, although his voice all but sang with prophetic disclosure" (*White Noise,* 64, 130).

In Lou Reed: "There's blacks with knives and whites with guns / Fighting in Howard Beach / There's no such thing as human rights / When you walk the New York streets. / A cop was shot in the head by a 10 year old kid name Buddah in / Central Park last week. / The fathers and daughters are lined up by / The coffins by the Statue of Bigotry" ("Hold On," *New York*).

I remember in the summers of the late 1970s and early 1980s, on the hottest days in New York, having the sense that the city literally was melting. The physical heat, the emotional heat, the heat of violence, injustice, and insanity were causing the city to dematerialize, and I was watching it, and part of it. And during Reagan's presidency, there was the sense that the country had decided to stop thinking, that thinking was no longer necessary, was conceptually obsolete, that we had entered a national age of post-thinking.

But I myself, from a very different political perspective, have an analogous urge to be stupid, to be post-discursive, a ghost of myself, an android replica, a Cy-berger. I want to make love to the android fashion models on the covers of *Vogue* and *Glamour.* I want to be stupid, and I want to be perfect. When I was ten or twelve, I played a mean trick on my sister Claudia. I pretended to her that I had become a robot and was no longer her brother. I spoke to her in a mechanical robot voice, called her "small one," and refused to acknowledge any relation between us. I looked like her brother, but I was not him. Jim did not exist anymore. Finally, Claudia started to believe my impersonation and became frightened and started to cry. And only then, when my trick was successful, did I suddenly realize what a terrible thing I was doing, betraying my sister's trust in that way. Looking back at this event now, though, I realize also that my cruelty represented a real desire to be not connected to my imperfect sister, to be free from my family's traumatic circumstances, and, in a larger sense, to be not human at all, to transcend all imperfections and traumas. My robotic attempt to achieve this transcendence, of course, was itself a disavowal of my own imperfection and humanity — that is, simultaneously an acknowledgment and a denial. As a robot, I could never be harmed, I could never malfunction, and I could never feel. The robot combines abjection (the robot's consciousness is more or less that of an insect) and transcendence. The robot survives the catastrophe with no injuries and no symptoms — except that it is itself the principal symptom.

Part of my theorizing, then, is the discourse of my robot self, walking invulnerable, transcendently abject, among the ruins of humanism, language, the self, the West, the inner city, the shopping mall, modernity, history, narrative, and all the other shattered objects of postmodern theory. This discourse is important because it is symptomatic; as symptom, it provides a true index, a tangible embodied link to the already blurred event to which it responds. The robot is not deluded; it is certainly the product of a genuine disaster. The temptations to be post-human are great and are everywhere, as omnipresent as catastrophe.

POSTMODERN CATASTROPHE AND
POST-APOCALYPTIC DESIRE:
"UNTIL THE END OF THE WORLD"

Until the end of the world . . . we tell stories. This is the message and the plot of the *Decameron,* the *Arabian Nights,* Melville's *The Confidence Man,* Frank Kermode's *The Sense of an Ending.* After the end, there will be something else — unimaginable: "heaven blazing into the head" — but until the end, there will be narrative, the verbal mark of temporality. There will be stories about the end, forestalling and invoking it, constructing moments that are conclusive, and thus definitive. The present, the world in history, is in flux and ambiguous; Kermode's expression is "in the middest." The apocalypse becomes a clarification, an alchemical precipitation into pure principles.

And yet, in providing such a definition, the end of the world ceases to be an ending: no longer a wall against which the suicide cars of history and personality collide, the end, in the imagination, becomes permeable, a boundary that can be straddled. The most important phrase in apocalyptic semiotics is Wittgenstein's invocation of Kant: "In order to draw a limit to thinking we should have to be able to think both sides of this limit (we should therefore have to be able to think what cannot be thought)" (27). Very few apocalyptic representations end with the End.[8] There is always some remainder, some post-apocalyptic debris, or the transformation into paradise. The apocalyptic desire *is* a longing for the end: John of Patmos's hatred of the world as Babylon, Henry Miller's wish to put dynamite in the world's anus, Michel Foucault's wish to see the traces of Man erased. Apocalyptic desire coincides with a total critique of the world, a critique that annuls any chance of reform. But apocalyptic desire is a longing also for the aftermath, for the New Jerusalem and for the frustrated humanist-anarchist visions behind Miller's destructive rants and Foucault's analyses.

This combination of violent hatred for the world as it is and violent desire for the world as it should be has characterized apocalyptic representations and apocalyptic social movements since their first recorded instances, in the Biblical and apocryphal apocalypses. Apocalyptic writings respond to social crisis (or, more accurately, to *perceived* crisis).[9] Apocalypse is not, then, as Kermode describes it, primarily an existential expression of a universal wish for narrative closure. The wish to end the world, or to represent the end of the world, arises in each case from more particular social and political discomforts and aspirations. In the wake of some catastrophe, the apocalyptic writer creates a greater and conclusive catastrophe. Surely, he thinks, the world cannot — and should not — have survived such destabilization and horror. And yet it has. The world, intolerably, continues. But it should, it *must,* end.

Apocalyptic representation stands in the midst of crisis and between two catastrophes: one historical (remembered and suffered), and one imagined (desired and feared). While the narrative closure peculiar to apocalyptic representation indeed places itself, as Kermode suggests, "in the middest," this position is less a biological or existential middle between birth and death than a historical middle between a destabilizing, traumatic historical event and an imagined obliteration that will erase all traumatic memory. Regardless of whether it imagines a wasteland or a paradise as its aftermath, the apocalypse ushers in a condition of permanent ecstasy outside of history and time.[10] The "betweenness" of apocalyptic discourse more resembles Zizek's description of the condition "between two deaths" — the first death being biological and the second symbolic. The second death, for Zizek, represents the annihilation of the whole symbolic order and of the possibility of using symbols. The apocalypse, in ending symbolization, ends at the same time both meaning and ambiguity. And the consequent "New Jerusalem" of understanding would be a condition of direct, unmediated apprehension. The imagined final catastrophe would result in "revelation" at last.

Of course, these escapes — from form, meaning, history — do not take place. And yet, the rhetorical gambit of much postmodern theory is that the "end," or some end, has, in fact, already taken place, perhaps without our knowledge. Baudrillard's description of postmodernity as a state of "simulation" posits a kind of revelatory end of representation in which the presumed depth of a signifier indicating a signified has been flattened to a single dimension of a network of signs without referents. The human subject in this state after the end of representation occupies a position on the network, a node in an endless exchange of information, engaged in an involuntary form of post-symbolic communication that Baudrillard describes as both ecstatic and obscene. Were the subject able to regain some theoretical vantage (the position of post-apocalyptic theorist), he would describe the world as Baudrillard does in "The Anorexic Ruins" (published in a brief collection titled *Looking Back on the End of the World*) as a world that has already ended: "Everything has already become nuclear, faraway, vaporized. The explosion has already occurred; the bomb is only a metaphor now. . . . In a certain way there is no life anymore, but the information and the vital functions continue" (34, 39).

Fredric Jameson, although he retains a Marxist orientation that Baudrillard has repudiated, shares with Baudrillard the panicked sense that postmodernity is a condition somehow "after the end." Jameson begins *Postmodernism, or, The Cultural Logic of Late Capitalism* by describing the postmodern as "an inverted millenarianism in which premonitions of the future, catastrophic or redemptive, have been replaced by senses of the end of this or that" (1). The most significant ending for Jameson is of history, in particular of narrative forms of representing history. Jameson's uses of the terms *pastiche* and *schizophrenia* help him to describe a "postmodern sublime" (akin to Baudrillard's "ecstasy") in which historical imagery returns cut off from its contexts, and the human subject, without coherent organizing narratives, finds itself "reduced to an experience of pure material signifiers, or, in other words, a series of pure and unrelated presents in time" (27).

Postmodernity as an end of narrative is a position associated most commonly with Jean-François Lyotard. Lyotard, of course, refers to the end of the "Big" narratives: salvation, emancipation, the dialectic, scientific knowledge. Nevertheless, in his recurrent emphasis on the sublime and unrepresentability as crucial, indeed privileged, concerns of the postmodern, Lyotard effectively problematizes narrative in general. While modernism, he writes, "is an aesthetics of the sublime . . . it allows the unpresentable to be put forward only as the missing contents; but the form, because of its recognizable consistency, continues to offer to the reader or viewer matter for solace and pleasure." The postmodern, on the other hand, "would be that which, in the modern, puts forward the unpresentable in presentation itself; that which denies itself the solace of good forms, the consensus of a taste" (*The Postmodern Condition,* 81). The unifying metanarratives break down, lose their legitimacy, and are replaced by a proliferation of local narratives or by the unpresentable witnessed in radically heterogeneous forms. The theorization of the postmodern, then, posits the end of narrative, and the end of the forms of identity and legitimacy that narrative (according to these theories) made possible.

But what in these theories of the postmodern has brought about this ending? Baudrillard, Jameson, and Lyotard all, with certain variations, attribute the apocalyptic shift primarily to economic and technological changes. Jameson is the most explicit in describing the postmodern as a product of a "third stage" of capitalism. The unrepresentable "sublimity" of the postmodern is due to the fact that late capitalism has not yet been adequately theorized, or, as he says, "mapped." In postmodern culture, as in the postmodern architecture that Jameson cites as examples, the subject cannot locate himself, cannot "map the great global multinational and decentered communicational network in which we find ourselves caught as individual subjects" (44). Furthermore, for Jameson, the representational means for this mapping does not yet exist; we require a "breakthrough to some as yet unimaginable new mode of representing" (54).

While Jameson intends to place this postmodern end of narrative in historical context, his historical narrative is primarily economic (as Baudrillard's and Lyotard's accounts combine economic, technological, and theoretical/ philosophical narratives). It is surprising that these and other theorizations of the postmodern that, almost invariably, portray postmodernity in apocalyptic or post-apocalyptic terms do not consider the effects of this century's catastrophic political events as factors destabilizing historical narratives. Considering that the most dystopic visions of contemporary science fiction can do no more than replicate the historical catastrophes of the twentieth century, it makes sense to reexamine and rehistoricize the theoretical bases of postmodern descriptions of the end of narrative.[11]

"1999 was the year the Indian nuclear satellite went out of control." Thus begins Wim Wenders's 1991 film *Until the End of the World*, a beginning that locates the film at the end of the century, the end of the millennium, and sometime just before — or just after — the end of the world. Wenders's film illustrates important apocalyptic, post-apocalyptic, and anti-apocalyptic sensibilities of the late twentieth century, showing their relations to technological change and to problematics of representation, and to the century's devastating historical catastrophes. *Until the End of the World* brings together notions of apocalypse as world-ending catastrophe (the object of ultimate terror) and apocalypse as revelation — that is, as direct unmediated access to some essential reality, an access or, perhaps, a union, which circumvents representation and narrative and thereby constitutes an object of ultimate desire.

These two senses of apocalypse — as cataclysm and as revelation — share a common movement toward a perception of the primal, toward immediacy, the unitary unmodified event, the absolute resolution. This is the urge to purify and unveil the world to its final transparent nakedness — an urge that is not, obviously, unique to the late twentieth century. What distinguishes the apocalypticism of this end of a century from those previous is, first, its sense that its apocalypse (whether as catastrophe or as revelation) may have already happened — that we live in a *post-apocalyptic* world — and, second, the manner in which technology now has informed, and is itself invested with, apocalyptic tendencies. In the film, the false apocalypse of the nuclear satellite's explosion inaugurates a very real sense of post-apocalypse in which the characters believe they have survived the end of the world. And in this post-apocalyptic world, the Farbers perfect the technology to record and transmit the neurochemical event of seeing: enabling the blind Edith Farber to see again, and the others to record and watch their own dreams. Hypermodern technology creates direct access to primary process, to dreams, which previously could only be remembered through narrative. Thus, Wenders imagines, one hundred years after the publication of Freud's *Interpretation of Dreams,* at the succeeding *fin de siècle,* the end of psychoanalysis as a narrative technique — an ending that is very much part of American cultural consciousness at the end of the twentieth century.[12]

This technological apocalyptic entry into primary process, then, occurs after the supposed end of the world; it occurs at the geographical end of the world, in a cave laboratory in the Australian wilderness, aided by technicians who are Australian aborigines, another primal ingredient in the technological-apocalyptic mixture. But before we explore Wenders's portrayal of the apocalyptic technologies of dreaming in the post-apocalyptic wilderness, we must look at the first half of the film, which chronicles Claire's journey through a series of postmodern cities — from Venice through Paris, Berlin, Moscow, Beijing, Tokyo, and San Francisco — before and until she reaches the temporal, geographical, and psychic ends of the world.

It is necessary to recall some of the complex plot of *Until the End of the World,* since narrative and the multiplicity of narrative are at issue in the discussion that follows. While an Indian nuclear-powered satellite is careening out of orbit and the world powers debate what to do about it, Claire, a young French woman, oblivious to the crisis, drives back to Paris from Venice. She is involved in an auto accident with two bank robbers, who entrust her with their loot. She returns to Paris with a fortune in cash, which the robbers, Raymond and Chico, will pick up later. They are able to trace Claire's movements with a hidden electronic device. On the way, in Lyons, Claire meets Sam Farber, who, calling himself Trevor McPhee, is fleeing for his life for reasons we do not yet know. Claire gives him a ride, lets him drive, and while she is sleeping, he steals a sizable portion of her stolen money. On arriving home, and surprising her husband, Gene, an English novelist (who never expected to see her again), Claire discovers the theft and leaves again in order to locate McPhee/ Farber. With the help of a German private detective (and an expensive computer tracking program that they purchase — with more of the stolen money — in Moscow), Claire pursues Farber, periodically catching and losing him again, across Europe and Asia to America and, finally, to Australia. Along the way, Claire falls in love with Farber and learns the reason he is being hunted. He is in possession of a special high-tech camera, invented by his father for the U.S. Department of Defense. This camera records not visual images but mental images — the "neurochemical event of seeing." These electronically encoded images can then be transmitted to a video screen or can be transmitted directly into another person's mind. Sam Farber's mother, Edith, living in hiding with her husband in remote Australia, is blind, and Sam is traveling around the world recording the images of Edith's family and friends so that she will be able to see them again. In Australia, as Sam and Claire fly to his parents' hidden home and laboratory, the falling nuclear satellite is detonated, cutting off all communications with the outside world and erasing computer memories — so that everyone at the Farber enclave believes that the world has ended. What happens there after the end I will discuss shortly in more detail. Let us return now to Claire's roundabout journey until the end.

The barely premillennial, only slightly futuristic world of 1999 through which Claire pursues Sam is a world of fluid identity, multiple languages, shifting genres, proliferating plots, and complex interlocking networks of information and capital. Detective Winters, the German who has modeled himself on American film private eyes, loves the hard-boiled cliché about names and games: "Winters is the name; what's your game?" And the portion of the film before the end of the world is very much concerned with names and games, or, more precisely, with names and *language* games. Claire has black hair; then, unexpectedly, she becomes blonde. Sam Farber we first know as Trevor McPhee. Claire refers to Gene, the novelist, the lover she abandons, as a "broken ladder," a name whose Wittgensteinian associations we will consider when discussing the end of the film.

Beyond these shifts of naming with regard to the characters, the film itself—in its first half—leaps from genre to genre. It is a mystery or thriller, and a comedy, and science fiction, and romance, and melodrama, and at times an extended music video. The world until the end of the world is a profusion of narratives and identities, and this portion of the film seems a comic picaresque through the symbolic and fluid proliferation that characterizes much of the theorization of postmodernity. Claire negotiates these fluid conditions of postmodern genre and identity through yet another fluidity—through the interconnecting global networks of information and capital that detective Winters uses to track Sam. The flow of money within the network *is* information. As Claire tells Sam, "Every time you use your credit card, the computer lights up." And, of course, money is required to enter the information network, and to ride its waves across the world.

Claire enters the information network by means of capital that has escaped from the network: the money stolen by Raymond and Chico. The various plots of the film, in fact, begin when Claire exits the map-zone provided by her car's computer and shortly afterward collides with Raymond and Chico and their stolen money. Both Claire and the money, at this moment, are, in effect, *heterogeneous* elements, elements outside the networks that now, in combination, have access to deeper levels of information and mobility within the networks. Wenders stresses the idea of the fluidity of possession, and the idea of theft as a prominent form of such fluidity. Claire's journey is financed by stolen money. Sam steals from her. The used-car dealer in San Francisco robs them both. And before the action of the film begins, there was the original, as it were, Promethean theft by Dr. Farber of the high-tech camera (which he invented) from the Defense Department lab (which owned the patent).

The most important point, however, of this emphasis on theft is that the whole postmodern picaresque, the journey to the end of the world, through the proliferation of genres and plots and cities, through the networks of information and capital, is financed by money that has been violently removed from the network. Without this money, Claire would be unable to take this journey. And furthermore, the postmodern fluidity that her journey reveals is visible precisely because Claire moves through it: from city to city, genre to genre, network to network. Without *her* movement, all the postmodern fluidity would appear as complex forms of stasis and repetition. And she is able to move only because she has miraculously acquired a fortune in stolen money.

The persistent comedy of the film's first half, its picaresque, its play of genres, becomes, in this light, a miraculous luxury, a veil across a scene of postmodern catastrophe of the sort described by Baudrillard, Jameson, and cyberpunk novels. If we remove the slapstick from the chase scene in the hotel in Tokyo, we are left with the grim conditions of the "coffin hotels" in William Gibson's *Neuromancer.* Likewise, the decor of the scene in Lyon, where Claire first meets Sam, resembles *Blade Runner* in its futuristic squalor. These are the sites of stasis inhabited by those who have no access to the privileged movement of the capital-information networks. For Claire, then, and, as Wenders implies, for the world of 1999 as a whole, postmodern fluidity is a function of capital liquidity — and the possession, under normal conditions (without the miraculous concurrence of heterogeneous subjects), only of multinational corporations. The postmodern is a veil thrown over a set of traumatic social relations.

"The world is *not* OK." This is what Edith Farber says when her husband, Henry, tells her that the world has not been destroyed by the fallen nuclear satellite, that the world is still OK. "The world is *not* OK," she replies. Edith has been blind since she was eight years old, since before the Second World War, just before she and her family together with Henry's family fled from the Nazis. When she sees again, thanks to the camera that Henry invented and then stole from the U.S. government, what she sees is a revelation: that the

world is ruined, that the apocalypse, which Henry and the others believe has
been averted, has, in fact, taken place. The postmodern world that she sees,
transmitted directly to her brain by the high-tech camera, is not the comic world
of proliferating genres: her revelation is that the world — even without an all-
encompassing nuclear disaster — is already post-apocalyptic, surviving like a
ghost in the wake of two catastrophes. The first is the present catastrophe of
the traumatic social relations governed by the global networks of information
and capital. The second is still, even in 1999, the historical memory of the
Holocaust.

According to Edith, Claire's journey across the world of 1999 repeats Edith's
childhood escape from the Nazis in the late 1930s. The two journeys correspond geographically, but beyond this resemblance, both are flights from catastrophe — or, perhaps, are flights between catastrophes. For Wenders, the
flight from the Nazis, the effects of the trauma of the Second World War and
the Holocaust, are still active in our construction of and responses to the contemporary postmodern world. This world, as he unveils it, is marked by catastrophe, so damaged that it seems to long for annihilation. Claire replays Edith's
flight from catastrophe as an end-of-millennium pursuit of apocalypse.

Claire's journey through the postmodern world reveals its roots in trauma,
its post-apocalyptic character, as well as the failures of its modes of representation. Claire's journey also indicates that the direction of contemporary post-
apocalyptic impulses is toward a definitive end — a real end of the world, an
end of history, an end of intelligence, and perhaps, in summing up all of these,
an end of representation. The post-apocalyptic sense almost always entails the
desire for another, more complete apocalypse, just as apocalyptic imagining
invariably follows some social and conceptual breakdown. In particular, our
contemporary, late-twentieth-century apocalyptic sense is intensively marked
by the post-apocalyptic responses to the historical catastrophes of midcentury
and to social and technological changes that are so vast, so unrepresentable as
to take on an apocalyptic character of their own. In the late twentieth century,
the unimaginable, the unspeakable, has already happened, and continues to
happen. And, paradoxically, while unimaginable, it is at the same time quite
visible. The apocalypse is on television all the time, as a fait accompli, as
"news." Our contemporary sense of fin de siècle, *fin de millennium* is in its
most extreme forms that of a world, in Zizek's phrase, "between two deaths."

The world is dead but does not know it is dead. It awaits the Second Death—
a term Zizek derives from de Sade but which appears in the Book of Revelation—which will be the obliteration of the symbolic order in its entirety: the
end both of the world and of the conceptual possibility of a world.

The Second Death, writes Zizek, "implies a distinction between . . . natural
death, which is a part of the natural cycle of generation and corruption, and
absolute death—the destruction, the eradication of the cycle itself, which then
liberates nature from its own laws and opens the way for the creation of new
forms of life *ex nihilo*" (*Sublime Object,* 134). The place between the two deaths,
an area simultaneously following and preceding an apocalypse, is the realm
of the living dead, the "phenomenon that fully deserves to be called the 'fundamental fantasy of contemporary mass culture'" (*Looking Awry,* 22). This is
also the zone of the return of historical trauma as social-somatic symptom.
Zizek cites the Holocaust and the Gulag, the "two great traumatic events," as
"exemplary cases of the return of the dead in the twentieth century. The shadows of their victims will continue to chase us as 'living dead' until we give
them a decent burial, until we integrate the trauma of their death into our historical memory" (*Looking Awry,* 23). The fascination or enjoyment of the living dead (that is, our fascination with them *and* their imagined enjoyment)
Zizek sees as embodiments of the death drive, which is "exactly the opposite
of the symbolic order: . . . the radical annihilation of the symbolic texture through
which the so-called reality is constituted" (*Sublime Object,* 132).

There is a certain confusion in these passages, as there is often in Zizek,
between the emphasis on enjoyment of the symptom, on the repetition of trauma
that ends in obliteration, and on the possibility of a narrative working through
of the symptom. Zizek's point, as I take it, is that the urge toward an annihilat-
ing enjoyment of the trauma's return—the death drive—can, and must, be
countered by some form of narrative working through, but that this therapeutic narrative is never complete or pure, is always itself subject to ideology or
fetishization, and thus, to some degree, is itself also a symptom. This, as we
saw, is a point made also by LaCapra. He says that the "nonfetishistic narrative
that resists ideology would involve an active acknowledgement and to some
extent an acting out of trauma"—in Zizek's terms, the enjoyment of the symptom. But, LaCapra continues, this narrative "would also attempt to conjoin
trauma with the possibility of retrieval of desirable aspects of the past that might

be of some use in counteracting trauma's extreme effects and in rebuilding individual and social life" (199). Wenders's film moves between these poles of emphasis—between the urge to annihilate a symbolic order altogether in a complete and fascinated merger with trauma, and the desire to rehabilitate narrative in an effort at working through trauma. And Wenders, like Zizek and LaCapra, shows that these opposing emphases are never entirely separate.

What Wenders presents when the film shifts to Australia is the coincidence of the apparent end of the world and the end of representation. The false, or deferred, apocalypse of the falling nuclear satellite coincides with the success of the Farbers' experiments. Farber's camera does not record optical images. It records, rather, the neurochemical event of seeing, the pattern in the brain of the person seeing, or dreaming. This technology is apocalyptic in that it bypasses mediation or representation. In the case of seeing, the camera bypasses the optical, the visual image, and provides a link directly from mind to mind. It does not represent an image, nor is it a form of communication. The camera overcomes all questions of epistemology, point of view, description, and memory. The two subjects see, as it were, with one mind, in the universal, instantaneous language of neural impulses.

In the case of dreams, the camera's apocalyptic potential is even more striking. We generally take vision to be the model for an "immediate" experience, and Farber's camera reveals the separations that vision must negotiate, and the apocalyptic possibility of a more direct form of seeing. Dreaming, on the other hand, is the quintessentially divided experience. Dreams are manifestations of primary process that are only available through narrative reconstruction. We know our dreams only through our remembering of them. And, as psychoanalysis describes, what we remember of the dream and how we tell it are always functions of repressions, censorships, new configurations of desire, and the ideological imperatives of language. As Freud's technique in *The Interpretation of Dreams* makes clear, we are separated from the primary process of dreams by several removes. The dream is from the first a censored production. Then we remember the dream, retell our memory, and finally confront the dream as text to be interpreted. The dream, as a general category, is, in effect, a genre. And although, as Lacanian psychoanalysis insists, the processes of narrative and interpretation are themselves thoroughly invested with the same unconscious markings as the dreams themselves, it is still—at least in Wenders's view of the *fin de millennium* — the dream, in its absolute distance, that stands for the apocalyptic truth of our desire.

Farber's technology permits direct access to primary process, without the mediations of memory and narrative. It circumvents representation in favor of pure *presentation*.[13] The technology eliminates the divide between conscious and unconscious, and thus between the self and the other that the unconscious holds forth as an ungraspable object. The self is united with its desire, which has now been revealed in its true form. This technological revelation of the dream is the film's true apocalypse, marking the end of genre, the end of narrative, the end of history, the end of the "world" as a site of action and discourse. And in the late twentieth century, the terror of nuclear apocalypse, the fascination with the televised vistas of "ordinary" catastrophes, and the postmodern, post-apocalyptic sense that the unspeakable has already occurred and continues to occur are linked with desires to end discourse and representation altogether: to reach the discursive "end of the world," which would be a union with the primary, the merging of all separations. Thus, in giving the nuclear end of the world a temporal and geographical identity with the conceptual, discursive end of the world — and by placing both of these ends under the sign of high technology — Wenders has sketched a model of the late twentieth century's apocalyptic fears and desires.

As it turns out, of course, Henry Farber's dream project is suicidal. Claire and Sam become addicted to watching their dreams, and their direct access to primary process results in a narcissistic, or solipsistic, madness, an imprisonment in a never-ending loop of primary feedback. And we should note that the content of their dreams is not of plenitude, union, and wholeness but, rather, of loss, separation, and trauma. Claire sees the image of herself as a small girl and asks, "Why do you leave her alone?"; then she sees herself pursued by a shifting face and a pair of hands. Their addictive fascination is not with the completion but with a primary lack, the traumatic disruption, that Wenders (along with Lacan and Zizek) posits as the foundation of the symbolic order.

Gene's novel — which is a chronicle of the events of the film and, we finally learn, also the film's narrative frame — rescues Claire from her dreams, and Gene explicitly states his belief in "the healing power of words, of stories." Wenders links this narrative power with the aboriginal Australians' psychic healing procedures, as he shows Sam being cured by the two Mabantua Old Fellows. Wenders appears, then, to valorize the mediations of narrative, of some version of the psychoanalytic "talking cure," over the apocalyptic possibilities of immediacy. It is worth noting that after Edith dies, Henry observes the Mabantua rituals for death but neglects those for mourning—that is, he rejects the narrative working through of the traumatic event and remains locked into the immediacy of grief, just as he, Claire, and Sam are subsequently locked into their unnarrativized dreams, and, indeed, just as the Farber family never escapes from continually reenacting their Oedipal scene. Wenders, like Freud, opposes a narrative working through against neurotic or apocalyptically psychotic repetitions.

The film's final vision, however, is the transcendent image of Claire weightless in a space station. Claire proved to be the most skillful user of the Farbers' camera—Henry says of her, "She's a natural." Her technological facility gets her a job with the ecological protection organization "Greenspace," and at the end of the film she sits installed as a high-tech angel protecting the earth from pollution. The image of Claire in space is *Until the End of the World*'s final apocalyptic gesture at the end of the millennium, an orbiting end of history, redeeming humanity and technology. It is perhaps a peaceful version of Reagan's Star Wars.

On one hand, this image represents a recuperation of apocalypse as *genre*. Claire's escape from earth remains within the control of narrative form. Gene, the novelist, appears with Winters the detective and Chico the thief to sing Claire "Happy Birthday" on an earth-to-space station conference call. But on the other hand, the vision of Claire as angel reveals an end-of-millennium anxiety—or desire?—that genre and narrative are already dead. Claire's private name for Gene is "broken ladder," a name that recalls Wittgenstein's apocalyptic reference to the ladder at the end of the *Tractatus:* "My propositions are elucidatory in this way: he who understands me finally recognizes them as senseless, when he has climbed out through them, on them, over them. (He must so to speak throw away the ladder, after he has climbed up on it)" (189). Gene, then, as the broken ladder, becomes the emblem for the failure and the inadequacy of representation, even in its role as therapeutic narrative. And Wenders ends the film with the problematic assertion that Claire, the transparency, the technological "natural," the post-apocalyptic cipher who has gone through the neuro-video event of primary process, will be the presiding genius of the next millennium.

SUBJECTS AFTER THE END:
SURVIVORS, GHOSTS, ANGELS

At the end of *Until the End of the World,* Claire has been installed as a guardian angel for humanity, both wired into and transcending all technological mediations. Wenders is an artist fascinated by angels. *Wings of Desire,* the film he made before *Until the End of the World,* told the story of angels who moved invisibly through the world, feeling infinite sympathy for the omnipresent human suffering, able to supply small touches of relief but without power to heal either individuals or the world. These angels are thoroughly other than human. They sympathize but do not understand, have never experienced suffering; the world to them is an austerely beautiful movie in black and white, given formal unity by the lines of human sadness and pain. They were always angels — though they can, if they choose, enter the spectacle they drift through, leave eternity, become human, live, and die.

Claire is different. She is a person and achieved her quasi-angelic status through an experience of alterity. She passed through the "end of the world," the end of representation, the "second death." Though installed in the heavens, a benevolent force directing ecological traffic, Claire's authority is not that of an angel — it is that of a survivor.

Since the late 1970s, the fascination with and authority vested in the figure of the survivor has been one of the defining features of the American post-apocalyptic sensibility. We see this fascination in the revival of interest in the testimonies of Holocaust survivors, in the changing evaluations given the Vietnam veteran, in the explosive issues surrounding child abuse and incest, in the bizarre world of the talk show, in court TV, in "real life" police and rescue shows, in accounts of "near-death" experiences and alien abductions, and in the pervasive public appetite for first-person accounts of all kinds. In all these settings, paramount value is placed on the figure and the testimony of the one who has experienced, who has passed through and emerged from an event seen as both catastrophic and revelatory. What the survivor has survived is some trauma endowed with cultural significance — some apocalypse.

The survivor and his testimony are invested with several distinct but related forms of authority. It is first epistemological, for the survivor has seen,
and knows, what no one else could see and know. This authority of knowledge,
or "epistemic privilege," confers a kind of ethical authority, for the survivor's
knowledge is often knowledge of a radical transgression of moral boundaries.
And ethical authority easily blends into political or spiritual authority, de-
pending on the cultural role the particular trauma has come to occupy. For instance, Second World War veterans were able to translate the authority of their
firsthand experience into a political force powerful enough to cancel the *Enola
Gay* exhibit at the Smithsonian Institution. Survivors' testimony often acquires
an aesthetic authority as well. The fictional representations of the Holocaust
to be discussed in the next chapter have seemed compelled to invoke the authority of the witness and often to assume the testimony's generic form. Finally, the authority that underwrites these others is ontological. The survivor
was *there,* was present at the event, went through the event. The survivor was
present, and his testimony seems to make us present, and thereby gives to us,
the listeners and readers, something of his epistemological, ethical, and spiritual authority.[14] It seems, then, understandable that even the eminent historian
of the Holocaust Raul Hilberg should assert that "any survivor, no matter how
inarticulate, is superior to the greatest Holocaust historian who did not share
in the experience" (in Linenthal, 216).

What is more striking is that since the mid-1970s, we have attributed these
qualities of survival not only to those who experienced a historically significant instance of political violence but also to those who experienced private
and family violence and, ultimately, almost any event whatsoever. Thus, Greil
Marcus writes of the phenomenon of "surviving the 1960s":

> Through the magic of ordinary language, "survival" and its
> twin, "survivor," wrote the 1960s out of history as a mistake
> and translated the 1970s performance of any act of personal
> or professional stability (holding a job, remaining married,
> staying out of a mental hospital, or simply not dying) into
> heroism. First corrupted as a reference to those "survivors"
> of "the sixties" who were now engaged in "real life," the word
> contained an implacable equation: survival was real life. (46)

A further implication of Marcus's observation, as survivors emerged from every sphere of American culture from the 1970s to the present, is that this culture has been viewed implicitly as a scene of universal trauma, a landscape of symptoms and ruins even amid the Reaganist optimism of the 1980s.

This process of universalizing the survivor was accelerated and made more concrete in the talk-show culture of the 1980s and 1990s, a phenomenon I will discuss in more detail in chapter 5. Two particular sites of trauma — gender relations and the family — began manufacturing survivors who testified to their catastrophes. I do not mean to minimize the real traumatic impact of sexual violence and family dysfunction and abuse but to show how trauma and survival have become regarded as universal and inescapable, and the survivor stands both as witness and as symptom.[15]

In this generalized sense of trauma and survival, the survivors are everywhere, marked with the imprints of catastrophe but without clear knowledge of what exactly the catastrophe was. We all were there, are still there, and we insistently re-create in every conceivable cultural form the catastrophes that inhabit us. We are therefore familiar with, or at home with, catastrophe, even as catastrophe is denied, externalized, and enjoyed as an aesthetic event. The pervasiveness of disaster "out there" is both a threat and a comfort. It is far away — as urban crime or foreign massacres and famines — but it may also lurk within our own families, or in the national "heartland," as in the Oklahoma City bombing.[16] That catastrophe provided extraordinary revelations about American cultural traumas and what it might mean to live after them. It showed first that fearful terrorists could be the most ordinary and patriotic Americans — not Arabs, as was believed at first. Timothy McVeigh, with his blond buzz cut and his guns, seemed the midwestern white American to the point of stereotype. Furthermore, the event took place directly in the middle of the country, not at its geographical or social extremities. On the evening news, a young girl at a counseling session at her church expressed the common feeling, "I could understand if it happened in New York . . ." In those centers of crime, where everyone gets what they deserve simply for being there, such an event would be conceivable, but not in the nation's heartland. The bomb exposed the contradictions in the American sense of national community. By ripping open the Federal Building, that emblem of such widespread national resentment, and showing its insides, the bomb revealed not the monstrous totalitarian conspiracy of right-wing paranoias but one's neighbors, and their children. What then was the source of trauma? The government and its supposedly liberal policies that put the nation on the road to social turmoil by favoring "outsiders"? Or some presence in the nation's social and historical heart that the bomb unveiled?[17] The survivor, then, is a figure both strange and familiar: the emaciated concentration camp victim and the middle-class American who may or may not have been abused as a child; the down-and-out Vietnam vet panhandler; the "Mister Jones" character ridiculed by Bob Dylan, to whom "something is happening and you don't know what it is"; the individual abducted by aliens then returned to his home; racial minorities; women; everyone. Lou Reed sings of a Vietnam veteran holding "a sign that reads, 'Please help send this Vet home.' But he is home" ("Xmas in February," *New York*), and Reed's description of the survivor as one who both is and is not home resembles Freud's well-known account of the uncanny as *unheimlich.* For Freud, both etymological and psychological archaeologies reveal the *unheimlich* to be ultimately inseparable from the *heimlich.* It is "that class of the frightening which leads back to what is known of old and long familiar" ("Uncanny," 220). The uncanny is a return of the repressed (241) and is connected as well to the " 'compulsion' to repeat" that Freud had discussed earlier in *Beyond the Pleasure Principle* ("Uncanny," 238). Thus, the uncanny, the appearance of *doppelgängers* and ghosts, is a form of symptomatic return of trauma.

In this light, the survivor is an instance of the uncanny, a kind of ghost. The ghost, after all, is the ultimate survivor, for it has actually died and continues to exist. And the ghost is, in effect, a pure symptom. It returns to tell a story, usually of the crime that caused its death, and yet, more than *bearing* a message, the ghost *is* the message. Its very presence — its survival — is a sign pointing back toward a repressed or an unresolved traumatic event. As an urgent, intolerable reminder of trauma, the ghost is often a symptom not only of an individual crime but also of an unresolved social sickness that extends into the body politic of the present. For example, literature's most famous ghost, Hamlet's father, is "doomed for a certain term to walk the night" for three related purposes. He first must purge his own sins; next, he appears to his son in order to narrate the tale of his murder and urge its revenge; but finally, his appearance goes beyond just personal and familial trauma and is a general sign that "something is rotten in the state of Denmark."[18]

Zizek has called the return of the living dead "the fundamental fantasy of contemporary mass culture" (*Looking Awry*, 22). He points to the more horrific imaginative instances, in George Romero's *Living Dead* and the *Friday the Thirteenth* movies, and Stephen King's *Pet Sematary*, and he theorizes these returns in two ways. First, in *The Sublime Object of Ideology*, he refers to the "second death," as we discussed with regard to Wenders's *Until the End of the World*, as the wish to obliterate the symbolic order and achieve an apocalyptic immediacy. Later, in *Looking Awry*, Zizek describes the "second death" in quite different, perhaps more conventional, terms as a form of working through or giving proper burial to traumatic material. The dead return, Zizek writes,

> because they were not properly buried, i.e., because something went wrong with their obsequies. The return of the dead is a sign of a disturbance in the symbolic rite, in the process of symbolization. . . . The return of the living dead, then, materializes a certain symbolic debt persisting beyond physical expiration. (23)[19]

And in this book, Zizek refers to the "living dead" in more explicitly historical terms than he did in *Sublime Object:*

> The two great traumatic events of the holocaust and the gulag are, of course, exemplary cases of the return of the dead in the twentieth century. The shadows of their victims will continue to chase us as "living dead" until we integrate the trauma of their death into our historical memory. (23)

Zizek never brings these two positions into harmony. The symptomatic repetition of the open wound and the horror and fascination it inspires seem to call out for some absolute ending, the final shattering of the obscene simulacrum of social harmony, if we invoke Baudrillard's vision, or of the obvious and monstrous injustices that seem like structural supports to social order. The Oklahoma City bombing and the riots following the Rodney King verdict appear as symptomatic actings out of traumatic social wounds that cannot seem to be worked through. Yet, most of the time most of us would prefer to try to construct a narrative of working through, an attempt to "get along," even though we cannot agree what such a narrative would be. And so our culture remains haunted by multitudes of ghosts, who are ourselves, the living symptoms of historical catastrophes, and we cannot determine how to respond to our traumatic histories.

A number of contemporary fiction writers—among them, Toni Morrison, Thomas Pynchon, D. M. Thomas, Maxine Hong Kingston, Philip Roth, and J. G. Ballard—have used ghosts to explore how historical trauma is transmitted and how it might be addressed or worked through. I will discuss Thomas's *The White Hotel* in chapter 3 and Pynchon's *Vineland* and Morrison's *Beloved* in chapter 6. For now, let me mention one feature that all these works share: all insist that the ghosts who return from some historical trauma return in, or as, bodies. That is, they are not merely incorporeal misty "presences" that appear and disappear. These ghosts eat and drink, suffer pain and heal, and make love; they "live" in the present, both affect it and are affected by it. Being somatic, these ghosts are, properly, symptoms; wounded, they wound in turn. They haunt the present because they live in it, and through them the past lives too. And to exorcise them would be another act of murder. It is, rather, the present that must change in order for the past to heal.

My friend David Fletcher sent me a chapter of a novel he is writing, titled *Expect a Miracle.* In it, the protagonist, who can neither free himself from his past nor make sense of the present, is visited, unseen, by his two dead siblings: his sister, who died of cancer, and his brother, who was killed in Vietnam. I tell David that I am struck by his use of ghosts, the haunting of the present by past family and political traumas. And he tells me, "No, you misunderstand; they're not ghosts, they're angels. They don't show the permanence of the past, but that the past *can* be overcome." And I wonder, what exactly is this distinction?

If, as I have suggested, the ghost is a symptom of historical trauma, the sign of its inevitable return and compulsive repetition, then what is the angel? And why are angels openly invoked, believed in, relied upon by so many people, making appearances on magazine covers and in movies, with their own TV series and long shelves devoted to them in the New Age sections of most bookstores — while ghosts, unless depicted as zombielike horrors in scare flicks, are mainly invoked by literary authors like Morrison and Pynchon and ignored by the general public? I have argued that ghosts are everywhere — that O. J. is the ghost of Rodney King, who is the ghost of Emmett Till of the Scottsboro boys, each a new reenactment of the ever repeating American trauma of race. Why then, contrary to Zizek's judgment, are angels, not ghosts, the objects of popular fascination?[20]

Angels do not come back from the dead. My friend David's fictional revenants have been purified by death, have lost their traumatic affect. They return not to haunt their brother and engulf him in the unhealed wounds they took with them into death; they return rather to reassure him. He already suffers those wounds himself. He is already haunted, but by the tragedies that destroyed them, *not* by them. They return to make him understand that everything is all right, that he can let go of the past — simply let it go: all is healed, all is forgiven. The angel, unlike the ghost, is beyond history and allows the person who is touched to step outside it too.

This is the angel's primary appeal: it is a form of grace, an acknowledgment that the past is *too* much, that the wounds of the past can never be healed, can only be transcended. The angel in American culture battles against the ghost, the symptom, and appears to triumph — a triumph of apocalypse over trauma, that is, of the utterly new beginning over the repetition of a history. The angel never returns, it always arrives, for the first time, from a place where every instant is a birth that annihilates its predecessors. That is why the angel can *save.* Contemporary angel narratives often involve rescue. Someone is drowning and is pulled back into the boat; only later does he realize it was not his friend that pulled him back. Lost in the Andes, two teenagers follow footprints back to a village and only later realize that no human could have been there to make them. The angel pulls you from mortal danger, instantly, without your knowledge or understanding.[21]

Unlike Rainer Maria Rilke's angels in *The Duino Elegies,* today's American angels are not terrifying. They are not figures for absolute alterity, ecstatic and awful, radically inhuman, catastrophic threats to our attempts at equilibrium. American angels are entirely reassuring; they are our friends.[22] As a popular book on angels tells us, "their closer presence is deeply encouraging — just the helping hand for which many of us have been praying. The angels are here" (Daniel, *Ask Your Angels!* 5). Particularly the much cherished "guardian angels" are seen as our most intimate companions, guides, and protectors. According to most contemporary angel books, angels are all around us and want to help us; all we need to do is to learn to see and hear them.

The methods proposed for finding and using angels are, in effect, forms of therapy. Angels explicitly address psychic needs. The back cover of *Ask Your Angels!* tells us to "draw on the power of angels to reconnect with our lost inner selves and to achieve our goals, whether they be better relationships, healing an illness, or recovery from addiction." John Randolph Price's *Angel Energy* adds that angels can "free us from disease and death, loneliness and unfulfillment, lack and limitation" (back cover). Both books, and most of the others I looked at, outline some version of meditation, some technique for relaxing, clearing the mind, and allowing a new perspective to nudge its way in. The new, uncluttered, pacific vision is designated by the authors as "the angel." The angel seems to be the same as other objects of meditation: God, Christ, the Cabalist throne of God, Buddha, Shiva, breath, spirit, and so on. And if the reader is able to achieve the meditative state, no doubt it will help him deal with his personal problems and fears.

But angel therapies — and angels in nearly all their popular contemporary appearances — only address the problems of individuals. To placate a ghost requires a community's effort; the angel saves only one, even if countless others perish. The lone survivor of a plane crash might say, "*My* angel saved *me,*" and thereby alert us to the selfish and self-delusory nature of his salvation. The American angel's triumph over American ghosts not only cuts the cords of history but also severs the individual from all social connections. These severings from history and society are, of course, impossible, too difficult even for angels. And they meet resistance also from the people being "saved," for even amid the impending privatizations of the 1990s (e.g., the threats to transform social security to personal investment funds — perhaps we should call them "guardian angel funds"), there remain desires for historical and social connection.

An episode of the TV series *Touched by an Angel* (fall 1996) illustrates these conflicts between wishes for personal, angelic salvation and a still perceived need to come to terms with historical and social disasters. An investigative reporter for a local television station, intent on uncovering an instance of child abuse by foster care providers, persecutes a loving and lovable elderly couple. The reporter utterly and, seemingly, willfully misinterprets everything she sees, and edits her report in a way that destroys the old couple's lives and livelihood. But what seems at first to be journalistic hubris turns out to be a compulsive reenactment of a tragedy from the reporter's past. Ten years before, her husband died in an accident as a result of lax safety standards at a local circus — abuses that she had known about but had not energetically brought to light. Continually blaming herself for her husband's death, she sees every case she works on as a chance somehow to undo her terrible failure and bring back her husband.

The two angels, who have taken undercover jobs at the television station, intend to help the reporter free herself from her past (as well as to save the lives and spirits of the elderly couple she has injured). The angels try by rational discussion to convince the reporter that she has mistaken a present situation for one in the past, but their "talking cure" is unsuccessful. The reporter is only healed when the angels reveal themselves as angels and give her direct reassurance that everything — life, the world, the cosmos — ultimately is good, and she is not to blame for her husband's death. The angels then save the old couple from their suicide attempt. The reporter recants her story and apologizes on the air, the old couple are given back their children, and everyone is happy.

All the individuals are healed by the angels' intervention, but, just as crucially, a social wound has been healed as well. And yet, the healing of the social wound of child abuse turns out to be the revelation that there really was no wound. The perception of the social trauma was really a mistake based on a personal trauma and its aftermath. Furthermore, the institutional means for uncovering and correcting social injustices — that is, the role of the investigative journalist — is also revealed to be rooted in personal pathology. *Touched by an Angel* evinces the desire that social wounds be healed. Its anxieties concern fundamental rips in the social fabric. But the angels come to tell us that everything is all right and that if we will see them and accept their healing as individuals, then social problems will fade like bad dreams.

The popular conceptions of angels in the 1990s show another form of the proposition that "one apocalypse requires another." It is another contemporary instance of the sense that some overwhelming, inconceivable event has occurred, some definitive collapse of order and value; that the wrong cannot be set right, healed, or worked through; that therefore the only alternatives are to complete the destruction, surrender to the night of the living dead, or to obviate the past and surrender to the belief that only my angel can save me.

Part II: Aftermaths of the Holocaust

3. Representing the Holocaust after the End of Testimony

In the previous chapter, I discussed the apocalypse as historical trauma — a catastrophic and obliterating event that actually has occurred and that generates symptoms that define the world that follows. In this chapter and the next, I discuss responses to the Nazi genocide of European Jews. The Holocaust is the paradigmatic instance of an apocalypse in history, and a study of its aftermaths and symptoms should provide the clearest understanding of post-apocalyptic sensibility and representation. To call the Holocaust an apocalypse is, of course, to impose on it a certain interpretation — as an impassable breach in history (both Jewish history and Western history), an unredeemable obliteration, and in some sense a revelation of some truth about European culture. Many Jewish thinkers, for instance, Emil Fackenheim and David Roskies, reject this interpretation, arguing for a continuity in Jewish history in spite of the genocide. Roskies criticizes the contemporary "apocalyptic tendency" among Jews to "allow the Holocaust to become the crucible of their culture" and thus ignore "the vitality of traditions of Jewish response to catastrophe, never as great as in the last hundred years" (9). Roskies's outstanding study of the continuity of Jewish literatures of catastrophe from chronicles of medieval pogroms through Yiddish poetry after the Shoah is a welcome reminder that *the* apocalypse did not take place and that Jewish thought and writing survived the Nazis' efforts to destroy them. At the same time, Roskies's entire project is evidence of the Holocaust's apocalyptic reverberations, and his focus on religious Jewish writers who consciously drew on historical and liturgical models of response to catastrophe simply discounts the responses of writers who found these models inadequate.

A few examples will suffice to illustrate ways in which the Holocaust has been regarded as apocalyptic:

Theodor Adorno:

> Our metaphysical faculty is paralyzed because actual events have shattered the basis on which speculative thought could be reconciled with experience.... Absolute negativity is in plain sight and has ceased to surprise anyone.... Auschwitz demonstrated irrefutably that culture has failed. (*Negative Dialectics*, 362, 366)

Arthur Cohen:

> Thinking and the death camps are incommensurable.... The death camps are a reality which, by their very nature, obliterate thought and the human program of thinking.... [The Holocaust was a] *tremendum* of the abyss, a phenomenon without analogue, discontinuous from all that has been, a new beginning for the human race that knew not of what it was capable.... We must create a new language in which to speak of this in order to destroy the old language which, in its decrepitude and decline, made facile and easy the demonic descent. (*The Tremendum*, 1, 25)

Elie Wiesel:

> Now, one generation after the event, one can still say — or one can already say — that what is called the literature of the Holocaust does not exist, cannot exist. It is a contradiction in terms, as is the philosophy, the theology, the psychology of the Holocaust. Auschwitz negates all systems, opposes all doctrines.... The past belongs to the dead, and the survivor does not recognize himself in the words linking him to them. A novel about Treblinka is either not a novel or not about Treblinka; for Treblinka means death — absolute death — death of language and of the imagination. ("Art and Culture after the Holocaust," 405)

Jean-François Lyotard:

> Suppose that an earthquake destroys not only lives, buildings, and objects but also the instruments used to measure earth-

quakes directly and indirectly. The impossibility of quantita-
tively measuring it does not prohibit, but rather inspires in the
minds of the survivors the idea of a very great seismic force.
The scholar claims to know nothing about it, but the common
person has a complex feeling, the one aroused by the negative presentation of the indeterminate. (*The Differend*, 56)

Edith Wyschogrod:

> The world of concentration and slave labor camps as concrete
> actualities emerges from a systematic effort to deconstruct the
> life-world — the sphere of micropractices which make human
> existence possible — to dismantle it and not merely to com-
> press its range. Here a space is created in which is changed
> not merely this or that component of experience, but the scaf-
> folding of experience itself. . . . Present experience is not com-
> parable to life before the advent of the death event of which
> the death-world is a part. The life-world, such as it is, now and
> in the future, includes in collective experience and shared his-
> tory the death event of our times, which is the death-world
> of the slave labor and concentration camps and the other means
> of man-made mass death. Once the death-world has existed,
> it continues to exist, for eternity as it were; it becomes part of
> the sediment of an irrevocable past, without which contempo-
> rary experience is incomprehensible. (*Spirit in Ashes,* 16, 34)

These and many similar passages point to an event in history whose traumatic impact seems to annihilate, along with a physical population, all previous ways of thinking and that transforms the world that follows so as to make
it incommensurable with what went before. At the same time, the new, post-
apocalyptic world is a world of traces and symptoms pointing back toward the
event. The event cannot be grasped or recovered, yet cannot be escaped. This
condition, an emotional and political relation to the historical trauma, stands
impervious to the Holocaust's ample documentation and its representation by
historians. An event like the Shoah can both exist empirically and historically,
as fact and narrative, *and* still continue an existence as unhealed wound and
symptom that blocks all reductions or amplifications to any concept or story
or set of documents.

The question again arises here, Is this not a condition of *all* representation? Are there not always simultaneously a capacity and inadequacy of symbols to link with the physical world? This idea of Holocaust representation as post-apocalyptic seems to invoke again a more general notion of representation as lack, and recalls Judith Butler's criticisms of Slavoj Zizek's overly broad descriptions of trauma. I admit this is probably true. Representing an apocalypse in history is just like representation in general . . . only more so. But this difference in magnitude seems to me significant, and not only in projecting the representation of the Shoah as a limit case of representation in general.[1] If every event and object encounters a similar friction in its entry into symbolic form, and there is never complete congruence between thing and word, event and narrative, nevertheless, not every event leaves cultural damage in its wake; not every event requires a continuing interpretation of symptom-filled aftermaths.

This chapter and the next will examine two types of post-Holocaust representation. In this chapter, after a short autobiographical segment that illustrates one aspect of post-Holocaust symptomography, I will discuss three recent and controversial novels that take as an important theme their distance in time from the catastrophic events that form their moral and aesthetic centers. In particular, these novels problematize the genre of testimony, that form of expression that indicates the speaker's presence at and witnessing of an event. The testimony of a dead author, preserved as text, becomes a post-apocalyptic remainder that unavoidably enters and compels further texts — testimonies to events they cannot witness. In chapter 4, I discuss certain texts by Jacques Derrida in which the Holocaust is mentioned or, I will argue, pointedly left unmentioned. In his early work, the Shoah is an absent referent that generates Derrida's frequent use of figures of rupture, decentering, and apocalypse. In his later work, the Shoah, now frequently invoked, serves, unfortunately, to blur important political-historical distinctions and to lead back toward the generalized apocalyptic tone of the earlier writing.

THE HOLOCAUST ON MY SNEAKERS

When I was nine or ten or maybe eleven (sometime between 1963 and 1965), I drew swastikas on my sneakers. It is hard to remember exactly why. They were fun to draw, getting the angles just right and putting it skewed so that the top line came down diagonally, the shape looking like some swirling razor pinwheel. Of course, I knew what the symbol represented: the Nazis, Nazi Germany, our enemies in the Second World War. And there was something else, but it did not seem relevant; a lot of dead bodies, it had something to do with being a Jew. But it did not quite register. We did not talk about it in my family or at temple. I knew about being slaves in Egypt — that came up every Passover. But the Nazis had no connection with my identity as a Jew, an identity I resisted because of boring services and Hebrew classes and its general irrelevance to my life as an American boy.

The Nazis, as I discovered in the encyclopedia, in war movies, and in TV series like *Combat!*, were above all an incredible military machine. They had the best organization, the best equipment, and definitely the best uniforms. Their problem was that they were too perfect. They would have everything figured out except they would forget or disregard or not be aware of one small thing. Really, what they represented was a belief in the world's comprehensibility, and thus its perfectibility. And so, in their arrogance and officiousness, and even their sadism, I saw a kind of pathos. The poor fools: the world would never work the way they wanted and planned it to work. They were *always* defeated by the resourcefulness and spontaneity of the Americans.

When I watched *Combat!*, I always rooted for the Germans (as I always rooted for the villains in James Bond movies). They had so much going for them and yet they always lost. How could they keep coming back week after week? In terms of casualties the situation was ridiculous. The Germans were easily getting mowed down at a thirty- or fifty-to-one clip in those shows. And they always died unheroically. In spite of superior numbers, firepower, position, they would be caught in some American trap, be thrown into confusion, picked off, blown up, and just die without any kind of death scene. The Nazis were the underdogs, like the old Dallas Cowboys in their doomed championship battles with the Green Bay Packers. The Cowboys of the mid- to late 1960s had the best scouting system, the best training methods; they revolutionized pro football strategy with their shifting formations, and they had the World's Fastest Human, Bob Hayes, at split end. But the Packers had guts.

In some inarticulated sense, I drew the swastikas on my sneakers because of the Nazis' status as doomed, futile dreamers of a world that can be ordered, freed of chaos and contingency — and in which the American bullies, Vince Lombardi and Sergeant Saunders, will finally be beaten.

There was more to it though. Even then, I think, there was something sexual. I remember one *Combat!* episode fairly clearly. Sergeant Saunders's unit is behind enemy lines on some secret espionage or sabotage mission. They encounter a German patrol and there is a skirmish, with the typical result: the Germans get wiped out. It is imperative that they all die, because if any escape, then the isolated American group is in big trouble. But one does escape. He is running through the forest away from his dead comrades, and then he is hit, in the left buttock. He grabs it, looks back, then continues to limp away as fast as he can. Miraculously, the Americans are not able to kill him. The German reaches his base, the Americans are surrounded, and their eventual triumph is that much more impressive.

As usual, the Nazis were in total control; and then they were surprised, shocked out of their complacency by a power of which they had previously no idea. It was their confusion, their fumbling with their weapons, their utter loss of control that fascinated me. The camera, I remember, often showed the Germans' faces at that moment, in the same way that pornography likes to reveal the woman's face as she reaches orgasm. The "combat" of *Combat!* was, in a certain way, sexual, as feminized Germans week after week were orgiastically massacred. And if one survived, he did not so much "save his ass" as he was saved *by* his ass. I identified with these beings, and these images of sudden reversals of power relations and the blurring between violent death and "petite mort" have helped structure (though with enormous transformations) my sexual fantasy life ever since.

Thinking back on it now, the most amazing thing is that my parents never spoke to me about my sneakers. I know they believed in encouraging me to be independent, and I guess they thought that whatever aberration the sneakers represented would pass. Finally, it was a friend of my parents, Bob Rosenberg, who spoke to me one day when I wandered into his shoe store at a local shopping center. I do not remember exactly what he said, but it was something like, "Don't you know what that means? Don't you know what those people did?" I remember how angry he was, and how ashamed I felt. Because I did know. I did, in fact, understand that there was a historical reality independent of my fantasies, and that the symbol could not be appropriated from its primary historical context without an appalling moral injury.

But these events took place during the early 1960s, when the cultural memory of the Shoah was in what appears now as a period of latency. The broad facts of the Nazi genocide were known — the Eichmann trial was only a few years in the past; the first writings of Elie Wiesel, Primo Levi, and other survivors had been published — but it seemed, on the whole, that there was nothing that anyone could, or cared to, say. For Jews, the memory was still too painful, and too shameful. In my family, two of my grandmother's sisters had been in slave labor camps, and their husbands hid in the countryside. But I never heard their stories. I had vague knowledge that terrible things had happened to Barbara and Aranka and Shiku and Bernie — but what? They never spoke about it; no one asked them. And this, I think, was typical. For most American Jews, the most important thing was that we were here, that we were Americans. The young people would be bar and bat mitzvahed, but there was no effort to teach either the Jewish religion in any depth or the Yiddish culture that had been exterminated in Europe and now lived in America only in the minds of these old, silent relatives.

And for non-Jewish Americans, the Holocaust had little relevance. Only twenty years after the war, the important facts were still the facts of victory, peace, and prosperity, combining uneasily with new anxieties regarding the Cold War and changes in race relations. The salient fact about the camps was the *liberation* of the camps; for Americans, the discovery of that horror coincided with its ending.[2]

What my story of the sneakers shows, though, is how the Holocaust, even during a time when it was seldom represented or discussed, could enter a mind and motivate behavior. The swastikas on my sneakers were symptoms of problems within my own family: these symbols of absolute evil displayed so obviously on my shoes, yet never mentioned, must have corresponded to the blatant yet unmentioned signs of damage embodied by my sisters. I chose unconsciously the most shocking symbolic analogy because somehow I knew that the original, historical trauma transmitted in the swastika was still active in spite of the silence surrounding it. The Holocaust in American culture (like the significance of my sisters in my family) was omnipresent, though unmentioned. Furthermore, as it took various symptomatic forms, it combined with contemporary concerns: that is, the Shoah was rewritten in terms of family, political, or sexual dramas. In addition to dramatizing the silence surrounding my sisters, I also acted out an angry, erotic fantasy of victimization and sadistic slaughter. The actual, historical genocide of the Jews being absent, the fantasy bizarrely — and yet appropriately, given the cultural images available — placed the murderers in the victims' positions.

David Grossman tells a similar story in his novel *See Under: Love.* A young Israeli boy in the 1960s, the son of survivors, hears constant references to the "Nazi beast," but his parents, still overwhelmed by pain, will provide no coherent narratives or details about their experiences. The boy knows that some terrible injury was done to his parents but cannot conceive what it could have been or who did it. In search of the "Nazi beast," his only clue, he collects stray animals — dogs, cats, birds — imprisons them in an abandoned basement, and conducts cruel "experiments" on them. In effect, he re-creates a concentration camp and inflicts his parents' suffering onto the animals. The survivors' trauma, inarticulated, forced out of memory, reappears in the child's symptomatic re-creation of genocide. Similarly, in Art Spiegelman's *Maus,* the survivor father refers to his wartime experience only elliptically, but these indirect references and ellipses tell Artie, the child, both nothing and too much. Spiegelman encapsulates his childhood relations with his father in the short prologue to volume one of *Maus,* when, instead of comforting Artie when he is abandoned by his friends during a childish dispute, his father tells him, "Friends? Your friends? If you lock them together in a room with no food for a week . . . Then you could see what it is, friends!" (6).

This is the world of the Shoah's "second generation," whether or not its members are actually children of survivors. It is a condition of silence, hints, ellipses; of enormous, inarticulable wounds whose features must be imagined; and of the coming into consciousness in a damaged world that appears prosperous and normal. And, somehow, explaining these invisible wounds are the figures of the defeated (yet still somehow omnipotent) Nazis and the absent shapes of the shamed, unspeaking Jews (whether dead or living). What is most noteworthy during this period is that the cultural fascination was with Nazis, not with Jews. The crucial questions were not, what was lost, what survived, how was survival possible? They were, rather, what was a Nazi, what were the nature and consequences of this form of power?[3]

In the mid- to late 1970s, this focus began to change. Interest in representations of Nazism continued in many social segments. In the video rental industry, for instance, a trip to any Blockbuster outlet will show that there are still far more video documentaries available concerning Hitler and the Third Reich than there are about the genocide. Overall, however, in the United States, an enormous transition occurred. There was a "boom" in representations of the Holocaust, as novels, films, histories, TV miniseries, museums, monuments, and college courses about the Shoah proliferated. This proliferation I regard as the "third generation" of Holocaust representation.[4]

I use the term *generation* partly in a biological sense. The first generation of Holocaust representation was that produced by survivors and victims. It is the work—more specifically, the early postwar work, the testimonial memoirs and fiction—of Elie Wiesel, Primo Levi, Charlotte Delbo, Jean Amery, Tadeusz Borowski, and their contemporaries, as well as the diaries kept by those who did not survive. In both the memoirs and diaries, the primary motive is to tell the world of the massive and barely credible suffering and injustice that the writer and his community have experienced.

The second generation is the generation that directly encounters the survivors. In age, they may be contemporaries. Or, they may be children or younger relatives of survivors. The characteristic of the second generation of Holocaust representation is that it responds to the presence of survivors and their ongoing testimonies. William Styron's *Sophie's Choice* falls into this category as it chronicles the protagonist's encounter with the Auschwitz survivor, as does Grossman's *See Under: Love* (in its first section about the young boy, though not in the rest of the novel), and Spiegelman's *Maus,* whose focus is the relationship between the survivor father and his son.

In the third generation, the direct living contact with the survivors is lost, or begins to be lost. It is at this point, during the late 1970s, the 1980s, and into the present, that the need for the survivors' testimonies has become felt most acutely, precisely at the time when the first generation has begun to age and die. The third generation of Holocaust representation takes place after the end of the possibility of testimony and witnessing, and this impossibility gives rise to the myriad and problematic forms that these representations have taken. We should note that these "generational" distinctions are fluid. In volume two of *Maus,* for instance, we learn that the book was actually composed after the father's death. We see Artie listening to his father's voice on a tape recorder and realize, if we have not already, that the book largely chronicles the difficulty Artie has had in making contact with Vladek's experience and representing it. The book really only begins after the father is gone. And its seemingly inappropriate form — the comic book to represent the Shoah — propels *Maus* out of any simple relation with the testimony it retells. Spiegelman responds to the "survivor's tale" in a way that makes it his own; his relation to these events that he did not experience constitutes his *Bildung,* and his bildungsroman takes a form that the testimonial material he received from his father could never have anticipated. Response, in the third generation, merges into appropriation. Vladek is dead; the Holocaust narrative now belongs to Artie. Likewise, Sophie dies, and it is Stingo/Styron who tells the story that becomes his story — of how he becomes who he is through his contact with the survivor and the Jew. This tendency to appropriate the experience of the absent, or deceased, survivor has been perhaps the most controversial characteristic of recent Holocaust fiction. I will discuss it in more detail later in this chapter. Now I want to return to the continuing, or renewed, role of testimony as Holocaust representations of all kinds have proliferated.

TESTIMONY AND FICTION

The transition to the third generation of Holocaust representations began in the mid- to late 1970s. As I discussed in chapter 2, in the aftermath of the social crises of the 1960s and, in particular, the war in Vietnam, there was a new interest in "survival" and "the survivor." Contributing to this general interest and of particular importance to the proliferation of Holocaust fiction, film, theory, and memorials have been the aging and deaths of the generation of survivors whose testimonial accounts have provided so much of our knowledge and moral understanding of the Shoah. The enormous value we have placed on the testimonies of these witnesses has led to a crisis in Holocaust representation as these witnesses have disappeared. The proliferation of highly problematic novels and films about the Holocaust illustrates our contemporary condition in which the traumatic impact of the Shoah is still felt but the event it-self has been lost to personal memory and exists today only as a set of texts. Holocaust representations after the end of testimony try to figure ways in which one can bear witness to texts.

Testimony has always occupied a privileged place in Holocaust writing. Just after the war, the legal testimony of survivors helped to prosecute Nazi war criminals; indeed, the very fact of living voices emerging from the geno-cide indicated a resistance to, and a victory over, the murderers. Gradually, tes-timony took on an even deeper significance, seeming to provide the principal access to this most inaccessible event. In chapter 2, I discussed the forms of authority — epistemological, ethical, spiritual, ontological — attributed to the survivor, and these attributions have been especially powerful with regard to those who witnessed any part of the Shoah. Those who were there and saw and experienced what appears to us living now as the limit case of modern evil have the unique power to make us see, to bring us into what almost seems a direct contact with the event by means of the survivor's presence or his words.

But this seemingly direct transmission of the presence and experience of the witness/survivor is complicated by the question of what exactly the sur-vivor went through. What the survivor witnessed, or suffered — and the word *martyr* comes from the Greek word for witness — was the event of mass death. And yet, the survivor did not die. This fact may seem obvious and scarcely relevant — of course the survivor did not die; otherwise he or she would not be a survivor and would not be giving testimony. The observation that the sur-vivor did not die in the genocide might even seem insidious, akin to the Holo-caust denier Robert Faurisson's objection that no living person has seen the inside of a gas chamber. But since we are considering not the empirical ques-tion of whether the genocide took place but rather the question of the wit-ness's moral and spiritual authority, the issue of the survivor's status as living and not dead becomes important, for these forms of authority come from the proximity to the genocide. Survivors themselves have testified to this anxiety. As Levi insists in *The Drowned and the Saved,* "we, the survivors, are not the true witnesses ... those who saw the Gorgon have not returned to tell about it or have returned mute, but they are ... the complete witnesses, the ones whose deposition would have a general significance" (83–84).

The only true witnesses, then, are the dead, and survivors attempt to speak *for* the dead. More crucial to a rhetoric of testimony, however, survivors attempt to speak *as* the dead. The survivor as living-dead, as returned from collective death, is the crucial trope of Wiesel's testimonial novel *Night*. First, near the beginning of the novel, Moche the Beadle returns to Wiesel's village in order, as he says, "to tell you the story of my death" (17). And as the novel ends, Wiesel, now himself a survivor, repeats this verbal gesture. Looking into a mirror for the first time since his deportation, Wiesel writes, "A corpse gazed back at me. The look in his eyes, as they stared into mine, has never left me" (119). It is this "corpse," who has seen the "Gorgon," who composes the testimony published under Wiesel's name. Wiesel presents himself as indelibly marked by the genocide and transformed into a pure vessel of testimony, no longer possessing a life, only a voice. The authority of testimony rests on the supposition of a symbolic death, as the witness passes through the Holocaust and emerges as his own ghost. An important corollary of this supposition is that the testimony of the living-dead witness provides face-to-face, unmediated access to what we in the post-Auschwitz world figure as the most radical, inconceivable alterity.

Critical and theoretical considerations of Holocaust testimony have largely shared this sense of testimony's authority as direct transmission of the Shoah, as imprint of mass death and absolute alterity. Indeed, recent discussions of Holocaust testimony often resemble the theological accounts of testimony given by Emmanuel Lévinas. Lévinas, in *Otherwise Than Being,* seeks to redescribe subjectivity in terms of an absolute ethical obligation toward the "other." The self maintains an utter openness toward the other, does not impose its categories on (or "thematize," as Lévinas puts it) the other. Lévinas sums up this attitude of openness as the "here I am" with which Abraham replied to God before the binding of Isaac. This, Lévinas writes, is "a transparence without opaqueness, without heavy zones propitious for evasion. 'Here I am' as a witness of the Infinite, but a witness that does not thematize what it bears witness of and whose truth is not the truth of representation, is not evidence" (146). Testimony is not representation because it is more intimate; it is identity; without being able to say what the other is, one nevertheless becomes it. "It is to exhaust oneself in exposing oneself, to make signs by making oneself a sign, without resting in one's every figure as a sign" (143). Again, Lévinas exempts testimony from the normal travails of representation. The witness does not write or utter the linguistic forms of testimony; he *is* that testimony. His entire existence is consumed by the need to be and to bear witness.

One enters this condition as ethical hostage to alterity through a shock, a trauma. The hold exerted by the other is "a traumatic hold" (141), and the self responds to "a non-thematizable provocation and thus a non-vocation, a trauma" (12). The "call" of the other cannot be described as a call; it is more like a grip, a stranglehold, something that knocks the self down, then inhabits and animates it.

Lévinas is writing about testimony to divinity, or to the human other taken as divine. *Otherwise Than Being* contains little in the way of historical reference, and Lévinas rejects any sort of "theme" that would link "the memorable past to the present" (147). It seems strange, then, that so many theorists of Holocaust testimony adopt Lévinas's assumptions and terms. Lévinas argues for the possibility of the impossible — "the approach of the other . . . the substitution for the other . . . the expiation for the other" (147) — and he posits this impossible possibility as the most basic ethical obligation ("a pre-originary susceptibility, before all freedom and outside every present" [146]). But whose obligation is he describing, and an obligation to do what? He describes a universal condition, "outside of every present." But his book is addressed to post-Holocaust readers. It is dedicated "To the memory of those who were closest among the six million assassinated by the National Socialists, and of the millions on millions of all confessions and all nations, victims of the same hatred of the other man, the same anti-semitism." Lévinas describes a philosophical-theological method of speaking for/as the dead, specifically for the victims of the Nazi genocide. For that is who, implicitly, the "other" is in *Otherwise Than Being*. When, like Abraham, one responds as Lévinas would have it, "Here I am," it is to *those* others that one must respond and open oneself and prepare to sacrifice whatever is most precious.

Those who survived the camps cannot, as Levi noted, bear witness to the deaths of those who did not survive. In that sense, then, they bear witness to the non-thematizable other, insofar as they claim to speak for/as the dead. But, then, it seems to me, that no survivor claims to speak from the other side of that boundary. Survivors bear witness to the living and the dying of those who perished, and to their absence. They sometimes speak of themselves as "living dead." But living dead is not the same as dead. And if the survivors cannot and do not testify to the experience of death, then to what do we who were not there testify? How do we satisfy the ethical obligation that Lévinas describes?

We bear witness to two things. First, to historical facts and statistics. We know what happened, both broadly and in many particulars. Historians, like Raul Hilberg, Yehuda Bauer, and Lucy Dawidowicz, have provided this information. Reading of the meticulous magnitude of sadistic insanity shocks us — in much the way that Lévinas describes — and makes us think, perhaps, that these others must speak through us now: somehow; we do not know how. Second, we bear witness to the accounts of survivors and victims, and the experience of traumatic gripping is more or less the same, except that it focuses on individuals in particular situations rather than on the massive, less apprehensible scope of the entire event. In both cases, we bear witness to previous acts of witnessing of what would seem to be the limit cases of brutality and horror.

But using Lévinas's framework, as so many theorists of Holocaust testimony do, whether explicitly or implicitly, brings with it certain confusions. It first implies that secondary testimony (testifying to others' testimonies) has the same status as the original testimony (the witnessing of the event). All the theorists I will discuss would deny this assertion on the face of it, but the assumptions that all testimony is testimony to an absolute alterity and that all testimony contains a transparency that bypasses representation require that conclusion. Lévinas's model of testimony also leads subsequent theorists to use the same terms for divinity as they do for evil. There is precedent for this. *Awful* and *awe* come from the same root. As we will see, these same terms will also serve for descriptions of trauma and the aesthetic sublime. It may be that such conflations are inevitable, a consequence of catachresis: there are only so many ways to articulate what one cannot say. And they are a consequence too of actual and widespread attitudes. But the generally unreflective links in terminology between the historical trauma of the Shoah, notions of absolute evil or horror, God, and the sublime need to be unlinked and examined if we are to come to a better understanding of the status of testimony in the third generation after the Holocaust.[5]

For Terrence Des Pres, who published the first major study of the psychology of Holocaust survivors, Holocaust testimony transmits the experiences of those who "return from the grave . . . pass through Hell. . . . The concentration camps have done what art always does: they have brought us face to face with ar-chetypes . . . they have given visible embodiment to man's spiritual universe" (176, 177).

Later writers, while revising many of Des Pres's conclusions and rejecting his overtly religious emphasis, have continued to emphasize testimony's po-tential for providing face-to-face immediacy. Lawrence Langer criticizes writ-ten memoirs as inevitably retaining the mediating devices of literary style and genre, then praises oral testimony as direct because nonliterary and sponta-neous. For Langer, oral testimony's discontinuities and incoherences repre-sent "the quintessence of the experiences they record" (*Holocaust Testimonies,* xi). Listening to the oral testimony of a survivor, Langer writes, "We are pre-sent at the birth of a self made permanently provisional as a result of fragmen-tary excavations that never coalesce into a single, recognizable monument to the past" (*Holocaust Testimonies,* 161). Langer shows how even inadvertent shifts in verb tense bear witness to the survivor's living death. "Because I was sure I am dead now," he quotes one survivor (*Holocaust Testimonies,* 190). Testimony, then, for Langer, is a direct, only barely mediated transmission of the experience of self-shattering into an analogously shattered language.[6]

Robert Brinkley and Steven Youra use Charles Peirce's concept of the semi-otic index to show how the Shoah can be transmitted directly into testimonial language. The index in Peirce's semiology is a direct trace or imprint of an event: lightning is the index of particular atmospheric conditions; a bullet hole is the index of the bullet's passage. Using Claude Lanzmann's *Shoah* as an example, Brinkley and Youra argue that verbal testimony can take on a similar indexical status. Witnessing, they argue, "works not by representing but by re-ferring, not through interpretive substitution but by pointing out" (115) Thus, the testimony as index has a referential force "that exists prior to any interpre-tive response," and its meaning is produced not by interpretation but "by the event that produced it" (121). The testimony, in effect, is the event. The wit-nesses do not "merely recall the past but participate in it again," and the film's audience "is made contiguous to the events" (122). Brinkley and Youra claim that *Shoah*'s status as indexical testimony is made possible by Lanzmann's rigorous empiricism, his refusal to place interpretation over fact. I would argue, however, that like Wiesel's, Des Pres's, and Langer's, their view of testimony as direct transmission of the inconceivable event is ultimately more theological than empirical. It is fitting that they end their essay by linking the Peircean index to Lévinas's account of "epiphany" as the direct encounter with the "face" of the other, unmediated by one's own conceptual frame.

Dori Laub and Shoshana Felman criticize the sacralizing of the Holocaust and its witnesses, but they too reinstate a theological perspective within their psychoanalytic descriptions. In her chapter on Claude Lanzmann's *Shoah*, Felman argues that this film "is the story of the liberation of testimony through its desacralization; the story of the decanonization of the Holocaust for the sake of its previously impossible historicization." The specificity of Lanzmann's questions, she writes, "resists, above all, any possible canonization of the experience of the Holocaust" (219). At the same time, however, Felman uses Lévinasian terminology of the "other" and the "face." The paradoxical task of testimony is to speak

> *from inside the very language of the Other:* to speak from within the Other's tongue insofar precisely as the *tongue of the Other* is by definition the very tongue *we* do not speak, the tongue that, by its very nature and position, one by definition *does not understand.* To testify from inside Otherness is thus to bear witness from inside the living pathos of a tongue which nonetheless is bound to be heard as mere noise. (231, Felman's emphasis)

This position "inside Otherness" is, once again, as for Wiesel and Levi, the position of the dead:

> [S]pokesmen for the dead, living voices of returning witnesses that have seen their own death — and the death of their own people — face to face, address us in the film both from inside life and from beyond the grave and carry on, with the aloneness of the testifying voice, the mission of singing from within the burning. (280)

Summing up this essentially theological description of testimony, Felman refers to Lanzmann's description of *Shoah* as "an incarnation, a resurrection" (214).

James Young has provided the most thorough critique of the epistemological and theological bases of testimony. He presents a poststructuralist analysis of testimony that relies largely on Derrida's description of "dissemination," the idea that any written text, once produced, can never return to its origin and thus cannot retain the authority that such a connection with its origin would imply. Testimony, Young argues, cannot constitute an exception:

> Once he withdraws from his words, the writer has in effect also withdrawn from the word's evidentiary authority, the only link it ever had to its object in the world. The writer's absence thus becomes the absence of authority for the word itself, making it nothing more than a signifier that gestures back toward the writer and his experiences, but that is now only a gesture, a fugitive report. (*Writing and Rewriting the Holocaust,* 24)

Young rejects any sense of an indexical relation between event and testimony. The witness, Young writes, would like "to show somehow that [his] words are material fragments of experience" and that he is a "walking trace" of events, but this is an "impossible task" (23). The testimonial text always, as soon as it is uttered, disseminates and spreads its meaning into an ever widening area of interpretation.

Young's argument, however, takes a crucial turn away from this Derridean analysis, and Young tries from another angle to complete the "impossible task" of linking word to event. The link between the experience of the Shoah and the survivor's testimony is lost irretrievably, and testimony's empirical status as evidence can never absolutely be maintained; therefore, for Young (following Hayden White), the testimonial text (like any historical narrative) is more a construction than an accurate representation of events. Nevertheless, in an almost Cartesian move, Young argues that testimony does at least give evidence of "the writing act itself," evidence that a particular person in a particular situation produced these words. The witness exists not because she experienced certain events but because she bears witness. Thus, Young continues, "even if narrative cannot document events, or constitute perfect *fact*uality, it can document the *act*uality of writer and text" (37, Young's emphasis).

Young's emphasis on the act of testimony is a move toward reestablishing its ontological authority. Testimony is still important because the writer was *there,* even if "there" may now be defined as the scene of writing or testifying rather than the scene of genocide. Young has thereby reversed one step of the process of textual dissemination, bringing the text back to at least an intermediate origin. But by implication, he must take the next step as well. Although of some theoretical interest in resituating the "author" banished by poststructuralism, the witness's being "there" at the moment of composing testimony is only relevant to a discussion of the Holocaust if the witness was also "there" at the event itself. Young recognizes this need when he observes that the key difference between fictional and nonfictional representations of the Shoah "may not be between degrees of actual evidential authority, but between the ontological sources of this sense of authority" (61). Finally, it would seem that the second part of Young's argument reverses the first part: the witness's original presence at the scene of genocide gives authority to his testimony even in the witness's absence.[7]

Given this massive, almost supernatural or prophetic authority of Holocaust testimony, what can we do now that the generation of witnesses is aging and dying? The reliance on testimony and witnessing that are no longer possible has since the late 1970s brought on a crisis in representation of the Shoah. There has been an enormous proliferation of Holocaust representations since this time, and this proliferation, both in sheer number and in variety of forms, is evidence of the cultural anxiety in the face of the loss of the link to the event provided by the witness. Some of these representations have the clear intention of preserving the testimonial link: the various video testimony projects, and in a different way the attempts to preserve memory in public memorials and monuments (as Young describes in *The Texture of Memory*).

In fiction and film, however, the products have been far more problematic. Most of the better-known Holocaust novels and films since the late 1970s — works such as *Sophie's Choice, Portage to San Cristobal of A. H., The White Hotel, The Ghost Writer, Maus, Time's Arrow,* and *Europa, Europa* — have been highly controversial. Alvin Rosenfeld and Saul Friedlander, in particular, have condemned many of these works.[8] Their criticisms have largely centered on how such works blur the historical and ethical significance of the Shoah, and combine accounts of the Shoah with autobiographical, aesthetic, comic, and erotic intentions that are distracting and misleading. While sharing their concerns, I believe it is more useful to read these problematic works in relation to the anxiety over the growing impossibility of direct testimony.

These controversial contemporary novels and films attempt to represent not the events of the Shoah itself but our contemporary relation to those events. And our relation is not to the events but to the textual testimonies to the events. There is certainly no shortage of documentation of the Shoah — of historical records and of textual and video testimonies. Recent Holocaust representations, I would argue, are still bearing witness — and in these works, the primacy of testimony and witness is still acknowledged — but they are now bearing witness not to events but to texts. And this is a historical moment when a Derridean account of "dissemination" becomes relevant. Young described all written testimony in terms of dissemination, arguing for every text's immediate separation from its original significance. What has actually occurred in our culture, however, is that this strictly linguistic sense of dissemination did not take place. Survivors and their testimonies, as I have described, retained their privileged status. The process of dissemination only began with the disappearance of the witnesses, with the physical and biological separation of the texts from their authors. Only at this point were we left with nothing but text, with no necessary connection to event or to meaning. And at this point, in the late 1970s, the proliferation of forms of Holocaust representation began.

The more controversial fictional responses to the Shoah of the past twenty years have adopted two related strategies. The first is an appropriation of a Holocaust narrative to personal or political concerns. In *Sophie's Choice,* for instance, the autobiographical protagonist and narrator links his exploration of the Holocaust to his personal struggles with his heritage in the racist South; the Holocaust becomes part of Stingo's bildungsroman. George Steiner's *Portage to San Cristobal* shows this process of appropriation on a broader scale, as all the characters in that novel construct their own Hitlers and their own Shoah narratives according to their various personalities, histories, and political motives. The most distinctive, most controversial, and, to me, the most brilliant feature of *Portage* is that Steiner has not exempted himself, as author, from the process of appropriation. The Hitler who finally speaks at the end of the novel is a Steinerian Hitler who delivers a distorted version of Steiner's own interpretation of the Shoah.

It is not an adequate response simply to condemn these narratives for *using* the Holocaust and incorporating it into other stories. Certainly, the phenomenon is troubling. To ensure a properly contextualized historical understanding of the Shoah itself, we must sever its narratives from extraneous contemporary concerns. What do Styron's problems as a southern writer or Steiner's as a European philosopher have to do with our understanding the Nazi genocide? Nevertheless, for a better understanding of our own history and culture in the wake of the Shoah, these accounts of appropriation are crucial. They show, above all, that the Shoah is the principal event that our culture lives *after*, and they show specifically how the transmitted memories of the genocide inform our thoughts and actions forty and fifty years later — after all, or almost all, the victims, survivors, perpetrators, and bystanders are dead, and only their texts remain.

The second strategy seen in these controversial fictions is an emphasis on the fictional text's relation to a testimonial text. Even in many of the most bizarre and problematic recent fictions, the testimonial text remains central. Thus, Zuckerman's fantasies in Philip Roth's *The Ghost Writer* emanate from his reading of Anne Frank's diaries. The extraordinary combinations of aesthetics, psychoanalysis, and eroticism in *The White Hotel* are both generated from and negated by a testimonial text inserted in the novel. In Emily Prager's *Eve's Tattoo*, the protagonist inscribes on herself that most indexical of Holocaust texts, the concentration camp tattoo. Both David Grossman's *See Under: Love* and Cynthia Ozick's *The Messiah of Stockholm* use the figure of Bruno Schulz as a murdered witness survived only by his symptomatic, obliquely testimonial stories. These emphases and inclusions of the testimonial text in contemporary fiction after the end of testimony accurately portray a more general condition. The ontological, epistemological, moral, and even aesthetic authority of witnessing remains after the possibility of witnessing is gone. The urge, the need, to testify to the events of the Shoah remains, but these events now exist not even in personal memory but only through the encounter with texts, particularly the texts of testimony.

I would argue, then, that the bizarre and problematic post-testimonial Holocaust fictions we are discussing are themselves forms of testimony: they bear witness to the continuing impact of Holocaust testimony in the form that it now exists, as text.[9] These post-testimonial fictions show the opposing forces that tear writing away from its experiential and historical sources and simultaneously bring writing back to these sources.

Dissemination and appropriation are words for tendencies or forces that separate writing from events and authors, and that relocate writing in other contexts. They are tendencies toward proliferation, implying an infinite production of forms and perspectives. But these processes, as I have described, are only half the story. What then brings Holocaust writing consistently back to the testimonial text, which is to say, back to the closest possible approach to the event itself? Or, to put it differently, what motivates the repetition and return of the testimonial text into post-testimonial fiction?

The terms I have used — repetition and return — give the answer away: I am referring to trauma. I propose that the presence of the testimonial text in Holocaust representations that otherwise use the most varied, ingenious, and bizarre literary forms shows the insistent return of the traumatic historical presence of the Shoah. Recall that the witness, whether living or dead, speaks as a kind of ghost, as the one who passed through, or closest to, death, and who carries death on him like a symptomatic mark and relates his testimony in language we take, or wish, to be connected indexically to the experiences it describes. The ghost, as I observed in chapter 2, is as much a symptom of past wounds as it is a speaking emissary. Like the return of trauma, the ghost is propelled from one time into another; its presence is a sign of some traumatic disorder in the past, some crime that has not been witnessed or put right, and is therefore a sign also that the present still suffers from that traumatic disorder. Trauma is what returns, and it returns as symptom, which is itself a reenactment of trauma. The existence of the symptom, like the presence of the ghost, is a sign that the trauma is still active, still has power to wound and disrupt.

But how can the traumatic symptom appear as text? In the Lacanian view of trauma that informs much current thinking (at least among literary scholars), trauma is associated with the Real and is outside and resistant to any symbolic expression. Trauma's initial effect is to disrupt understanding, language, identity — to rip apart the symbolic order, to efface memory. The traumatic event is always reconstructed in retrospect; when it occurs, it is only a silent or screaming gap, wound, or void. Testimony, as Felman and Laub describe it, is at least in part an attempt to remember and tell the traumatic event and thereby work through it. But testimony is also partly the inability or refusal to work through; it is a remembering of the trauma that seeks to eternize its traumatic impact. Recall Wiesel's powerful repetitions in *Night* of phrases beginning with "Never shall I forget..." which conclude, "Never shall I forget these things, even if I am condemned to live as long as God Himself. Never" (43). This litany is no working through; it attempts to transmit trauma untransformed, in as close an approximation to the original wound as language can convey.

Symptoms, as Freud described them, are somatic, and Freud contrasted the somatic symptom, the unconscious acting out, against the verbal, and thera-peutic, remembering and working through. But language, obviously, can act out as well, can compulsively repeat, can haunt future uses of language. Lan-guage, like the body or the psyche, can be wounded and can wound. A text can be traumatized and can transmit trauma. A text can disrupt the symbolic order in which it appears, and can force readers to restructure that order in light of the traumatic disruption.[10]

But is a traumatic return as a text that bears witness to trauma the same as the firsthand experience? Obviously not. To bear traumatic witness to a testi-monial text is not the same as to have been there at the event. It is something, but it is not the same. It is all we have, and it is not enough. To read the testi-mony of the witness compels further testimony.[11] The contemporary writer is affected by the trauma transmitted through the testimonial text, but in his own place and manner. He is less traumatized than the original witness. It may be that literary ingenuity comes to substitute for the ghostly presence: literary in-genuity and the literal return of the ghostly text.

Such, at least, is the wish and the need of works like *The White Hotel, Maus*, and *The Messiah of Stockholm*. And here lies the tension of Holocaust writing after the end of testimony. The act of writing is separated from the ontological authority of witnessing. The text that bears witness to text tends toward infi-nite proliferation at the same time as it is shattered, transfixed, and reordered by the trauma transmitted by the testimonial text. This textual trauma, more-over, retains some of the original traumatic unreadability. It remains, in La-canian terms, linked to the Real; that is, it shatters the symbolic order, the forms of understanding, in which it appears. The traumatic real is incommen-surable with narrative and representation, and therefore the traumatic text may be confused with some other discourse of the incommensurable — as a form of the sublime or of the sacred. These three discourses of the incommensurable—the traumatic, the sublime, and the sacred—tend to merge. A traumatic discourse may be represented in terms of the sublime (as a shattering aesthetic experience) and then interpreted as sacred. I believe this process underlies much recent theorizing about Holocaust testimony, as well as recent Holocaust fiction.

EVE'S TATTOO: SHARING THE TRAUMATIC MARK

Eve's Tattoo, by Emily Prager, is the story of a young American woman who in 1989 has a concentration camp prisoner's identification number tattooed on her arm. The action is shocking, grotesque, and yet it seems, in extreme form, the quintessential third-generation gesture. It is an attempt somehow to reach into and through a Holocaust testimony and arrive at a complete identification with the Holocaust witness. The goal, of course, is impossible; what results from the immersion in testimony is a proliferation of narratives, each of which refracts and intensifies contemporary concerns through the medium of an ultimate, and unexperienced, catastrophe.

The quality that stands out about Eve before she gets the tattoo is that she is *unmarked,* either physically or morally. Strikingly young looking, she is an ingenue even at the age of forty. By profession she is a writer of satirical sketches of the superficiality of American life, and yet she seems herself to be an object for her satire. She is a feminist and a moralist who feels acutely her lack of moral bearing or marking. She is, in short, a late-twentieth-century, educated American who envies the moral and spiritual authority of the Holocaust witness—the authority of those who were *there* at the site she feels continues to define the moral contours of her culture. Marking herself with the tattoo, she feels, enables and authorizes her to identify with the Holocaust victim.

Eve's tattoo of the ID number begins a sequence of identifications. On assuming the victim's number (which she saw in a photograph of an anonymous woman prisoner at Auschwitz, or Birkenau), Eve gives the victim a name, "Eva." Eve, in effect, merges with Eva, or Eva completes Eve. Eve's relationship with "Eva" is, Prager tells us, "the strongest bond she had ever formed" (48). Furthermore, Prager gives us evidence that she, as author, strongly identifies with her character. Emily and Eve are the same age. Both write satirical columns in similar magazines. (In fact, both share the incongruous position of being feminists writing columns in a "men's magazine"; Prager writes for *Penthouse*). Finally, there is the obvious fact of the name "Eve": the first woman, the mother for whom all women are daughters, with implications both of Edenic innocence and loss of innocence. Prager has written a fiction illustrating a particular kind of identification with Holocaust victims; she hints that she herself shares in this identification, even as she analyzes and criticizes it; and she suggests an even broader identification, either with or involving all the "daughters of Eve." As we will see, the novel is divided in its concerns between its obsessive identifications with and narrative returns to the Shoah, and its links to the contemporary concerns of feminism (and also, to make the matter more complex, Catholicism). From being primarily the mark of a Jewish victim, Eve gradually transforms the tattoo into a kind of Catholic-feminist stigmata.

Eve's first explanation for getting the tattoo seems disingenuous. It is, she claims, akin to an MIA bracelet, simply a form of commemoration for the missing and forgotten. But a tattoo is clearly much more significant—in being more permanent, more intrinsic—than a bracelet, and Eve broadens her explanation by referring to the tattoo as a "testament." It represents her bearing witness to the unknown woman in the photograph who bore that number and, by extension, to all women who were murdered by the Nazis. The tattoo is the physical presence to which Eve bears witness. It is a somatic mark, mute and nonrepresentational. It is also a text, something written that reaches beyond itself. And yet as a sign, this mark can only have one meaning: the inscribed person was there, in the camp. No one else would possibly have this mark. This presumably absolute singularity of meaning—tattoo as presence—is what makes Eve's gesture so shocking and transgressive. Eve was *not* there; she has no right to appropriate this sign. She was not a witness and therefore cannot testify. Her bearing the tattoo is, as her boyfriend shouts at her, an "affront."

But Eve feels the need to testify, for reasons she cannot satisfactorily articulate. She can only be, as Geoffrey Hartman puts it, a bystander. She can do nothing but watch and feel, at several removes, these events whose representations so cry out for an intervention that did not come. She must, she feels, do something whose traumatic effect is in some way analogous to the representations she viewed with such helpless horror and sadness. As a sign that shows the desire and the impossibility of identifying with the victims, the tattoo is an appropriately absurd or shameful mark of this futile testimonial aspiration. Eve's tattoo aspires to be the form of testimony closest to the Peircean index as described by Brinkley and Youra: a direct unmediated mark that emerges out of a traumatic event and points toward it. In bearing the tattoo, Eve imagines Eva inside her, her alternate self who was there in Auschwitz. This incorporation of the victim goes far beyond any kind of memorializing. It is an attempt at ontological duplication: to slide back through the chute of the indexical, to ride the physical symptom back to the original site of trauma.

But in the present, what does the tattoo do? It disrupts. It demands attention, like an open wound. Conversations cannot continue in its presence. Identities fluctuate, or even fall apart. Current political events—the fall of communism, the decay of American cities, the spread of AIDS—appear as already reinterpreted through this mark, the index of "Eva," the revenant. The tattoo is a hideous insertion into contemporary social life, a grotesque destabilizing emergence like the Lacanian Real that leaks in symptomatic forms into a symbolic order at the points where ideological defenses are most vulnerable. Everyone knows what the crude numbers on the forearm mean, but what are they doing on the arm of a young blond woman in New York in 1989? They open a chasm.

Notions like the Peircean index and the Lacanian Real are inimical to narrative. They point outside of language and are encountered as marks, traces, cries, wounds, scars. But only the most traumatized, or iconoclastic, person can let these symptomatic insignia remain inarticulate. Thinkers as disparate as Kermode and Zizek agree that the unspeakable chasm, the void, the trauma, the apocalypse will be crossed by means of narrative. People *will* create closure for the wound. The index with its silent gesture (like Ozymandias's pillar or the ghost of Christmas future), the "grimace" of the real (in Zizek's phrase) *must*, through some combination of psychological, ideological, and structural urgency, be filled out or covered over with language.

The tattoo generates narratives. Eve explains the tattoo and eases people's shock by telling the story of the life and death of "Eva." In each story, though, to each different audience, "Eva" is a different woman, for Eve tailors her stories to fit her listeners' needs. To her New York upper-middle-class friends at a dinner party, Eva is an upper-middle-class German Jew. To a group in a veterinarian's waiting room, Eva is an animal lover who saves the pets of deported Jews. To her uncle who is dying of AIDS, Eva is a nurse who tries to help

Jews in a boxcar and mistakenly is trapped inside with them. To the nurses/nuns at a Catholic hospital, Eva is a Catholic nurse who resists the Nazi euthanasia program.

Eve's stories cover over the tattoo's traumatic, destabilizing impact with a more comfortable identification with the fictional, but plausible, Holocaust victims she describes. After her first narration, Eve exults that

> everyone had identified. For a few minutes the tattoo had jolted them from the lethe of middle-class life and they suddenly looked not sophisticated or cynical, not fed up or bored, not played-out or wired, just human, exposed, their expressions softened with an empathy they would never have acknowledged that they could feel. (29)

But Eve's stories are designed to produce empathy not so much for others but for people like themselves, and the jolt her listeners feel comes from the realization that disaster *could* happen to people like them. Their "lethe" is an amnesia concerning their own lives; their historical amnesias, I believe, remain largely untouched by Eve's stories.

As Eve's stories address her listeners' anxieties, they also establish a new, more intensified site for Eve's concerns as a feminist Catholic. The tattoo, typically the mark of the condemned Jew, becomes on Eve a feminist emblem. The tattoo, Eve says, "is about the fate of women" (12); it is "the emblem of a different perspective, the perspective of women, all kinds of women" (13). This is, on one hand, a valuable gesture. The writing and criticism of Holocaust testimony have, with some important exceptions, been dominated by male writers. The American perspective of the camp experience has been shaped more by Wiesel and Levi than by Charlotte Delbo or Ida Fink.[12] Eve's tattoo, then, is a testament to the women who perished in the Holocaust: women of all the European nationalities, religions, and ethnicities who fell under the Nazis' power; as Prager writes in the book's dedication (with her verb tense again emphasizing her concern in the present), "For the women who resist, and the women who don't."

With women as the central subjects and victims of the Shoah in this novel, what becomes of the Jews? I described earlier the novel's sequence of identifications. Eve uses the tattoo to try to achieve a total identification with the

Holocaust victim; Prager, the novelist, seems to strongly identify with her character (while still commenting on the futility of Eve's undertaking); Eve constructs stories that encourage an identification of her audience with fictional
Holocaust victims. This last form of identification, through narrative, seems
to vitiate the first—the identification through incorporation that Eve's tattoo
initially proposes. And yet, I believe, this most traumatic identification, which
resists narrative in favor of immersion, resurfaces in the very identification
that is not included in the sequence: an identification with the Jews.

Jews, in a disguised, indeed evasive, way, constitute the real marks of trauma
in *Eve's Tattoo*. They are not at all like tattoos. They are not fixed or inscribed.
In fact, in their ability to hide and transform themselves, Prager's Jews assume
some of the stereotypes of anti-Semitic propaganda. It may be that an anxiety
about anti-Semitism, only faintly articulated, lies near the center of this novel.
Eve, in several of her "Eva" narratives, tries to understand how women could
become Nazis, especially considering the open misogyny of much Nazi legislation and ideology. One factor she never considers is hatred of Jews. Late in
the novel, however, Eve is forced to confront her own, relatively mild anti-
Semitism, and from this hint, we may begin to interpret the exceedingly odd
ways in which Prager portrays Jews.

What is a Jew in *Eve's Tattoo*? A Jew is not a Jew; a Jew hides himself. A Jew
is a man, or at least (as we shall see) is not a woman. A Jew is a sexual promise,
or reward. And a Jew, unlike Eve, does not need stories to reach or cover over
a site of trauma. The Jew emerges out of that trauma and uses stories to remove
himself further from the trauma, and yet never can remove himself. The Jew
in *Eve's Tattoo* does not fit, either historically, narratively, or sexually. Both
attractive and horrible, the Jew seems to be a *third gender.* Finally, I believe, it
is her portrayal of the Jew, not of the tattoo, that destabilizes Prager's fiction.

The two principal Jewish characters—Charles (Eve's boyfriend) and Jacob
Schlaren (the Yiddish transvestite)—are both extremely unsettling. Charles is
a French Jew who has exiled himself from Judaism. His parents collaborated
with the Nazis, turning in their neighbors in exchange for their own lives.
Charles, therefore, feels himself unworthy of being a Jew and so converts to
Catholicism. Eve does not know he is Jewish until she receives the tattoo.
Then, his violent reaction gives him away. The tattoo shocks him into a reim-
mersion in his parents' betrayals. Charles requires no story to explain the tat-

too, for he already has a story that he wants to forget, that he hoped his conversion had erased. Charles, as secret Jew, refuses to participate in the link of identifications, refuses to assume any but a consciously false identity for himself. It is noteworthy, and troubling, that the greatest moral opprobrium in this Holocaust novel falls on Jews. There were, of course, a small number of outright Jewish collaborators, and much has been written about the morally troubling negotiations between Jewish ghetto leaders and the Nazi authorities. It is strange, though, to put Jewish collaboration at the center of Jewish identity in a novel that, at least on the surface, pushes Jewish identity to the margins.

Charles's evasiveness and his guilt point to some more fundamental anxiety in the novel regarding Jewish identity. Another of Charles's features that problematizes Jewishness is his sexuality. Prager portrays Charles as the ideal lover: he is strikingly handsome and beautifully dressed; he is gentle and passionate and sexually intoxicating. And these qualities, particularly his sexuality, Prager links to his Jewishness. When Eve does not know Charles is Jewish, she remarks to him that she had always believed that Jewish men made the best lovers—until she had met him. Charles, with a single comment, demurs and concurs, saying that her earlier opinion was certainly correct (50). When Eve gets her tattoo and Charles reveals his Jewishness, he immediately withdraws from her sexually. The traumatic sign, the tattoo, rather than discovering "Eva," reveals the Jew, or as Eve says, the "Jew in quotes." Thus, Eve's attempt to incorporate the Shoah reproduces and combines historical and contemporary traumas in ways she could not anticipate or control. The number on Eve's arm, in effect, *summons* the "Jew," and a whole array of traumatic associations: the "Jew" as evasive and hidden, as sexually exotic, as responsible for his own victimage.

Finally, in the novel's climactic scene, Eve encounters an actual Holocaust survivor, Jacob Schlaren, who both reinforces and problematizes the status of the survivor as moral/spiritual authority. When Eve meets him, she feels ashamed. In his presence, the tattoo becomes suddenly false and presumptuous because, as she says, "you experienced it" (145). Contact with the one who was *there* discredits her gesture toward presence, identification, and the traumatic indexical. But this authority, this presence, that Schlaren embodies is not at all straightforward. Like Charles's, Schlaren's identity and Jewishness are elusive, and are connected with an elusive sexuality. As a child, Schlaren's mother disguised him as a girl, so that they could better pass as gentiles. Having been captured and about to enter Auschwitz, the mother wisely had him return to being a boy. After the war, Jacob uses the skills he acquired in childhood and becomes a famous transvestite actor in the Yiddish theater.

Schlaren for Eve becomes a kind of Tiresius: he has been both man and woman, living and dead, gentile and Jew. Surely he can tell her everything she needs to know. But he cannot, or does not. He wants instead to learn her gestures ("You're so feminine. I wish to study you," 146). He reveals an anti-Christian prejudice that parallels Eve's vague anti-Semitism. At the same time, he accepts her; he does not require a story from her. Her need to expiate her "survivor" guilt in such a bizarre way does not require an explanation. His story and his transformations are stranger than any that Eve had imagined. Nevertheless, Schlaren refuses to answer Eve's final question.

> "When Christianity works, it's about love. What's Judaism about when it works?"
>
>   "I don't wish to tell you," he said, smiling. "That's another difference between us." (155)

This unanswered question reappears near the end of the book, and its implied answer helps explain Prager's vision of the tattoo, its function and ultimate futility. Almost immediately after her conversation with Schlaren, Eve is hit by a truck. Her arm with the tattoo is broken and ripped open. When the arm is repaired, the tattoo is gone, "in its stead, a neat row of suturing staples" (176). Thus, miraculously, the "symptom" has disappeared. The image of suturing implies an artificial, perhaps premature, closure of a wound that needs to be healed more gradually. And yet, the tattoo was always more an "acting out" than a "working through" of trauma. Eve's contact with the real survivor shattered her fantastic identification, and the truck completed physically the psychological exorcism of "Eva." There is, however, no satisfactory answer to Eve's predicament. She must bear witness, and cannot bear witness. To make the attempt will be inevitably to "act out" an impossible identification, and to be silent is merely to suture a still open wound that wounds her even though it is not hers.

But what is the answer to the question — the secret essence of Judaism (that unstable and destabilizing identity) evaded by the shifting Jewish Tiresius? In the contexts of *Eve's Tattoo,* what Judaism is "about" is memory. When Eve refers to the unanswered question, she and Charles, with whom she is happily reunited, are discussing a recent possession of Charles's: a Jewish armband from the Nazi period. A friend had brought it to show Charles, then forgotten it. And Charles, meaning either to return it or throw it away, instead retained it. Why, he asks Eve, did he keep it? And then Eve recalls the question that Schlaren refused to answer. The armband is a piece of "memorabilia," an aid to memory at a time when memory is fading. What Judaism is about, I believe Prager is implying, is memory. Memory is not symptom, or index, or incorporation, or any ideal of complete, immediate identification or presence. It is elusive, evasive, and can be only partially retained or transmitted, and Prager's figure of the "Jew" is elusive and destabilizing because of its connection to memory. Memory, in its elusiveness, undermines Eve's attempt to create a permanent inscription of trauma, and Eve's gesture of the tattoo is revealed as absurd and pathological, itself the symptom of a trauma becoming lost to memory and to the possibility of testimony. And yet, in the gesture's violent effrontery, its naive moral will, its misguided emphases, its troubling conflations of historical trauma with contemporary political concerns and with unresolved personal crises of sexuality, guilt, and identity, *Eve's Tattoo* presents an accurate picture of contemporary relations to the Shoah in the third generation.[13]

Trauma and History in *The White Hotel*

The story of *The White Hotel*'s plagiarism controversy has become familiar. In a small acknowledgment on the novel's copyright page, D. M. Thomas noted his use of material from Anatoli Kuznetzov's "documentary novel" *Babi Yar,* "particularly the testimony of Dina Pronicheva." Shortly after publication, a correspondent to the *Times Literary Supplement* (March 26, 1982) pointed out enormous similarities between the two texts—indeed, passages from *Babi Yar* that had been lifted nearly verbatim. The writer blamed Thomas both for plagiarism and for a deficient imagination. In the next week's *TLS* (April 2, 1982), Thomas explained his reasons for adhering so closely to Kuznetzov's text. There were more letters attacking and defending the novel in the weeks that followed. Gradually, the issue faded, and subsequent critical attention to *The White Hotel* has focused more on its representations of women and of psychoanalysis.

I want to return to this instance of repetition, not as it pertains to copyright infringements or to an author's lack of imagination but as another return of, and to, a testimonial text. Chapter 5, "The Sleeping Carriage," where the repetition occurs, is the traumatic, revelatory, apocalyptic center of the novel. It contains the moment of horrible unveiling when the protagonist, Lisa Erdman, is killed at Babi Yar and when, at the same moment, we finally understand the puzzles that the rest of the novel had posed, that is, the causes of Lisa's mysterious "neurotic" symptoms on account of which she had sought the help of Freud. Thomas wrote to the *TLS* that as his protagonist approaches her death, along with thousands of other Jews, "the only appropriate voice becomes that voice which is like a recording camera: the voice of one who was there" (383). To represent the catastrophe at the center of *The White Hotel,* Thomas requires the ontological authority of the testimonial text. And, I will argue, his insertion of this text is a gesture, necessarily textual, of trauma that tears apart the carefully constructed texture of the rest of the novel.

James Young, in an excellent discussion of this novel, points out that Kuznetzov's account is itself a borrowing and an elaboration of an earlier account (that is, the transcript of Pronicheva's testimony at a war crimes trial), and that Thomas's version is only the latest in a series of textual transmissions:

> Thomas is actually relying on Kuznetzov's own novelistic reconstruction of [Pronicheva's] account. Kuznetzov's declarations of his work's explicit factuality notwithstanding, Thomas is ultimately invoking a secondhand rendering of a third party's memory, which had been massively censored in the Russian, then rewritten (i.e., "uncensored") by Kuznetzov on his immigration to the West, and then translated. (*Writing and Rewriting the Holocaust,* 56)

Young's conclusion is that this is "hardly the stuff of 'authentic' or unmediated testimony" (56). But Young's poststructuralist critique of testimony, as I argued earlier, misses the more important issue of the insistent repetition itself, and the textual consistency that endures through all the mediations. Thomas reads Pronicheva's voice, however translated and mediated, and continues nearly intact the transmission of this voice that, like the voice of Wiesel, survived as its own ghost. The voice returns again and again, saying the same thing but in different texts and contexts, and readers now bear witness to it as the closest trace of the event to which it once bore witness. Presence is momentary, though one may never escape from it. And yet, some things persist. Massive suffering and injustice explode from representational frames sometimes as single voices. They are rewrapped, and again they explode. This has been known for a long time: Genesis 4:10: "What have you done? Your brother's blood cries out to me from the ground."

Thomas wants somehow to bear witness to the event, to the crime. And so his novel bears witness, through literal repetition, to Pronicheva's testimony. But this witnessing remains the horrified, helpless witnessing of the bystander. The literal repetition is the literary mark of trauma, the "kernel" that Zizek writes of that continually destabilizes its symbolic surroundings. Through this witnessing, nothing can be changed. Yet, at the same time, because of the textual, traumatic repetition of chapter 5, neither can anything remain the same. *The White Hotel* is a series of narrative or philosophic frames, or imagined possibilities (expressed partly as literary genres) of what life might be. "The Sleeping Carriage" with its testimony of the Babi Yar massacre shatters all of them.

The White Hotel is composed of a prologue and six chapters, each written from a different narrative position, in a different genre and style. The prologue is a series of letters exchanged between Freud and his fellow psychoanalysts Hanns Sachs and Sándor Ferenczi; the succeeding chapters consist of two erotic narratives (one in verse, the second an elaborated version in prose) attributed to Lisa Erdman; chapter 3 is a case history of Lisa written by Thomas's recreation of Freud; chapter 4 is a more conventionally realistic, or novelistic, narrative of Lisa's career and marriage after her psychoanalysis. Then comes the chapter, informed and structured by a survivor's testimony, depicting Lisa's murder at Babi Yar. The novel ends with a very puzzling chapter, which I will try to explain at the end of this discussion, in which Lisa and other characters somehow rematerialize in a kind of heaven that resembles Palestine.

The traumatic repetition of the testimonial text in chapter 5 negates, as I said, the chapters that precede it. But what exactly does the traumatic intrusion wipe out? In a broader sense, what do these chapters present that, in Thomas's view, the Shoah obliterates? The answer, I believe, is, all that is of value in Western culture. The prologue and first four chapters try to portray and embody what Thomas judges the best, most precious things that Europe has produced. These are, first, the astonishing technical and emotional achievements of Western art, from classical opera to the realist novel to modernism; second, "the beautiful myth," as Thomas puts it, of psychoanalysis, that is, psychoanalysis not as a form of scientific therapy but as a shared narrative endeavor toward exploring subjectivity and personal history; and finally, and perhaps underlying these others, the human subject itself. *The White Hotel* is, in its largest sense, a trial of Western culture. Its highest and most subtle achievements are placed beside the testimony of a victim of its greatest horror.

Thomas's view of these achievements, and of their relation to the Nazi genocide that he considers their negation, is complex. They are, first of all, marvelous. Thomas's skill in reproducing the varied genres and styles that make up this novel is evidence of his admiration for their histories. He makes us realize anew as we read what powerful instruments are the realist novel, the Freudian case history, the techniques of modernist fragmentation and surrealist combination, and what a wonderful, precious creation is human subjectivity, with its frail integrity, its overwhelming sensations and emotions, its efforts to know itself, to know others, to imagine a moral order for the world.

The achievements of the West are presented as instances of extraordinary artistic and erotic creativity, intellectual subtlety, and moral insight. Indeed, Thomas constructs these as sites of plenitude, harmony, and innocence: as Edenic, though in a peculiar sense. The psychoanalyst Sachs, in a letter to Freud in the prologue, says of Lisa's poem, "her phantasy strikes me as like Eden before the Fall — not that love and death did not happen there, but there was no *time* in which they could have a meaning" (10). This assessment is important and needs interpreting, for it applies not only to the erotic poem but to all the sections of the novel before the catastrophe of chapter 5.

"LIKE EDEN BEFORE THE FALL"

The aesthetic-moral achievements of the West are wonderful and innocent. Several very powerful critiques of *The White Hotel* have argued that the novel, either intentionally or inadvertently, implicates Western aesthetics, technology, subjectivity, and, in particular, psychoanalysis in the logic of fascism. Taking up the kind of arguments proposed by Adorno and Horkheimer in *The Dialec-*

tic of Enlightenment, Zygmunt Bauman in *Modernity and the Holocaust,* Lyotard in *The Differend,* Derrida in *Of Spirit* and "The Force of Law" (which I
will discuss in the following chapter), and, ultimately, Heidegger in his postwar writings, Mary Robertson, Linda Hutcheon, and Laura Tanner suggest, in
different ways, that *The White Hotel* demonstrates how fascism is a product of
Western modernity and how psychoanalysis shares with fascism a logic of
domination. Hutcheon writes of Lisa's murder at Babi Yar, "The voyeuristic
male soldiers reassert their patriarchal power over woman as object in perhaps a more immediately effective way than Freud's equally patriarchal inscription of her as subject. But the two are not unrelated" (176). And Robertson asserts that Babi Yar in the novel makes "all the previous psychoanalytic
sleuthing and artistic game playing seem at the least morally frivolous, if indeed they are not somehow responsible for history's nightmare" (462).

These writers are correct on two major points. First, they recognize the formally disruptive effect that chapter 5 has on the novel as a whole. As Tanner
observes, "the reader shares Lisa's perspective and listens to her voice until
that voice, like the reader's consciousness, is assaulted by an act so harsh that
it fragments the mediating forms of the novel as clearly as it destroys Lisa's
own body" (145). Second, it is absolutely right to see in *The White Hotel* a
critique of psychoanalysis. Psychoanalysis in this novel, after all, does not
work. Freud's study of Lisa's symptoms, for all its ingenuity and (I believe)
humaneness, is completely wrong. As Hutcheon, Robertson, Tanner, and other
critics correctly point out, Lisa's symptoms are not *hysterical,* they are *historical.* Even though, late in his career, Freud tried to envision cultural and historical applications of psychoanalysis (and Thomas presents the analysis of
Lisa as taking place at the time Freud was writing *Beyond the Pleasure Principle*), he never moved successfully or coherently beyond variations on individual etiology, and Thomas's portrayal reflects this limit in Freud's technique.

But this critique of Freud's historical blindness does not lead Thomas to the
conclusion that psychoanalysis is implicitly fascist. What is striking in Thomas's
presentation is that he creates a psychoanalysis relatively free of the patriarchal domination for which it has been justly criticized. This revised psychoanalysis is not so different in its fundamental assumptions and practices from
that which was developed by Freud. It still assumes that repressed sexual events
and/or fantasies resurface as somatic or behavioral symptoms, and that the talk-

ing cure and the transferential relation between patient and analyst will help recall and work through the traumatic memory. What Thomas changes is the nature of the transference, making it more a relation between equal researchers who share a goal. Thomas perfects psychoanalysis in its own terms, developing the potentials for cure laid out by Freud as far as they will go—up to the limits imposed by a blindness to history. And so he constructs psychoanalysis as an Eden.

Specifically, in the fictional case study, "Anna G.," Thomas rewrites the case of Dora (*Fragment of an Analysis of a Case of Hysteria*, 1905), an account of one of Freud's most notorious failures, as a success. In this early case study, Freud shows himself to be grossly insensitive and domineering in his treatment of a teenage girl whose father apparently is trying to give her to the husband of his mistress as some form of recompense. While Freud believes her claims that Herr K. made sexual advances to her—and Dora was particularly outraged that no one else would believe her—he nevertheless makes himself complicit with Herr K. and Dora's father in bullying Dora toward *accepting* Herr K.'s advances. Freud diagnoses Dora's hysterical symptoms not as responses to her impossible situation in relation to the two families but as signs of repressed sexual desire for Herr K. Freud observes in a postscript that he failed at "mastering the transference" (140), but the greater problem seems to be his failure at mastering his own countertransference. If Dora resists his suggestions as she resists her father and Herr K., it is because Freud sides with the other men in her life in regarding her as an object to be desired and controlled. Freud appears even to identify with Herr K. as he regards this young woman "in the first bloom of youth... of intelligent and engaging looks" (38), and is as frustrated by her resistance to his analysis as is Herr K. by her resistance to his desire.[14]

In the case of "Anna G." almost all these problems disappear, and we see psychoanalysis working at its best. Lisa, in contrast to Dora, is an adult. She has her own income, no father threatens her, and she is mature enough to reject those of Freud's speculations that seem least useful (e.g., her possible homosexual feelings toward Madame R.), while using the analysis to create a stronger and more self-conscious subjectivity. Thomas imagines an analytic situation based on mutual affection and respect. The transference between Lisa and Freud works, not perfectly, but as well as can reasonably be hoped, as desire motivates and inspires the analysis but does not distort it as was the case with Dora. When Lisa writes to Freud that "whatever understanding of myself I now possess is due to you alone" (193), she is exaggerating; nevertheless, by any standard, her experience in psychoanalysis helped her in everything — except the ability to foresee her death.

Furthermore, Freud does not try, as he does with Dora, to dictate Lisa's desire. Although, as Tanner points out, Lisa's sexual writings contain Freudian imagery (Tanner, 138), they still are focused on Lisa's own desire, pleasure, and anxiety. Thomas's Freud publishes his patient's writings together with his own (as the historical Freud did not), and so while he interprets Lisa's poem and prose narrative, these writings also speak for themselves, beyond Freud's analysis. And in an important and ironic gesture, while in "Dora" Freud inscribes male desire — Herr K.'s and his own — over Dora's sexuality, Lisa writes her poem of sexuality over a text of male desire, on the score of Mozart's *Don Giovanni*.

"NOT THAT LOVE AND DEATH DID NOT HAPPEN THERE"

The Edenic sites also contain catastrophes, but the catastrophes, the individual and mass deaths, somehow do not disrupt the fundamental harmony. These juxtapositions seem most bizarre in Lisa's writings in chapters 1 and 2, as she and her lover make love without being disturbed by the fires and avalanches taking place nearby. But the plenitude that all the chapters up until "The Sleeping Carriage" convey, both formally and thematically, accommodates awful events. Lisa's friend Vera dies in childbirth; Freud loses his daughter and grandson; and there is, of course, Lisa's mysterious illness, which subsides after her psychoanalysis but never disappears. Lisa, reading a newspaper story about a serial murderer who has been executed, reflects that *"somewhere* — at that very moment — someone was inflicting the worst possible horror on another human being" (179). And later she expresses her dismay more generally that good and evil in life seem so intertwined. "The idea of incest," she writes in a letter to Freud, "troubles me far more profoundly as a symbol than as a real event. Good and evil coupling to make a world" (192). These sites of plenitude, "white hotels," or Edens, that Thomas constructs, *contain* their horrors; that is, they are not punctured or negated by them. Thomas has Freud lament after the death of his daughter, "Were one given to mysticism, one might well ask what secret trauma in the mind of the Creator had been converted to the symptoms of pain everywhere around us. As I was not so given, there was nothing for it but 'Fatum and Ananke' " (110).

Freud accepts the symptoms because they do not shatter the homeostatic balance of the world itself. They are not genuinely traumatic. As he theorizes in *Beyond the Pleasure Principle,* biological death is not a trauma; in fact, it is quite the reverse, for it ends all agitation and restores the condition of inorganic stasis toward which all life instinctually moves. "Fate and Necessity" is the death drive. In this most leveling and universalizing sense, these Edens of Western culture contain death and catastrophe out of a mature acceptance of mortality. Biological organisms tend toward both reproduction and extinction. Therefore, in Lisa's "Gastein Journal," every disaster is portrayed as an act of God or nature, and so there is no breach of social harmony. The aristocratic English officer and the Russian revolutionary become allies in investigating uncanny events, and a Catholic priest and Protestant pastor "could agree at least that God's love was beyond analysis" (69). The one disruptive element is Vogel, the German lawyer, who expresses his pleasure that "there were a large number of Yids among the victims" of one of the disasters. The other characters, however, regard this statement as "unspeakably offensive" and reject Vogel's anti-Semitism, while at the same time remaining sympathetic to Vogel himself, who had suffered losses of his own (84). As Lisa writes, "The spirit of the white hotel was against selfishness" (86).

"THERE WAS NO *TIME* IN WHICH THEY COULD HAVE A MEANING"

The fatal limit of all the Edenic "white hotels" of the first four chapters is their blindness to history. They accommodate disaster through a naturalizing, static vision that corresponds to the late Freud's biological theory of the death drive, a theory that, as I discussed in chapter 2, turns away from a view of trauma that acknowledges the importance of social and historical events. The Fall, then, is into the trauma of history, literally, into the ravine at Babi Yar. Then, all at once, the cultural achievements Thomas re-creates in the prologue and first four chapters—psychoanalysis, the subject, the realist and modernist narratives—find their meaning in an absolute loss of meaning.

Through the traumatic repetition of the testimony from Babi Yar, Thomas uses the Shoah as a touchstone for Western modernity, revealing in it an innocence that is nevertheless culpable, culpable precisely because of its innocence. The West's cultural achievements are technically marvelous and, as Thomas presents them, deeply humane. But they do not see the abyss that opens in front of them because they do not recognize the historical possibilities of their own destructive obsessions. The "landscape of hysteria" Thomas refers to in the author's note (vii) is shown in this novel — and specifically through the traumatic eruption of testimony in the text — to be not an individual but a social and historical terrain.

The White Hotel is neither an outright condemnation nor an exculpation of Western culture. It is an examination of the effects of a historical trauma, its ability to enter texts long after its occurrence and to destabilize and reconfigure contemporary historical perspectives. We can *only* see the achievements of the West, Thomas insists, through the perspective of the Shoah. *The White Hotel* confirms Walter Benjamin's sweeping insight about the interconnection of civilization and barbarism — but more obliquely than Benjamin intended. Even Benjamin's prophetic *Theses on the Philosophy of History,* written on the eve of war, could not anticipate the Holocaust. The *Theses* lament the defeat of socialism, and their view of barbarism comes from a critique of class oppression, the "anonymous toil" that forms the material basis for cultural masterpieces. And the undifferentiated wreckage witnessed by the angel of history has been assimilated into the narrative of progress.

But the Shoah has *not* been assimilated (except in the Reagan-Fukuyama "end of history" scenarios, as I will discuss in chapter 5). Benjamin's *Theses* can be read as yet another "white hotel," filled with images of harmony and horror, and failing to see the absolute horror just over the ridge. But how could it see? It saw and did not see. Its author, like the inventor of psychoanalysis, realized his personal danger just at the last moment but, unlike Freud, did not succeed in escaping. And where would the messianic chips resurface — not after a failed revolution, but after the near annihilation of an entire people? This is Thomas's question as well after the shattering textual witnessing of chapter 5. After such destruction and loss, where does memory reconstitute itself, where does the possibility of any form of redemption appear?

Thomas provides an exceedingly puzzling answer in *The White Hotel*'s final chapter, "The Camp." In this chapter, Lisa arrives by train in a kind of heaven, a dry, rough country that resembles Palestine. All the other dead are there too: her stepson, her mother and father, her friend Vera, her Jewish neighbors from Kiev, Sigmund Freud. These dead seem very much alive. Their existence is corporeal; they eat, drink, sleep, menstruate, have sex; indeed, they still suffer from the injuries they suffered from in life, or died from. Lisa has her pains in the pelvis and breast. Her mother's face is still scarred from her death in the fire. Freud suffers from cancer of the jaw.

These physical ghosts appear in one sense to be the historical symptoms I discussed in the previous chapter: traumas of the past physically (and socially and politically) inhabiting the present. As readers we know this, especially as we see on the novel's final page that "heaven" is rapidly filling up as more and more trainloads of "immigrants" arrive, and the makeshift tents that will house them "stretch away to the horizon on every side" (273). But these victims — and they are not, remember, survivors — do not haunt the world, for Thomas has segregated them in an enormous, imaginary refugee facility, the imaginary Palestine that Jews were often promised before they were murdered. In this heaven, the dead do not remember their death, do not know they are dead. And, slowly, their wounds are healing.

The world of "The Camp" strongly resembles, in its generosity, guiltless sexuality, and odd juxtapositions, the world of Lisa's erotic poem and narrative. At a camp dance, for instance, "there was a happy communal spirit" as "married couples did not stick selfishly together but made sure the many widows and widowers were brought into the fun" (261). Afterward, as Lisa strolls with the British lieutenant, we see juxtaposed, in a manner entirely characteristic of "The Gastein Journal," the image of the "beautiful bed of lilies of the valley" with the observation that the lieutenant "did not mind that she was bleeding" (261). When Lisa is reunited with her mother, they drink milk from each other's breasts (268), an event that, again, repeats incidents from Lisa's writings.

The camp is a place of reconciliation, though these processes are slow and never complete. Lisa's reunion with her mother is awkward at first but turns out to be successful; her relations with her father will take longer to repair. In

a larger social context, even the serial killer, Kurten, is slowly being rehabili-
tated. And as these social and familial reconciliations take place, physical healing occurs as well. Lisa's symptoms diminish, and Freud slowly recovers from
his cancer. The spirit of the camp, like that of the "white hotel" in Lisa's journal, is "against selfishness" (86).

But what, we might ask, is going on here? What kind of perverse comedy
has Thomas perpetrated? These people do not recover, they do not reconcile,
they do not heal. They do not live. They died in *the camps*. Why are we provided with this sick consolation — including the pointed and pointless irony
of the chapter's title — where no consolation is possible or perhaps even per-
missible? After Babi Yar, after the genocide, and after the shattering of the
white hotels of Western culture, why now has Thomas added yet another one?
For "The Camp" is another white hotel, another site of plenitude in which subjectivity and morality and *personal* histories are explored, private wounds examined and treated, while history and its far greater traumas are not recognized.

This chapter of consolation, coming after the shattering transmission of the
witness's testimony and the awful death of the novel's sympathetic protagonist, shows both the futility and inevitability of these consoling fictions, these
white hotels. "The Camp" is painful to read because it combines such a vision
of insight, love, and potential social harmony with the now certain knowledge
that these qualities and all who possessed them are lost. Since "The Camp" is
so consciously a consoling fantasy, it both consoles and does not. Seeing the
oblivious dead trying to remake their lives after the end is a reminder of their
deaths. The fantasies of healing cause pain because we know that the dead
will not heal, however much we wish them to. For on this point Thomas recognizes our desire: we want Lisa to live. It is unacceptable that she die at Babi
Yar. And so, Thomas lets her live, although we know she died and that there is
no heaven.

"The Camp" shows that Thomas cannot imagine any link between the wonderful knowledge contained in white hotels and the historical understanding
that might protect them. Lisa laments at the end, "Why is it like this? We were
made to be happy and to enjoy life. What's happened?" (274), and still cannot
see, after the event, what she could not see before it. "The Camp" shows with
a horrible, ironic, sentimental perversity how impossible it is to register the

traumatic, apocalyptic impact of the Holocaust. Even the ghosts, in Thomas's view, have forgotten to haunt us. They, like the living, try to resume their private lives even as the camp expands beyond the horizon.

FORGERIES AND FALSE MESSIAHS

Cynthia Ozick's *The Messiah of Stockholm* shows more clearly than any other recent novel the problematic status of Holocaust testimony at a time when it can exist only as text, when testimony becomes the creation of texts in response to texts. And these new texts, these testimonies to testimonies, inevitably spin into countless directions, as the traumatic impact of the Holocaust merges with the private concerns of individuals, their own obsessions, and their artistic ambitions. Ozick's protagonist, a Swedish orphan named Lars Andemening, invents an identity as the son of a Holocaust victim, the Polish-Jewish writer Bruno Schulz, and thus invests himself with the moral authority of the dead and with the genius of a seemingly prophetic writer. Lars's greatest obsession is with Schulz's *missing* text, titled *The Messiah,* the novel his adopted "father" was working on when he was shot. If he could find this text, his identification — both moral and aesthetic — with his "father" would be complete. The missing text, precisely because of its absence, becomes more than a text: it is the experience itself, forever unavailable and yet continually appropriated. It is the book, I believe, that every post-testimonial Holocaust fiction in some way attempts to be. It is always titled *The Messiah,* and if found — as it is, later in Ozick's novel — it is always a forgery.

Lars is obsessed with origins. Heidi Eklund, the bookseller who is the only person to whom Lars confides his secret identity as Schulz's "son," calls him "a priest of the original" (99). Lars learns to read Schulz in the original Polish, as if in this way he will make direct contact with what his "father" saw and knew. And although this transmission from the past is, and can only be, textual, Lars imagines a contact that would be direct and immediate. In his sleep, he sees through Schulz's "murdered eye," joining Schulz as witness. Lars wakes from this merging as from death. Ozick writes, "He had no dreams. Afterward his lids clicked open like a marionette's and he *saw*" (8). What Lars sees through Schulz's eye, however, is not the Shoah, not the murder of the

Polish-Jewish writer by the SS, but rather the literary aftershocks of the Holocaust. On waking, he writes inspired book reviews of novels by Eastern European writers following in Schulz's difficult legacy.

Lars is caught in a contradiction. He desires a direct transmission from the Holocaust—direct in terms of both biology and experience. And yet, even in his nocturnal experience of the eye, the transmission is textual. Lars's vision is a vision conveyed through his intimate, obsessive understanding of Schulz's fiction. Schulz's stories, of course, are not exactly testimony. And yet, like Kafka's fiction, in retrospect we interpret these stories as a prophetic witnessing to a world about to disintegrate into horror. Schulz, the author as Holocaust victim, becomes for Lars the ultimate source of authority. Schulz's text becomes sacred. Immersion in that text (and Ozick describes Lars's experience as he writes his visionary reviews as "a crisis of inundation," [8]) is a direct contact with the inconceivable alterity of the Shoah. Or rather, it is and it is not. For what Lars's experience with Schulz's text and Schulz's imagined eye inspires is a desire for the real and ultimate text that can transmit the reality of the Holocaust as no existing text can do. Lars wishes for a text that somehow would *be* the experience of witnessing, that would truly, directly, physically testify.

That text, the missing text, would give all the answers. If found, that text would be the messiah. Ozick's narrator and her characters continually use religious terms when referring to the purported manuscript of Schulz's lost novel. "There on the table lay the scattered Messiah . . . resurrected; redeemed" (104). When Adela (a young woman who astonishes Lars by claiming to be his sister, Schulz's daughter, and, as proof, actually produces what she says is the lost manuscript) shakes the bag that contains the supposed manuscript, they hear "the sound of fifty wings" (71). Heidi uses the language of origin, essence, and witnessing, calling the manuscript "the original. The thing itself. I saw it with my own eyes" (53).

Ozick, in her essays and interviews, has always been critical of all forms of idolatry, and especially the idolatry of literature. (And Lars is said to have "thrown himself on the altar of literature," 7.) This manuscript of a messiah, so overloaded with redemptive imagery, seems clearly to be false, a forgery. Indeed, the plot that Ozick invents for the manuscript is about the destruction of idols. Her "Messiah" can be read as a cautionary tale against false messiahs and fetishized texts, especially those that claim to provide some communion with victims of the Shoah. As Ozick said in a 1993 interview, "If a [Holocaust] novel must be written, let it be written by a true witness" (391). There is no murdered eye we have access to, no messianic text to be discovered.[15]

The Messiah of Stockholm as a whole, however, suggests more complicated relations between text and event. In Lars's relationship with Heidi, there is a recurring dispute. While Lars is obsessed with Schulz's textual legacy (and with his own status as Schulz's only true son and authentic reader), Heidi rejects what she calls his "ceremonial mystification" (33) and always turns their conversations back to the "catastrophe of fact" (32). As opposed to Lars's quotation from Schulz that "reality is thin as paper," Heidi counters, "What's real is real" (37), and "Death's reliable" (42). Heidi claims not to like or understand Schulz's writing at all, describing it as full of "animism, sacrifice, mortification, repugnance! Everything abnormal, everything wild" (33). This last adjective, *wild,* however, sets off resonances in the novel, for Schulz's murder was part of a larger massacre labeled by the Gestapo the "wild action" (38).

Heidi wants to move away from text toward fact, but her language connects that fatal, wild action to the incomprehensible, wild text. Somehow, the wildness of violence and of immediacy — which resists textualization — enters the text, and this linkage based on the word *wild* becomes the central connection in the novel. Ozick emphasizes the link, or thread, between *fact* and *text:* "Whatever they touched on, Heidi rattled her links — everything belonged to the shooting. Everything was connected to the shooting." But a paragraph later, Lars complains, "You get me off the track. You make me lose the thread." Heidi replies, "The thread? The thread? What's this thread? What's this track?" And Lars answers, "My father's books. His sentences" (39). For Heidi, the significant connection is to Schulz's murder; for Lars, it is to Schulz's texts. For Ozick's novel, it is both. The text contains and transmits the wildness of the event. And, I will argue, the psychoanalytic term for the "wildness" is trauma.

This wildness, this trauma, however, is misapprehended by Lars, who feels it most acutely, as something sacred: "the *wilderness* of God" that he receives through his imagined father's eye (69, my emphasis). Ozick shows here, and later in her brilliant imagining of Schulz's missing *Messiah,* how the sublime, the divine, and the traumatic — those three versions of the inconceivable, the unrepresentable, and the shattering — can be conflated. The trauma of witnessing, now separate from the witness, receives an aesthetic representation that tries to recuperate and transmit its power, and the sublime representation is interpreted finally in theological, salvational terms.

Ozick reinforces the link between literary language and the "catastrophe of fact" — the fundamental traumatic link between a "wild action" and wild language — in her description of the "messianic" manuscript. It consists, she writes, of

> intricately hedged byways of a language so incised, so *bleeding* — a touch could set off a hundred slicing blades — that it could catch a traveller anywhere along the way with this knife or that prong. Lars did not resist or hide; he let his flesh rip. Nothing detained him, nothing slowed him down. The terrible speed of his hunger, chewing through hook and blade, tongue and voice, of the true *Messiah*! (105, Ozick's emphasis)

The manuscript is a symptom — a physical manifestation of past injury — and is also itself a continuing trauma. It is both wounded and wounding, not only representing catastrophe but also transmitting it.

Within the manuscript, the figure of the messiah itself has qualities both of a somatic organism and a text. "It was as if a fundamental internal member had set out to live on its own in the great world — a spleen, say, or a pancreas, or a bowel, or a brain" (109). And yet, "more than anything else, the Messiah . . . resembled a book." It is, as Lars reads it, "the authentic Book, the holy original, however degraded and humiliated at present." The messiah's body is inscribed with "peculiar tattoos" that resemble cuneiform, and that compose an "unreadable text," "an unknown alphabet" (110). Lars had previously noted that the mixed-up pages of the manuscript could be read in any order, that they resembled "the mountain ranges growing out of the chasm of the world," and that in them he experienced "everything voluminously overlapping, everything simultaneous and multiform" (106). This would seem to be a description of an aesthetic sublime. Later, again like an experience of trauma, the manuscript wipes out the memory of itself, and yet Lars feels certain that the vision of the manuscript must have originated in the same murdered eye that inspired his literary texts (115).

The Messiah as Ozick presents it through Lars's perceptions is the ultimate and original text of the lost witness: a text that is more than a text, immediate and unreadable, presenting and transmitting its wounds as if from body to body; it is sublime, an aesthetic object with the overwhelming power of a force of nature; and it is sacred and redemptive — it is the Messiah. In showing Lars's response to the would-be messianic text of Schulz, Ozick shows our own contemporary response to the loss of the generation of witnesses. As the "originals" disappear, we feel increasingly the need to create the text — the missing text — that will place us at the Shoah, that will be the "eye" of the Holocaust and allow us also to witness with the witnesses. And thereby, Ozick suggests, we conflate catastrophe with redemption, with aesthetics as the means that allows this conflation.

Is then the text a forgery and a false messiah? Obviously it is the latter. The text itself makes that clear. The creaking, messianic, organic, textual contraption, having destroyed the idols of the town of Drohobycz (where Schulz lived, and the locale of all his stories), collapses and gives birth to a bird that completes the destruction. The text contains no redemption, only destruction. The messiah is by definition a false messiah. There is no other kind. And certainly no messiah has come from out of the Shoah.

But the question of the status of the manuscript as forgery is trickier. Lars quickly concludes that Dr. Eklund (Heidi's mysterious husband, possibly Adela's real father) composed the manuscript. But Dr. Eklund and his colleagues, Heidi and Adela, though admitted con artists, maintain to the end that the manuscript is authentic. "*I* could make that? I, I?" Dr. Eklund protests:

> A seraph made it! Idiocy —*I* could make that? Instinct's the maker! Transfiguration, is this your belief? Conspiracy gives birth to a masterwork? You had your look, you saw! You think what's born sublime can be connived at? How? How, without that dead man's genius? What is there to empower such an impersonation?...Do you think there is a magical eye that drops from heaven to inspire? Barbarian, where is there such an eye? (127–28)

Lars himself, by this time, acknowledges that there is no eye, no direct transmission from the witness, from the dead to the living. And who *could* produce such a brilliant imitation of Schulz's fiction? The stolid Dr. Eklund would not seem a likely candidate. But Dr. Eklund's argument immediately breaks down, for we as readers know that the manuscript text *is* a forgery, an imitation. Ozick, not Schulz, composed this astonishing apocalyptic fiction that seems, like Schulz's work, to speak prophetically from the borders of the Holocaust. So, even if there is no magical eye, there is nevertheless some form of transmission from the dead to the living.

And there is more to Dr. Eklund than we or Lars initially see. After Dr. Eklund's outburst at Lars, denying his authorship of the manuscript, Ozick suddenly redescribes Dr. Eklund so as to locate him entirely in the shifting site of trauma that moves between event and text, between the witness to event and the witness to text. First, she refers to his eyes: "His naked eyes spilled catastrophe." Then Ozick brings back the word that had previously stood at the boundary between event and text: *wild.* Dr. Eklund's "big scraped face with its awful nostril-craters rambled on, a worn old landscape lost to any habitation. Wild, wild" (128).

The forger and his text seem to share the same terms and features that Ozick had identified with originality and authenticity. The forger's face, like the action in which Schulz was killed, and like Schulz's language, is "wild." His eyes, like the fantastic murdered eye, overflow with catastrophe. Neither Lars nor Dr. Eklund shares the ontological privilege of witnessing the Shoah, yet both produce texts that transmit its trauma. And they do so by testifying to the text of the absent witness. Both Lars's fantasies and Dr. Eklund's forgery paradoxically bear true witness to Schulz's traumatic text. The "wildness," that is, the incomprehensible traumatic nature of Schulz's death and his language, provokes a wild, traumatic response in Schulz's readers. The bleeding testimonial text continues to wound, and the texts it inspires bear the wound as they bear witness to it.

Ozick's novel is a warning against such forgeries, against a sanctification of the Holocaust and the urge to identify with Holocaust victims and survivors, against making the Holocaust the sole locus of meaning and the generator of lost "messiahs." But at the same time, *The Messiah of Stockholm,* like other problematic recent Holocaust fiction, shows that the continuing traumatic impact of the Holocaust on contemporary culture continues to demand responses. These responses will be partly symptoms — evidence of the scars and still open wounds the Shoah has left on Western culture — and partly the working through of these symptoms. They will be forgeries, false testimonies to events their authors never experienced: and they will be the most real and necessary responses we can make.

In his essay "False Documents" (1977), E. L. Doctorow proposed that history and fiction were indistinguishable, that there was a larger, more pervasive category—narrative—in which both fiction and history could be subsumed. Defending his own historical fictions, like *Ragtime,* which combine historical reference, literary allusion, and imaginative elaborations on both, Doctorow wrote, "There is no history except as it is composed. . . . [H]istory is a kind of fiction in which we live and hope to survive, and fiction is a kind of speculative history, perhaps a superhistory, by which the available data for the composition is seen to be greater and more various in its sources than the historian supposes. . . . I am thus led to the proposition that there is no fiction or nonfiction as we commonly understand the distinction: there is only narrative" (24, 25, 26).

Doctorow's position here exemplifies important directions in poststructuralist theory of this time. From the late 1960s through the 1970s, thinkers like Jean-François Lyotard, Jacques Derrida, Michel Foucault, Gilles Deleuze, Hayden White, and Linda Hutcheon critiqued the hierarchies and distinctions among forms of discourse. More important than any distinctions between discourses were overriding commonalities described in terms of ideology or episteme or writing or metaphysics or narrative. Although insistently anti-foundational, all these thinkers nevertheless identified shared conditions of possibility that shape phenomena and the ways we perceive and represent them.

But Doctorow's essay contained a further note, an unassimilable, heterogeneous fly-in-the-ointment that threatened to reinstall the distinctions he had otherwise exploded: "I am well aware that some facts, for instance the Nazi extermination of the Jews, are so indisputably monstrous as to seem to stand alone" (24). The general leveling of distinctions among discourses *can* have exceptions. Certain historical events force up again the epistemological and ethical barriers between fiction and history, and for Doctorow the prime instance of such an event is the Holocaust. Doctorow's wavering is momentary. He returns immediately to his "apology for narrative."[1] But this stutter, this drawing back from a poststructuralist description of narrative, brought on by the proximity of memory of the Shoah, is also characteristic of poststructuralist theory from the late 1970s to the present. Not only for Doctorow, the creator of "metafictions," but for thinkers like Lyotard, Derrida, and White, the Holocaust has become a touchstone or limit case for poststructuralist theory.

While immediately after the Second World War, the Shoah became a central theme in the work of Theodor Adorno and Hannah Arendt, their example was not taken up in the years that followed. In critical theory, literary criticism, sociology, and even in academic history — as in the culture at large — thinking about the Holocaust experienced a moratorium, a kind of latency period. With the exceptions of the work of Jewish theologians like Emil Fackenheim and Richard Rubenstein and the idiosyncratic literary and cultural theorist George Steiner, the Shoah was not a major issue in American or French intellectual life of the 1960s.[2]

Given this general and understandable avoidance of such a recent and overwhelming horror, it is not surprising that poststructuralist theory in the late 1960s and early 1970s (both in France and the United States) also neglected the Holocaust. What becomes striking in retrospect, however, is that this neglect of the central, most traumatic violence of the century coincided with a rhetoric that was intensively apocalyptic, filled with invocations of rupture, decentering, fragmentation, irretrievably lost identity, the shattering of origins and ends. How could a discourse so attuned to rhetorics of obliteration entirely overlook that act of overwhelming obliteration in its still recent past? And why, a decade or so later, did the Holocaust come so suddenly to occupy explicitly a discourse that previously had seemed to describe its violence while not mentioning its name?[3]

The reasons are both general to European and North American culture and specific to literary theory. As I observed earlier, memory of the Holocaust was largely suppressed, disregarded, or transformed during the 1950s and 1960s. In both Europe and America, the principal cultural concerns lay elsewhere, and it is not surprising that philosophers and literary theorists did not address the Shoah directly. The Shoah became an important theoretical topic at exactly the same time as it returned to general public consciousness. There were also, however, specific disciplinary factors behind poststructuralism's move toward Holocaust theory. First, the publication in 1987 of Victor Farias's *Heidegger and Nazism* placed this scandal of modern philosophy back into a critical spotlight. Thinkers for whom Heidegger had long been a crucial point of reference — Derrida, Lyotard, Lacoue-Labarth — for the first time began to address his Nazism and its implications for his, and their, philosophy. In the United States, the revelation, also in 1987, of Paul de Man's collaborationist journalism provided the greatest single impetus for poststructuralism's move toward theorizing the Holocaust. In addition, in the late 1980s, poststructuralist theory was criticized for ignoring history, and the trend in literary theory was toward New Historicism.[4] Finally, the threat to historiography posed by the Holocaust "revisionists" like Robert Faurisson and Arthur Butz instigated some of White's and Lyotard's writings.

For a number of reasons, then, the Nazi genocide of Jews became a central topic of concern and urged poststructuralist thinkers from the late 1970s to the present to reconsider (though not necessarily to change radically) positions they had taken in the 1960s and early 1970s.[5] In the rest of this chapter, I will examine perhaps the most difficult and elusive case, that of Derrida. In Derrida's early work, certain key terms — *trace, differance,* and so on — serve to illustrate general characteristics of language, especially how language manufactures illusions of presence, voice, and immediacy that are the basis of the hierarchical, metaphysical divisions that govern Western thought and society. Derrida also uses these terms to show the inherent instability of these hierarchies, and he presents language as both generating and preserving but also destabilizing the bases of metaphysical thought. In Derrida's later work, *differance* and *trace* are replaced by other key terms, like *cinders* and *shibboleth,* that refer, sometimes obliquely, sometimes directly, to the Shoah. But, as I will argue, the later terms function in Derrida's texts in the same way as did the earlier ones. The cinder *is* the trace. If this is so, the Shoah retrospectively reappears in the earlier work as an absent, or repressed, historical referent. At the same time, Derrida's use of the cinder as trace shows his continual ambivalence toward historical reference and his continuing urge to conflate distinctions that seem to him merely the dual components of metaphysical hierarchies. Through this discussion of Derrida, I will suggest that the catastrophes, apocalypses, and ruptures that dominated poststructuralist thinking in the 1960s and early 1970s are disguised figures for the Holocaust, and that poststructuralism's eventual turn toward the Shoah allows us to rethink poststructuralism as a post-apocalyptic genre that has begun to remember its catastrophe.

I am not, however, arguing or suggesting in any way that Derrida's thinking or poststructuralism in general is openly or covertly or unconsciously in sympathy with Nazism. Derrida, like many other thinkers, is struggling with the aftermaths, the "traces," of the Shoah, and many of his suggestions for figuring their transmission — for example, as "shibboleth" or "cinder" — are useful and evocative. Elaine Marks, one of the few writers to consider directly (though briefly) Derrida's references to the Holocaust, is right in remarking that a work like *Cinders* stresses that "in 1987, what remains are words, like traces, with their secrets, their etymologies, their histories" (45). In this regard, Derrida's project is much like those of the fiction writers I discussed in the previous chapter. I disagree, however, with Marks's assertion that Derrida does not tend to "negate or minimize the event" (45). It may be that this process is inevitable. The shibboleth, in putting the wound into writing, makes it universally available, no longer singular, and thereby deprives it of the power to wound further. But, as I argued earlier, it seems to me that the text still maintains more traumatic force than Derrida allows. Derrida presents powerful descriptions of how an event like the Holocaust can be past and present at the same time. In doing so, however, and particularly as he discusses Heidegger, Derrida blurs important political and historical distinctions that need to remain clear.

The apocalyptic tone of Derrida's work of the 1960s and early 1970s is unmistakable. "Structure, Sign, and Play," the essay Derrida delivered at the International Colloquium on Critical Languages and the Sciences of Man at Johns Hopkins University in 1966 (and the moment we commonly take to be the "inauguration" of deconstruction), begins,

> Perhaps something has occurred in the history of the concept of structure that could be called an "event," if this loaded word did not entail a meaning which it is precisely the func-

tion of structural — or structuralist — thought to reduce or to suspect. Let us speak of an "event," nevertheless, and let us use quotation marks to serve as a precaution. What would this event be then? Its exterior form would be that of a *rupture* and a redoubling. (278, Derrida's emphasis)

And the essay ends with a nearly Yeatsian image of the impending birth of a monster:

Here there is a kind of question, let us still call it historical, whose *conception, formation, gestation,* and *labor* we are only catching a glimpse of today. I employ these words, I admit, with a glance toward the operations of childbearing — but also, with a glance toward those who, in a society from which I do not exclude myself, turn their eyes away when faced by the as yet unnameable which is proclaiming itself and which can do so, as is necessary whenever a birth is in the offing, only under the species of the nonspecies, in the formless, mute, infant, and terrifying form of monstrosity. (293)

Derrida's text stands between two apocalypses. One, some "event" that cannot really be called an "event," which evidently has no name, which is only in some approximate sense "historical," has *happened.* The other, even less imaginable and less assimilable to any concept of history, is about to happen, cannot help but happen, has already germinated and gestated and is now, through its birth, already transforming every conceptual system. Derrida's tone is really more post-apocalyptic than apocalyptic. It is retrospectively portentous; the thing that *will* happen *has* happened, has as good as happened. The center on which all structure depends will be lost — but really it already has been lost, indeed has always been lost.

This sense of an imminent, apocalyptic breach that, in reality, has already occurred reappears throughout Derrida's work of this period. In a typical passage in *Of Grammatology,* for instance, Derrida writes, "The age of the sign" which is "essentially theological . . . perhaps will never *end.* Its historical *closure,* however, is outlined." Deconstruction tries to "designate the crevice through which the yet unnameable glimmer beyond the closure can be glimpsed" (14). In this after-the-end (or closure) scenario, signification obviously becomes quite problematic,[6] and Derrida makes use of certain crucial terms (often puns and neologisms) to try to put into words (and to thematize the impossibility of doing so) the apocalyptic break that will occur, is occurring, has occurred. These key terms — *trace, writing, supplement, differance, dissemination, pharmakon, hymen* — in showing the radical indeterminacy of language, mark the place of the monstrous birth of the "yet unnameable glimmer beyond the closure."

Derrida's discussion of *differance* best shows the apocalyptic, and post-apocalyptic, function of these key terms and of his thinking in general. The substitution of the *a* for *e*, a change that can be perceived graphically but not phonetically, renders *differance* an unnameable entity of writing. As Derrida insists, *differance* is "neither a word nor a concept" ("Differance," 3). When spoken, it is indistinguishable from *difference,* and its meaning is simultaneously "to differ" and "to defer." In other words, *differance* is never a single, coherent linguistic thing. It is a label given to an unnameable process by which every linguistic sign reveals itself to be utterly separate from its referent, and divided and inconsistent in itself. *Differance* reveals that language can never indicate a "here" or a "now." It is always, inevitably, later and distant. The thing, the event, can only be known through traces that it leaves. No origin will ever be recovered intact; only scattered fossils can be inferred. *Differance* is the process by which these traces that have no origins are generated, and these traces without origin are what constitute the world. *Differance,* as Derrida describes it, is the reason the world is the way it is — irremediably nonunitary, divided and differing from itself in every particle, ungraspable in itself and having, as it were, no self to grasp. What is primary and original is *differance,* which cannot be an origin, which is by definition not-present.

Language creates the illusions of presence and identity: that one can know who one is, where one is; that one can tell a true history of events; that events, understood as discrete occurrences that can be narrated, indeed take place in the way that language presents them. These metaphysical presuppositions of presence, identity, and history furthermore form the basis for all social institutions, Derrida suggests, for these rely on narratives of origins and ends for their legitimacy. *Differance* apocalyptically destroys these social and linguistic presuppositions, strips them and reveals them to be illusions created by metaphysics in language. Derrida ultimately presents this apocalypse of language and representation as having social and political consequences:

> First consequence: *differance* is not. It is not a present being,
> however excellent, unique, principal, or transcendent. It gov-
> erns nothing, reigns over nothing, and nowhere exercises any
> authority. It is not announced by any capital letter. Not only
> is there no kingdom of *differance,* but *differance* instigates
> the subversion of every kingdom. Which makes it obviously
> threatening and infallibly dreaded by everything within us
> that desires a kingdom, the past or future presence of a king-
> dom. ("Differance," 21–22)

Derrida's apocalyptic language here and throughout the essay is peculiar in that it suggests an apocalypse without an event. *Differance* is an ongoing apocalypse, a continual revelatory destruction built into the structure of language.[7] Indeed, Derrida several times explicitly denies the relevance and efficacy of events and of the histories in which they might be written. *Differance* makes events and history possible. And yet, like the "event" referred to in "Structure, Sign, and Play," *history* in "Differance" can only be written in quotation marks. " 'History,' " for Derrida, is a flattening, a "final repression of difference" (11). Trying to go back, through narrative, toward an event, one finds only traces of traces of the event — it is never there.

Is then this event that was never there ("a past that has never been present," [21]) a variety of trauma? "Differing" and "deferring," the two operations of *differance,* imply, as Derrida points out, a logic of *nachtraglichkeit,* Freud's term for the inevitably retrospective narrative re-creation of the forgotten origins of neurotic or traumatic symptoms. As we saw in chapter 2, Freud expressed ambivalence regarding the occurrence and significance of events. In each of his attempts to theorize trauma, he initially emphasized the traumatic event but later attributed symptom formation to broader biological, even cosmic disorders. Derrida, in referring to Freudian *nachtraglichkeit,* agrees with the Freud who de-emphasizes the event and its consequences, though he points then not to a biological determinism but to the structural, linguistic process of *differance* for the production of traces (in psychoanalytic terms, symptoms).

But Derrida must combat the implications still contained in the concept of "trauma" of an actual history, of a shocking particular event that initiates a series of consequences (however reconstructed after some period of delay), and that is not itself a structural effect implicit in the processes of symbolization.

That which apocalyptically explodes every structure emerges from within the structure. There is no need for, indeed, no possibility of, any external traumatic event. The structure and its deconstruction both are effects of the same non-origin, non-process of *differance*. Thus, early in the essay, Derrida inserts a brief but important attack on Lacan's view of trauma. *Differance* "exceeds the order of truth at a certain precise point, but without dissimulating itself as something, as a mysterious being, in the occult of a nonknowledge or in a hole with indeterminable borders (for example, in a topology of castration)" (6). This statement refers to a larger, ongoing controversy between Derrida and Lacan (in the late 1960s to early 1970s), and is crucial in "Differance" for its attack on "castration" as a parodic shorthand for trauma. While it is a mistake, in my view, to reduce trauma to some notion of real or imagined castration (though both Freud and Lacan seem at times to do so), Derrida uses this easy dismissal of castration to help achieve the far more problematic dismissal of all traumatic events.

Without the intrusion of the event into a symbolic structure, "the present becomes the sign of the sign, the trace of the trace. It is no longer what every reference refers to in the last analysis. It becomes a function in a structure of generalized reference." And yet, this presence of a present moment, inevitably differing and deferred, eventually returns in the "form of presence," which is to say, "in a text," as "an effect of writing" (24). This seems to be the process we examined earlier in the recent problematic fictions about the Holocaust. But Derrida's position here is unequivocal. He is not trying to understand how events of the past both destabilize and restructure the present, and how testimonies to traumatic events take problematic forms when they become testimony to textualized accounts of traumas. Derrida's argument, rather, seeks to level this, or any, historical process to a universal process in which each particular instance is fundamentally the same as every other; the textualization of the most trivial event is the same as that of the most overwhelming. What destabilizes and restructures is always *differance*, not the "events" or "histories" that are its traces.

Derrida's general, structural apocalypticism, which is always-already post-apocalyptic, is closely attuned to the atmosphere of French political opposition in the late 1960s. While Derrida was not personally involved with the insurrections of 1968,[8] his stress on all-encompassing symbolic-social systems and their complete overturning was very much in the "spirit of '68." There are, of course, many theories as to the origins and significance of the student and subsequent labor uprisings of May 1968, but most observers and historians have agreed on a few important features. First was the widespread perception that French political life was in a condition of stalemate. The impressive economic and technological developments since the Second World War seemed only to contribute to a growing social impasse. Class stratifications remained largely intact, and workers felt demoralized by the impersonality of their modernized sites of working and living. Likewise, students felt stifled by the increasingly huge and impersonal university system that they saw as a replica of France's centralized political administration, "a bloc impervious to change" (Brown, *Protest in Paris*, 52). The Fifth Republic's constitution had given the president unprecedented power, and the opposition parties were divided. Overall, there was a sense that meaningful reform was vitally necessary, and yet was impossible given the bureaucratic rigidity of French society and government. Thus, the alliance in 1968 between students and workers — an alliance filled with contradictions and soon to be dissolved — was based largely on shared frustration and disgust with the rigid, hierarchical, centralized, and impervious power of de Gaulle's state. The state could not be reformed: it could only be instantly, spontaneously, and apocalyptically swept out of being.[9]

In addition to the immediate political situation, recent French history was also at issue in the rejection of authority in the late 1960s. The American war in Vietnam, protests against which served as an initial impetus for the 1968 uprising, evoked memories of French imperial crimes and failures in Indochina and Algeria. And beneath these memories were others, even more traumatic, of French collaboration with the Nazis and participation in the deportations of Jews in France. The students proclaimed, "We are all German Jews." This statement's absurd exaggeration shows the intrusion of traumatic histories into the general disenchantment with French postwar modernization and prosperity. In attempting a kind of total revolution against a state that appeared as a total and permanent entity, revolutionaries portrayed the French state as the direct correspondent and suppressor of these traumatic histories — successor to Vichy and to the power of empire.

Thus, when Derrida writes that *"differance* instigates the subversion of every kingdom," his apocalyptic enthusiasm should be seen in part in the context of the spirit of '68.[10] And we can read this context also in Foucault's and Gilles Deleuze and Félix Guattari's total critiques of Western culture in *Discipline and Punish* and *Anti-Oedipus.* All these critiques, like Derrida's, address ongoing, structural features and do not rely on events or practices that emerge at any particular historical moment.[11] It is striking then that near the end of "Differance," Derrida introduces a specific date, 1946, in reference to an essay by Heidegger. Heidegger's essay, written in this year, is about forgetting. It is not, of course, about any particular events that might be forgotten but about the broader, more "essential" forgetting of the ontological difference between particular beings in the world and Being as such, untouched by human agency, subjectivity, or perception. As long as human attention is focused on distinctions among beings and the ontological difference is forgotten, then no space can be cleared for Being itself to come into presence, and truth (as unveiling, *aletheia*) will remain veiled. Derrida takes Heidegger's thinking a step further, calling into question the primacy of the ontological difference, and its forgetting. The ontological difference itself, the coming to presence, and forgetting of Being all are effects of *differance*. Like everything else, the sign "Being" is a trace pointing to other traces. The crucial forgetting and rediscovery is not of Being and its distinction from beings but rather of *differance*.

Derrida pushes forgetting back a step further — or rather brings it up to date. Heidegger, in 1946, chooses amnesia, chooses to regard the distinctions among "beings" as trivial (i.e., the distinctions between Nazism and liberalism are insignificant since both are presencings of Being as technology). Derrida, in 1967, forgets Heidegger's forgetting. He, in effect, accuses Heidegger of not forgetting enough, and then completes the job: forgetting what Heidegger forgot and Heidegger's forgetting of it. "1946" cannot be considered a *trace* in Derrida's text — a trace pointing only toward other traces. It seems to function quite explicitly as a *symptom*. It points back toward a traumatic event that has been repressed.[12]

In the text of "Differance," the inscribed date "1946" is an anomaly. Its appearance in 1967 fixes the site of several overlapping amnesias: Derrida's forgetting of Heidegger's forgetting of the Holocaust, and Derrida's forgetting of the Holocaust. Derrida wants to claim that it is not this date (and the memories and amnesias it covers over) that destabilizes any text or "kingdom" but that, rather, *differance* is the (non)agent of an always-already occurring apocalypse. In later writings, however, the "date" and other historically loaded terms become central to his post-apocalyptic sense.

In "Shibboleth" (1984), discussing Paul Celan, Derrida presents the writing of a date in a poem as the sign of a wound that when written, is both transmitted and effaced. "Whether one knows it or not, whether one acknowledges it or conceals it, an utterance is always dated" (313), and the date is "a cut or incision which the poem bears in its body like a memory.... To speak of an incision or cut is to say that the poem is entered into, that it begins in the wounding of its date" (317). The date is the mark of something unique, unrepeatable—Derrida compares it to a circumcision. It is a particular wound, suffered at a particular moment. Apparently reversing Derrida's earlier critiques of presence, the date as wound would seem to be a mark of presence, an indexical pointer toward an actual event. And Derrida's thinking about the date (especially as a variant of circumcision) seems also to contravene his attack on Lacan's view of trauma as symbolic castration. And yet the event, of course, has gone, has passed, and so the date in the text marks a ghostly return: "the possibility of a recurrence, and the recurrence of that which precisely cannot return.... A date is a spectre" (317).

As in Derrida's earlier, apocalyptically charged work, in "Shibboleth" a catastrophe has taken place, but now it is the particular, historical catastrophe—the Shoah—that is always near the center of Celan's fragmented poems. What was evaded in the reference in "Differance" to Heidegger in 1946 now seems to be faced. There are, however, crucial similarities between the earlier, as it were, "undated" work and the later work that addresses the historical specificity of the Holocaust. Recall the apocalyptic function of the term *differance*. "Neither a word nor a concept," its phonic instability (the indistinguishable *a*) illustrates how it eludes and destabilizes linguistic structures. It stands as a (non)originary, (anti)structural (non)basis of all signification even as it subverts all signification.[13] This function serves for all Derrida's earlier key terms (*trace, dissemination, pharmakon, hymen,* etc.), which denote a general, structural working of language; and it serves again, in almost exactly the same way, for the later key terms that point specifically toward the Holocaust.

The term *shibboleth* in Derrida's essay on Celan indicates the process by which a unique, unrepeatable traumatic event comes to be textualized, and thus repeatable. Shibboleth is a password, what allows passage from the singular (and, necessarily, nonlinguistic) into the shared realm of language. But shibboleth does not convey any single meaning for the event. As the event enters language, it becomes apprehensible as it loses its singularity. As text, it is reproducible, multiple, deconstructible. The shibboleth suggests very well the process we saw taking place in recent Holocaust fiction, the proliferation of forms that occurs when writers bear witness to trauma as text. As passage from the unique wound to the shared text, shibboleth shares crucial features with *differance*. First, it depends on a phonic instability. Its initial consonant sound can be pronounced either as *s* or as *sh*. As written, the initial *sh*, like *differance*'s final *a*, is indeterminate. Second, since shibboleth is a process that makes language possible, Derrida wants to place it outside the structure of language. "The word shibboleth, *if it is one*, names . . . any insignificant mark, for example the phonemic shift between *shi* and *si*, once it becomes discriminative and decisive, that is, divisive" (322, my emphasis). Like *differance*, shibboleth is not, strictly speaking, a word, for in its ultimate indecipherability and arbitrariness it "marks the multiplicity within language, insignificant difference as the condition of sense in language" (323).

Derrida uses a similar strategy in presenting the term *cinder*. In the book *Cinders*, Derrida traces the recurrences in his writings, over fifteen years, of an odd and ambiguous phrase he first used at the end of *Disseminations: "Il y a là cendre"* (There are cinders). The accent over the *a* in "là" changes its meaning from the definite article *the* to the demonstrative *there*. So, the phrase can also mean, "there are cinders *there*," in a specific place. Either, "cinders exist; cinders there are," or "cinders are there, right there." Cinders in general, or certain specified cinders. But, as in *differance* and *shibboleth*, the accent mark does not affect pronunciation, and the phonemic indeterminacy points toward a general instability of meanings. Further, as with the other key terms, *il y a là cendre* points toward the linguistic construction of presence, of "thereness," through the arbitrariness of the accent mark. The cinder, Derrida writes,

> is nothing that can be in the world, nothing that remains as
> an entity. It is the being, rather, that there is—this is a name
> of the being that there is there but which, giving itself, is
> nothing, remains beyond everything that is, remains unpro-
> nounceable in order to make saying possible, although it is
> nothing. (73)

The cinder would seem then to be another version of *differance,* another de-
structive/constructive, apocalyptic condition of possibility that itself does not
quite, in any proper sense, exist.

Derrida's use of the indecipherable "il y a là ..." also emphasizes the continuing importance of Heidegger in Derrida's thinking, for "il y a" is the French
translation of "es gibt," one of the most crucial phrases in Heidegger's writings. "Es gibt" (in English, "there is"), for Heidegger, is the process of giving,
is the gift, whereby entities become present in the world. It is not simply that
they are there, as the English idiom implies; rather, they are given, sent, permitted to come into presence. Being is a gift, and the summit of human responsibility is to maintain an openness in which the gift can be received. But what is
the "it" ("es") that gives? Heidegger, in "Time and Being," describes a process
that underlies both "beings" and the more essential "Being"—that is, as Derrida will later do in "Differance," Heidegger preempts the "ontological difference." This "it" that gives makes possible "beings," "Being," and even time.
And "it" is not any kind of event or occurrence, since such would have to take
place in time. "It" is "the extending and sending which opens and preserves"
(*Time and Being,* 20), out of which Being and time are possible. Heidegger
calls this nonevent, nonentity *ereignis,* translated as "appropriation," and it is
the "giving" whereby any particular thing comes into being as itself, as what
it is. One of *ereignis*'s chief qualities is to withdraw and conceal itself as it gives,
so that we perceive and live among, and as, its gifts but never encounter "it."

Ereignis seems to designate simultaneously a Creation and a Fall, a plenitude and a loss. That which makes presence possible is never present, however endlessly we chase it. And so we are, tragically—partly owing to *ereignis*'s self-concealment and partly to our own blundering refusals to create an
opening for its "unconcealment"[14]—cut off from full presence and genuine
Being. Derrida tries to arrive at "the other side" of this Heideggerian nostalgia,
to begin from the premise that full, undivided presence never existed and is

structurally impossible: that entities come into being from an originary division that is always further dividing, and therefore never originary.[15] But he returns, in *Cinders,* to the problematics of "es gibt" and "il y a," where what is "given," what is "there," can only be ashes. And in "Shibboleth," the "date" is something which is "given," a "datum"; "not something which is there, since it withdraws in order to appear, but perhaps *there are* (*gibt es*) dates" (315, Derrida's emphasis)—which, as we have seen, is tantamount to saying, there are singular, unrepeatable wounds.

What terms like *differance* and *trace* performed in Derrida's earlier work, the terms *date, cinder,* and *shibboleth* accomplish in the more recent texts. They mark sites of unrepresentibility out of which representation emerges, sites of absolute rupture that impel transmission, sites of the destruction and generation of structures, sites, in short, of an apocalypse that has already happened and whose effects continue to be felt. But while the earlier terms marked an ongoing, structural apocalypse, the later terms seem explicitly to indicate a historical apocalypse, the Shoah. The synonym for *cinder,* Derrida writes, "would tell of the all-burning, otherwise called holocaust and the crematory oven, in German in all the Jewish languages of the world" (*Cinders,* 57). And Derrida even maintains that the older terms are "better named by 'cinder'" (*Points,* 208), and that

> the best paradigm for the trace . . . is not, as some have believed, and he as well, perhaps [Derrida refers to himself in the third person in this passage], the trail of the hunt, the fraying, the furrow in the sand, the wake in the sea, the love of the step for its imprint, but the cinder (what remains without remaining from the holocaust, from the all-burning, from the incineration the incense). (*Cinders,* 43)

Given this distinct and self-conscious shift in terminology, we can recontextualize the structural post-apocalypse of early deconstruction into a response to the Shoah, seen as an apocalypse within history. The nameless apocalypse that, in Derrida's early work, was never not and always-already occurring can now be recognized as the Holocaust—at that time still so close, and in the midst of other "apocalyptic" upheavals unable to be recognized. In this light, Derrida's Heideggerian blurrings of empirical distinctions, the placing of "events" and "histories" in quotation marks, and the subsuming of all these under the universal function of *differance* mark Derrida's texts of the middle to late 1960s as traumatized responses to the still overwhelming impact of the Holocaust.

And yet, Derrida's newly specific and historical sense of apocalypse as Shoah remains oblique in his writings. Derrida insisted in an interview that *Cinders* referred to the Shoah "in an altogether direct way. The text names, for example, the crematoria or genocides by fire, but also all the genocides for which the genocide by fire is a figure, all the destructions whose victims are not even identifiable or countable" (*Points,* 392). Derrida's phrasing here is astute. The odd figure, "genocide by fire," subtly displaces "holocaust's" connotations of divine sacrifice by fire. Derrida retains the fire (which produces the cinder), while rejecting any implication of divine sanction. And Derrida rightly observes, and probably rightly accepts, that the Shoah has become a figure for all genocides. At the same time, Derrida seems overly concerned with illustrating his own figures and themes: the cinder, the disappearance of the presence of the event, the Holocaust as exemplifying a universal process of disappearance. Indeed, in all the later writings, in which some term designating the Holocaust replaces a general, structural term as the figure of apocalypse, there remains a vagueness, a tendency to universalize and to blur important distinctions.

In further clarifying the cinder, for example, Derrida notes that "in every experience there is this incineration, this experience of incineration which is experience itself. Of course, then, there are great, spectacular experiences of incineration — and I allude to them in the text — I'm thinking of the crematoria, of all the destructions by fire." But underlying these, there is incineration "as the elementary form of experience" (*Points,* 209). Regarding the function of the "date" in "Shibboleth," Derrida writes, "And I will not speak here of the *holocaust,* except to say this: there is the date of a certain holocaust, the hell of our memory, but there is a holocaust for every date, somewhere in the world, for every hour. Every hour is unique, whether it comes back or whether, the last, it comes back no more" (336). The shibboleth, as the possibility of translation from the singular and unrepeatable date as wound into the shared world of language, is a universal process, as is the phenomenon of the cinder as the physical trace of vanished experience. The historical event of the Nazi genocide functions in these texts as a limit case, a particularly vivid and exemplary instance of a universal process. Thus, what seemed to be a historicizing of a previously ahistorical analysis of language turns out to reaffirm the universal and ahistorical assumptions of the earlier writings. Every utterance, as Derrida notes, is "dated," but ultimately it does not much matter what the date is.[16]

Part of Derrida's problem with "dating" seems to stem from a constitutional reluctance to connect personal or social histories to philosophical discourses. When asked in interviews to speculate on how his personal experiences — his "dates," his wounds — might have influenced his thinking (in other words, to speculate on his own shibboleth), Derrida refuses, sometimes with annoyance. "I wish that a narration were possible," he says, but to do so he would have "to invent a language, to invent modes of anamnesis," and this he cannot do. "So, having said that, am I going to take the risk here, while improvising, of telling you things that would resemble a narration? No!" He will answer, he says, "precise factual questions," but "I don't feel capable of giving myself over to . . . variations on my memory, my inheritance" (*Points,* 203). In the midst of the excesses of contemporary celebrity culture, this reticence is admirable. At the same time, Derrida by no means shies away from his own celebrity, and this irritated refusal to remember, this claim to lack a language for remembering (a shibboleth), seems disingenuous. If, as I have suggested, Derrida in his later works has redefined deconstruction as locating the effaced date/wound in the text, then the "risk" of improvising variations on memory should be no greater than the risk of refusing to do so.

In another interview, Derrida does not refuse to answer the question of whether "there is a date, a traumatic incursion, so to speak, that leads you to philosophize?" Instead, he immediately translates the question from the personal to the most general context.

> J.D.: Me?
>
> Q.: For example . . .
>
> J.D.: No, the question should be addressed in general, does a philosopher . . .
>
> Q.: It is to be understood in a general fashion but, obviously, if you could say . . .
>
> J.D.: By date, do you mean a singular moment or experience?

Q.: Yes, the singular experience of the wound, if I take up
again the terms of *Schibboleth,* that sets off this process of
philosophical reflection. (380)

The interviewer then refers to Lévinas's dedication to *Otherwise Than Being*
(to the victims of the Shoah, whose presence is constantly felt though never
otherwise mentioned throughout that book), and Derrida takes the opportunity
to shift the conversation to a discussion of Lévinas. In his reply, Derrida repeats the strategies of his writings. Any particular text transmits its own singular wound, but *all* texts transmit their wounds — this is something in the nature of texts, and wounds — and in speaking about one, you speak about all.
There are no meaningful distinctions that can be drawn between the "dates"
of one text and those of another.

Derrida is correct, and is extraordinarily insightful, regarding the spectral
quality of the textualized wound — its liminal state between presence and non-
presence, the loss of singularity as wound enters text. As D. M. Thomas, Cynthia Ozick, and Emily Prager showed in their fictions, in this moment just at,
or just after, the end of testimony, we remain haunted by wounds, by historical traumas, that enter texts *as* texts. The consistent veering back toward universal, structural processes on the part of terms with specific historical referents
suggests powerful moral and historical tensions in Derrida's writings. Derrida's recognition of the belated impact of the Holocaust after thirty or more
years of relative silence and his sense of an ethical need to focus on it and respond to its renewed historical urgency come into conflict with his wish to
contain its impact within the terms of his previous thinking. That this thinking
was in many ways a dialogue with Heidegger that ignored Heidegger's Nazi
sympathies makes the tension even more difficult to manage.

The publication in 1987 of Victor Farias's *Heidegger and Nazism* marked a
traumatic return of an old, known problem. As with so many discourses relevant to the Shoah that emerged in the 1980s, there were no new revelations in
Farias's book. Heidegger's Nazi sympathies and actions were known, but their
consequences seemed until that time vague and indecipherable, and could not
be thought about clearly. He was a Nazi, but stopped being a Nazi. He was a
Nazi, and never recanted or explained his involvement, but he misinterpreted
what Nazism meant. He was a Nazi, but Hannah Arendt excused him. He was

a Nazi, but *Being and Time* provided the most brilliant analysis of the existential condition of human "thrownness" and the struggle for authenticity. He was a Nazi, but his later work provided the most compelling critique of the logic of Western technology and its relation to all forms of representation. This attitude of disavowal toward Heidegger's Nazism (he was but he was not; he was but it had no real consequences) was not a sign of evil or complicity on the part of philosophers. It was part of the general inability to address the Holocaust that was prevalent in Europe and America until the late 1970s — perhaps a general splitting of the social ego in which the Holocaust was known but not acknowledged.

Farias's book, probably more on account of its timing and polemical tone than of its content, forced Heidegger's Nazism to the center of philosophical, and public, attention. While in 1967 Derrida could refer to a Heidegger text of 1946 and only discuss Heidegger's remarks about "Being" and "beings," and not what it might have meant for Heidegger to be discussing the ontological difference in 1946, after 1987 such an omission was no longer possible. In December 1987 came the revelations of Paul de Man's collaborationist wartime writings. And along with these two traumatic returns, deconstruction and post-structuralism were under attack by New Historicist and other politically left-wing literary scholars for lacking a sufficient sense of history, politics, or ethics — criticisms that previously only had come, and now came again with renewed force, from conservative positions.

Derrida's most comprehensive, though still oblique and troubling, response to all these philosophical, critical, and political confrontations was made in an essay in 1989 that he delivered at two conferences — first at "Deconstruction and the Possibility of Justice" at the Cardozo Law School (October 1989) organized by Drucilla Cornell, and six months later at "Nazism and the 'Final Solution': Probing the Limits of Representation" at UCLA (April 1990) organized by Saul Friedlander. In this essay, "Force of Law: The 'Mystical Foundations of Authority,' " Derrida first redefines deconstruction as a discourse of "justice" that is not reducible to — indeed, that destabilizes — any given set of laws. "Law," he argues, is invariably put in place not by justice but by a violent force, and so must in every case have this basis in force exposed, deconstructed, by a notion of justice that is radically other, that is, not predicated on force or violence. In the second part of the essay, Derrida discusses an essay from 1921 by Walter Benjamin, "Critique of Violence," which establishes similar distinctions between the violence that initiates and is perpetuated by law and what Benjamin calls "divine violence," an apocalyptic or messianic force that will expose and overturn legal violence. Benjamin makes no distinction between different types of legal violence (i.e., between the laws of a liberal democracy and that of a dictatorship), placing them all under the aegis of certain shared forms of representation. Derrida links Benjamin's essay with conservative, proto-Nazi discourses of the 1920s, and makes the provocative point that even Benjamin, who has attained an almost sainted status in contemporary theoretical discourse, has affinities with Nazism. Heidegger's presence is strongly felt in this context but is only mentioned once, with reference to the affinity of his thinking with Benjamin's. Equally provocative, and also not mentioned, are the connections between Benjamin's distinctions, which Derrida criticizes, and Derrida's own, which strongly resemble Benjamin's.

"Force of Law" is a strange, difficult performance that bears out Peter Dews's observation of "an extreme tension and torsion at work" in Derrida's writings after what Dews calls his "ethical turn" (6). Derrida's first goal in this essay is to defend his work against charges that it can say nothing positive about ethics or justice, that it is capable only of pointing out the impossibility of coherent discourses on these topics, and that deconstruction verges perhaps on nihilism, a total critique of Enlightenment thought that points to nothing other than the "monstrous birth" alluded to at the end of "Structure, Sign, and Play." In "Force of Law," Derrida embraces the Enlightenment: "Nothing seems to me less outdated than the classical emancipatory ideal. We cannot attempt to disqualify it today, whether crudely or with sophistication, at least not without treating it too lightly and forming the worst complicities" (28). He reaches this alignment by describing an idea of justice that uses utopian language reminiscent of Walter Benjamin and Ernst Bloch. Law, which was invariably founded in and perpetuated by violence, must be deconstructed by a notion of justice that is "an experience of the impossible," an "aporia" (16). Justice is an imaginative site that does not exist in the world but that establishes the measure by which all existing laws are seen to be unjust. Deconstruction, as Derrida now defines it, takes place "in the interval" between law and justice, and is the practice that reveals the hidden violence within every law (15). Just as *differance* functioned politically as "the subversion of every kingdom" ("Differance," 22), so in this essay the interval of deconstruction is where "transformations, indeed juridico-political revolutions take place" (20).

The deconstruction of existing legal norms is possible because of the impossible, utopian, undeconstructible ideal of a justice not founded on violence. To explain this further, Derrida adds the language of Lévinasian ethics to that of Frankfurt School utopianism, calling this ideal of justice "infinite" and "irreducible . . . because owed to the other." Since it is "without calculation and without rules, without reason and without rationality," justice is "a madness." And deconstruction is

> mad about this kind of justice. Mad about this desire for justice. This kind of justice, which isn't law, is the very movement of deconstruction at work in law and the history of law, in political history and history itself, before it even presents itself as the discourse that the academy or modern culture labels "deconstructionism." (25)

Justice, because it does not exist as such in the world, is the desire for justice. Justice is "the very movement of deconstruction," and "deconstruction is justice" (15). We can say then that *justice* in this essay takes on the apocalyptic function of *differance, trace, cinder,* and so on, and at the same time operates like Benjamin's "messianic chip," Bloch's sense of the utopian content in every ideological production, and even Lévinas's ethical obligation to the other. The first section of "Force of Law" is a sort of theoretical collage that seeks to rescue deconstruction from accusations of immorality by placing it alongside what are widely perceived as several of the most profound ethical-political theories of the past fifty years. The problem with Derrida's position here, aside from the possibilities of calculation and cynicism, is one we have seen throughout his whole career. In separating absolutely the utopian, undeconstructible form of justice from any existing legal system, in denoting justice as the radical other of law, Derrida provides no criteria for distinguishing one existing legal system from another. From the perspective of justice, all laws are equally culpable, all are implicated in processes of force and violence. If this really is so, then we have no way to claim that liberal democracy is better than fascism, except perhaps by degree. And yet, even the argument "by degree" is problematic, for how can one discern a degree of something that is infinite and irreducible? Derrida does not claim that existing systems of law are mixtures of justice and violence, that they contain kernels of justice that can be identified and augmented. This would be closer to Bloch's position, or Benjamin's in the "Theses on the Philosophy of History." Derrida's claim is that justice is absolutely other than law. Derrida would argue, I think, that he intends this alterity as a continual impetus toward the radical transformation of existing legal and political systems, all of which—including our own—*are* terribly flawed. He transfers the deconstructive motif of undecidability from the realm of mere signification to that of ethical decision: one cannot decide, there are no rules (for justice is heterogeneous to rules), but one is obligated to decide what is just. And yet then, following this deciding of the undecidable (and here Derrida uses the logic of the shibboleth and of dissemination), what *had* been justice now is inscribed and offered for repetition as a law, and so is "no longer *presently* just, fully just. There is apparently no moment in which a decision can be called presently and fully just" (24, Derrida's emphasis). The formulation of justice as the other of law has now become another critique of presence. Justice is not, but *il y a/es gibt* justice. Justice is another ghost, another trace, another cinder that annihilates the presumed foundations of the existing order. We cannot determine what is just but are obligated to decide. And our decision is false as soon as we utter it, for justice is not here. It is what we desire and is the way we try to reach it. But it recedes, like the trace, like *differance,* continually differing and deferred.

The second half of "Force of Law," in which Derrida presents and critiques Benjamin's 1921 essay "Critique of Violence," mirrors the first half, for Benjamin's distinctions between "mythic" and "divine" violence closely resemble Derrida's distinction between law and justice. In this section, however, what is at issue is the representation of the Holocaust seen as the limit case of any discussion of justice. Benjamin, like Derrida, critiqued all existing systems of law and government as being founded and preserved by violence. Benjamin then distinguished two separate categories of violence. "Mythic" violence was the worldly, political violence that founded and upheld the state. It was mythic in that it relied on some narrative of origin for its legitimation. In relying on a mythic history—in effect, on ideology—mythic violence was entirely of a piece with a culture's whole system of representation and language. Ultimately, for Benjamin, representation (both symbolic and political) was inseparable from violence. No form of government, law, or language could escape complicity — even identity — with the mythic violence that founded and upheld the state. Opposed to mythic violence, and outside any system of representation, was what Benjamin called "divine" violence. In the terms of Benjamin's Marxist-messianic thinking, divine violence was the violence of the revolution, of the general strike, of the political act that rejected and obliterated existing forms of representation (again, in both the symbolic and political senses) and immediately summoned the apocalyptic future.

In his critique of the violence of representation, Benjamin bitterly criticizes parliamentary democracy for attempting to disguise its violent nature under pretenses of rights and liberties. Derrida, in this regard, links Benjamin to the conservative legal scholar Carl Schmitt (who later became the preeminent jurist of the Third Reich) and places Benjamin's essay in "the great anti-parliamentary and anti-'*Aufklarung*' wave on which Nazism . . . surfaced . . . in the 1920s and the beginning of the 1930s" (64).[17] Furthermore, although Derrida does not mention it, Benjamin's critique of representation seems to anticipate Heidegger's critiques of "framing" and of the "world picture," and of Heidegger's sense that *all* Western culture — whether democratic, communist, or fascist — was part of a supervening representational logic of "technology" that concealed the truth of Being.

Derrida goes on to speculate on how Benjamin, had he lived, would have evaluated the Nazi genocide of the Jews. Derrida suggests that Benjamin, proceeding from the argument in "Critique of Violence," would have regarded the Shoah primarily as a consequence of representation. The final solution would be "the extreme consequence of a logic of Nazism" that is itself thoroughly implicated in the mythic violence that sustains every modern state and that is therefore part of "the fall of language into communication, representation, information" (58–59). And because Nazism would be "the final achievement of the logic of mythological violence" (59), which Benjamin sees as all pervasive, there could be no position within this logic from which to judge Nazism and the Shoah. "No anthropology, no humanism, no discourse of man on man, even on human rights, can be proportionate to either the rupture between the mythical and the divine, or to a limit experience such as the final solution" (61).

As Derrida imagines Benjamin's posthumous thinking, the only language capable of evaluating the Holocaust would be some prelapsarian language of naming, of pure witnessing, that would bypass the "fall" into representation.

Derrida's portrayal of Benjamin's thinking resembles almost exactly his critique-cum-defense of Heidegger in *Of Spirit*. In that book, Derrida criticizes Heidegger for falling back on the metaphysical notion of "spirit" to justify his embrace of Nazism (as opposed to a more "vulgar" biologically based Nazism)[18] and failing to realize that Nazism is already implicit in the metaphysics of spirit. Since for Derrida all Western thinking is implicated in metaphysics, his critique of Heidegger's Nazism finally becomes all encompassing:

> We have here a program and combinatory whose power remains abyssal. In all rigor it exculpates none of the discourses which can thus exchange their power. It leaves no place open for any arbitrating authority. Nazism was not born in the desert. We all know this, but it has to be constantly recalled. And even if, far from any desert, it had grown like a mushroom in the silence of the European forest, it would have done so in the shadow of the big trees, in the shelter of their silence or their indifference, but in the same soil. (109)

For both Heidegger and Benjamin, there can be no "arbitrating authority" for evaluating the Holocaust, for all existing and conceivable discourses are themselves complicit in the genocide, or at least in its ideology.[19]

Derrida, of course, is right that "Nazism was not born in the desert," and that no one can speak from a position of absolute righteousness, without any shadow of racism or murderous intention. And it is certainly a rhetorical coup to link Heidegger and Benjamin in this way. Indeed, Derrida's final criticism of Benjamin at the conclusion of "Force of Law" is that Benjamin is "too Heideggerian, too messianico-marxist or archeo-eschatological for me" (62) — a criticism that seems disingenuous given Derrida's persistently Heideggerian and apocalyptic intonations. Derrida seems to be saying: all of you who heap such venom on Heidegger, and on de Man, for their participation and collaboration in Nazism and for their subsequent silence, look at the sacred Benjamin, he is just the same. If you condemn Heidegger and de Man, you must also condemn Benjamin. And you must also condemn yourselves, for all of you speak the same language. In fact, even I (and this is the most clever, one

might say the most Kierkegaardian, part of Derrida's strategy) have acknowledged my own complicity with these discourses by constructing my "deconstruction as justice" argument along lines that uncannily resemble the argument of Benjamin's that I proceed to condemn.

The problem with these equations is obvious. Benjamin's critiques of parliamentary democracy from the 1920s sound jejune and dangerous today and
partake of a "politics of cultural despair," in Fritz Stern's phrase, similar to
other extremist discourses of that time, from both the Left and Right. But it is
certainly possible, and necessary, to distinguish between Benjamin's critique
in 1921 and Heidegger's act of joining the Nazi party in 1933 or de Man's
writing for a collaborationist newspaper during the war. Benjamin was never
a Nazi, nor a Nazi collaborator or sympathizer. He was a Jew who died fleeing the Nazis. It is embarrassing to state the obvious, yet Derrida fails to do
so. His sense of justice is too distant, too far deferred, and stands in absolute
opposition to every known form of law.

This continual sense of distance, non-presence, difference, and deferral
(marked by the shifting sets of apocalyptic terms — *differance, cinder, justice*)
I have interpreted as Derrida's responses to the traumatic events of the Shoah
in the changing contexts of French culture from the 1960s through the 1980s.
The figures of some nameless apocalyptic rupture that characterize Derrida's
early work can be seen in retrospect as naming the Holocaust. Later, Derrida
recognizes the Holocaust as a crucial theme in his thinking and tries to theorize how such a singular and traumatic event enters Western discourses, including his own. He seems unable, however, to bring together his sense of the
traumatic effects of a particular event with his broader concerns with the conditions of possibility for the occurrence of events as such. Although the Shoah
provides the terms for much of his later thinking, ultimately it cannot be distinguished from any other event. Derrida is incapable of historical distinctions
since, for him, history (always in quotes) remains the effect of some larger
process within which particular distinctions blur. Finally, the crises in poststructuralist thought brought on by the Heidegger and de Man controversies
made the tensions in Derrida's thinking still more acute. Simultaneously criti-
cizing and defending these figures, he adopts what seems to me a Heideggerian position in which all Western discourses are complicit with Nazism. In
this situation, there can be no firm position from which to pass judgment. Only

an apocalyptic revelation of justice, of the other, would provide such a vantage point. But this aporetic need for further apocalypse was produced by a previous apocalypse within history, the Shoah.

Apocalypse has been a constant preoccupation through all the turns in Derrida's thought. The foregoing analysis has shown that Derrida's thinking is also, and primarily, post-apocalyptic, for its apocalypse is a historical event, and Derrida's work begins in and continually returns to attempts to respond — even by avoiding, disguising, blurring that response — to the most traumatic historical event of Derrida's lifetime. The "date," or the "wound" in Derrida's writings, as in so much American and European discourse from the 1960s through the 1980s, remains fixed around Auschwitz 1944.

Part III: American Post-Apocalypses

American Apocalypticism, Post-Apocalypse, and Reaganism

The European settlement of America had an apocalyptic sensibility from its inception. Columbus himself wrote, "God made me the messenger of the new heaven and the new earth of which he spoke in the Apocalypse of St. John . . . and he showed me the spot where to find it" (in Boyer, 225). Later, the English inhabitants of New England portrayed their colony as a "city on a hill," an apocalyptic break with the past, the unveiling of a new social order and a new relationship with nature. The new, morally purified world would be free from the power of money — from the "vain, luxurious and selfish EFFEMI-NACY" of England's commercialized society, as the eighteenth-century English preacher John Brown wrote (in McCoy, 32) — as it would be free from inherited social status. Even as Puritan influence waned, the American apocalyptic sense continued in secular and political forms. As Tom Paine wrote in *Common Sense*, "We have it in our power to begin the world over again. A situation, similar to present, hath not happened since the days of Noah until now. The birth-day of a new world is at hand" (120).[1]

The American apocalyptic sense, however, always encountered conflict. The vast American wilderness could be seen as Edenic but also as demonic. And the non-Christian inhabitants made implausible the premise that a New Jerusalem could simply be placed onto a virgin land. The American sense of apocalypse was from its beginning split into two contradictory senses: first, that the apocalyptic break from Europe had successfully been achieved; second, that an apocalyptic struggle with native, or natural, powers was still to come. Even the Puritan jeremiads, as Sacvan Bercovitch points out, insisted that a final, uniquely American redemption was contained in embryo in the flawed Puritan communities. At the same time, as Richard Slotkin has observed, "The mythic tales and polemics [of the frontier] are rife with visions of border wars that turn overnight into preludes to Armageddon and with proposals for genocide and wars of extermination" (13). A sense of achieved, or at least potential, post-apocalyptic perfection coexisted in the developing American apocalyptic ideology with a violent terror of some darkness that both loomed outside and dwelled within.

This has been an explosive ideological coexistence. And it has been complicated further by the actual and evident imperfections of American history — slavery and its legacies, the violent injustices committed against Native Americans, the war in Vietnam. Like any country, America's history contains traumatic events and national crimes that can only with great difficulty be assimilated into a narrative of national perfection.

In recent years, the related emotional and political trends that have come together as "Reaganism" have been the most conspicuous and politically powerful instance of this American post-apocalypticism. In the view of the Reaganist or neo-Reaganist Right, the United States was perfect in its inception, has always been perfect, and is perfect today — or would be but for the efforts of identifiable enemies at home and abroad. The external, or internal but non-intrinsic, threat — whether of communism, liberalism, drug addicts, welfare mothers, immigrants, or the federal government — must be eliminated, but there is no inner flaw, no need for introspection or self-reckoning. And what may seem to be flaws, unspeakable traumas, and irredeemable tragedies can nevertheless be fit into optimistic and redemptive narratives. In a 1984 speech, Reagan invoked the story of American immigration:

> That's the great thing about America, we all come from some-
> place else. We all have roots that reach somewhere far away.
> Even the Native American Indian apparently came across
> from Asia when there was a land bridge leading to North
> America tens of thousands of years ago.[2]

In this astonishing conflation of immigration and the conquest of the West, Reagan entirely elided the destruction of Native American cultures. The central and founding crime of American history is stirred into an utterly distorted "melting pot" in which dispossessed Native Americans apparently share the same national experience as those who dispossessed them. And of course, another important group with "roots that reach somewhere far away" — that is, African Americans — are not mentioned at all. In Reagan's narrative, the Indians are no longer the "bad guys" resisting white America's "destiny" because the unequal struggle for possession of the continent never took place. Reagan's narrative is a post-apocalypse that has repressed its apocalyptic moment. The Native Americans now are immigrants just like the rest of us, and therefore could not possibly have been, or continue to be, victims of any injustice. Equilibrium has been restored: America *is* perfect and has *always* been perfect.

But the burden of this repression is unbearable. And so, in order to uphold that conviction of perfection, Reaganist ideology has felt the need to precipitate and reprecipitate, distill and redistill the purity of the national moral categories. Again and again, Sylvester Stallone, Bruce Willis, Sigourney Weaver must confront the Other, the Alien, the Terrorist. Reagan and his Republican successors and their Democratic allies must confront the un-Americans among us. And the militias grasp on to the Second Amendment as on to a sacred, purifying talisman and train in the wilderness for Armageddon. It is so hard to maintain that national sense of unique perfection. For the apocalyptic break with the past, which is the premise of all subsequent American myths, never really happened. The United States is a morally mixed nation, like any other. The burden of maintaining a perfect history is too heavy for any culture. And the insistent denial of the traumatic events of our history has brought about the need for these repeated apocalyptic purgings, both real and imaginary, as if *this* time we will finally get right what always was right, and somehow never was right.

Reagan's interest and belief in the biblical apocalypse is well known. In 1970 he remarked, "For the first time ever, everything is in place for the battle of Armageddon and the second coming of Christ," and a decade later, on the verge of becoming president, he added, "We may be the generation that sees Armageddon" (in Dugger, C1). Also well documented is his nostalgia for a preurbanized, preindustrial America. This nostalgia, in fact, is often seen as the ideological center of Reaganism — the wish to return to a peaceful world of family farms and white fences that merges into a 1950s suburbia of newsboys on bicycles and kind men delivering milk.[3] The nostalgic vision of perfect social harmony seems incompatible with apocalyptic expectation of divine judgment and world cataclysm, but Reaganist ideology was uniquely able to reconcile apocalypticism and nostalgia by emphasizing the long-standing sense of American post-apocalyptic perfection, of America as the ongoing fulfillment of prophecy. In 1846, the year after the term *manifest destiny* was coined, J. Sullivan Cox wrote in *The United States Magazine and Democratic Review*,

> Something of the same spirit now glows in the bosom of every member of this western commonwealth in America. Call it what you will, destiny, or what not; it is leading us as a cloud by day and a pillar of fire by night. It beckons to us from the dim and shadowy distance, and bids us, All Hail! It illumines our faces with hope, lights our eye with enterprize. Who can define it? As well define infinity, space, eternity; yet who so heartless as not to feel it. It has been called manifest. Its effects *are* manifest. They are seen in the throbbing pulse of America. It whelms and controls us, yet who would stem its rushing stream. (in Tuveson, 126)

Reagan's attitudes toward American history and even the rhythms and figures of his language emerged from the same apocalyptic-post-apocalyptic tradition that informed Cox's article. In a 1984 campaign speech, Reagan said,

> It was a second American revolution [he says of his first term], and it's only just begun. But America is back, a giant, powerful in its renewed spirit, its growing economy, powerful in its ability to defend itself and secure the peace, and powerful in its ability to build a new future. And you know something? That's not debatable. (238)

Cox and Reagan are alike in their dismissal of alternate views: "That's not debatable"; "Call it what you will." Their tones, at the same time colloquial and absolutist, invoke an infallible prophecy whose results are already far advanced.

Given this sense of inevitable prophetic fulfillment, Reagan's anti-Soviet, Cold War polemics could sound simultaneously alarmist and complacent. Reagan's 1964 speech in support of Barry Goldwater ended with a ringing apocalyptic Cold War exhortation: "You and I have a rendezvous with destiny. We will preserve for our children this, the last best hope of man on earth, or we will sentence them to take the last step into a thousand years of darkness" (36). The most serious threats that Reagan described in his speech, however, came not from the Soviet Union but from liberal "big government" at home, from Johnson's Great Society. "A government can't control the economy," Reagan argued, "without controlling people" (27). In Reagan's portrayal, the country was one step away from being a fully accomplished welfare state that, being indistinguishable from Soviet communism, would consequently acquiesce to any Soviet military threat.

And yet, in spite of the speech's consistent tone of crisis, Reagan at the same time emphasized that fundamentally nothing was wrong with the country — except in the minds of liberal social engineers.[4] He refers to Rice County, Kansas, which had recently been declared a "depressed area." "Rice County, Kansas, has two hundred oil wells, and the 14,000 people there have over thirty million dollars on deposit in personal savings in their banks. When the government tells you you are depressed, lie down and be depressed!" And he continues,

> We have so many people who can't see a fat man standing
> beside a thin one without coming to the conclusion that the
> fat man got that way by taking advantage of the thin one! . . .
> We were told four years ago that seventeen million people
> went to bed hungry each night. Well, that was probably true.
> They were all on a diet! (29)

Poverty and the social antagonisms entailed by economic disparities are simply denied, are made into jokes. And so, in Reagan's vision, the United States stands paradoxically in a position of imminent and fatal crisis demanding immediate response and, simultaneously, in a relaxed posture of "if it ain't broke don't fix it" satisfaction.

Twenty years later, as president, Reagan condemned the Soviet Union as an "evil empire," and like many post–Second World War premillennialist thinkers,[5] Reagan linked the prophecies of the Book of Revelation to the crises of the Cold War and saw the struggle between the United States and the Soviet Union as a fundamental cosmic struggle. And yet, for Reagan, American victory over communism was a foregone conclusion and the Soviet threat seemed oddly negligible. It had already happened. As Reagan told the graduates at the Notre Dame commencement in 1981, "The West won't contain communism, it will transcend communism. It won't bother to dismiss or denounce it, it will dismiss it as some bizarre chapter in human history whose last pages are even now being written" (in Erickson, 153).

Reagan's Cold War position was complex. He regarded the Soviet Union as a genuine threat and initiated an enormous arms buildup to combat that threat. At times, he interpreted the American-Soviet rivalry in biblical apocalyptic terms. But, at the same time, as the Notre Dame speech indicates, Reagan saw the Cold War, and the apocalypse, as already over. His Strategic Defense Initiative was another post-apocalyptic gesture — an object that when installed, would instantly usher in the millennium. The Notre Dame speech and the SDI proposal share the prophetic logic I discussed in chapter 1. Once the prophetic words have been uttered, the event may as well have occurred, for it must occur. In the mind of the believer, it *has* occurred. He has seen it and described it. The physical manifestation is merely the echo — not even the confirmation — of the prophetic revelatory word. Prophecy, then, not cataclysm, is literally the apocalypse. Everything that follows the revelation is post-apocalyptic. The Reaganist post-apocalypse relies on a teleological view of American history, in which America's end (both its destination and its destiny) is contained in its origin. Reagan's Cold War effort was a paradoxical struggle to install what already had always existed. As columnist Sidney Blumenthal wrote, "Reagan challenged us to stay the same" (260).

America, for Reagan, was an "achieved utopia."[6]

I have spoken so far of Ronald Reagan as an independent individual, located in an American tradition of apocalyptic and post-apocalyptic thinking but still an autonomous and original contributor to that tradition. Such a depiction is misleading. While Reagan undoubtedly had his own opinions on America's history and its future, the Reaganist text and Reaganism as the dominant political direction of the 1980s are complex mixtures of several political and historical sources. When I speak of "Reagan" or of "Reagan's view of history," I refer to the ideological phenomenon of Reaganism. Reagan the individual is not irrelevant to Reaganism. His particular image and skills were essential to its success. What Reagan articulated, however, went beyond any sense of personal vision. Reagan's "message" was, rather, a confluence of diverse political directions whose emblem and engine were, and still remain, the cheerfully apocalyptic actor/ex-president.

What Stuart Hall wrote about Thatcherism, that it "has remained a plurality of discourses — about the family, the economy, national identity, morality, crime, law, women, human nature" (53), is true of Reaganism as well. And these discourses engaged, or aroused, particular constituencies, all of whom could support Reagan. As Thomas Byrne Edsall writes, "In Reagan, the [Republican] party long identified with the rich found a leader equipped to bridge divisions between the country club and the fundamentalist church, between the executives of the Fortune 500 and the membership of the National Rifle Association" (270). While Reaganism was, as Edsall points out, a "revolution led by the affluent" (282), one of whose results was an astonishing redistribution of wealth to those who were already wealthy,[7] its supporters came from many classes and out of an assortment of motives and convictions. They opposed "big government" (i.e., the remnants of Johnson's Great Society programs), supported a strong military (and continued to believe with Reagan that the Vietnam war was "a noble cause"), opposed abortion, supported what appeared to them to be "traditional family values," supported a vague but powerful ideal of American community, opposed affirmative action programs for African Americans, supported severe penalties for violent crimes, opposed gun control, believed in traditional gender roles, supported prayer in the public schools, and opposed defacing the American flag. And among those who adhered to one or several or all of these Reaganist positions were the traditional country club Republicans, Christian fundamentalists, and the white ethnics (Reagan Democrats), southerners, and neoconservatives who had formerly been liberals.

Nevertheless, among these diverse positions, which encompass economics, military strategy, religion, sexuality, and law, there is a common referent, a particular historical period that animates the Reaganist spectrum. All the Reaganist themes returned to the 1960s and attempted in some way to undo the incomplete changes of that decade.[8]

The 1960s have been described as a site of trauma, and even apocalypse, by writers both of the Right and the Left. Kevin Phillips, writing that the 1960s experienced social and moral upheaval "on an unprecedented scale" (20), quotes Robert Nisbet that

> it would be difficult to find a single decade in the history of
> Western culture when so much barbarism — so much calcu-
> lated onslaught against culture and convention in any form,
> and so much sheer degradation of both culture and the indi-
> vidual — passed into print, into music, into art and onto the
> American stage as the decade of the Nineteen Sixties. (18)

The neoconservative writer Michael Medved wrote of his own political journey from 1960s radical to 1980s conservative as "part of a considered and inevitable response to the trauma of recent history" (in Collier and Horowitz,
23). On the left, Todd Gitlin and Tom Hayden both portray the origins and the
endings of the 1960s in traumatic and apocalyptic terms.[9] Hayden refers to
the "messianic sense" that prevailed in the formation of the SDS at Port Huron
in 1962 (74), and Gitlin writes of the apocalyptic mood of the late 1960s, as
political positions hardened and radicals spoke of being ready to do "whatever it takes" to end the war and bring down the government (*The Sixties,* 244).

But the 1960s were apocalyptic not only because of their own political di-
visiveness and turbulence. They were apocalyptic also because they provided
a critique of American history as a whole. The civil rights movement did not
merely attack contemporary racial injustices; it addressed the entire history of
American racial oppression. It forced past traumas into the current scene. Likewise, the protests against the Vietnam War linked that war to all other American and European imperial abuses, including the slave trade and the destruction
of Native American cultures. The social movements of the 1960s produced an
echo chamber of trauma and apocalypse that attacked the core of the American perfectionist, post-apocalyptic sense. The particular political crises of the
1960s were magnified as returns of all the repressed or denied traumas of American history.

Susan Sontag expressed this widespread sense of the continuing traumatic
content of American culture in her contribution to the 1967 *Partisan Review*
symposium "What's Happening to America?" (reprinted in *Styles of Radical
Will*). Sontag wrote, "America was founded on a genocide, on the unquestioned
assumption of the right of white Europeans to exterminate a resident, techno-
logically backward, colored population in order to take over the continent."
The country's energy is "the energy of violence, of free-floating resentment

and anxiety unleashed by chronic cultural dislocations which must be, for the most part, ferociously sublimated" (*Styles of Radical Will,* 195). And, for Sontag,

> the unquenchable American moralism and the American faith in violence are not just twin symptoms of some character neurosis taking the form of a protracted adolescence which presages an eventual maturity. They constitute a full grown, firmly-installed national psychosis, founded, as are all psychoses, on the efficacious denial of reality. (196)

Finally, Sontag added,

> there is a profound concordance between the sexual revolution, redefined, and the political revolution, redefined. That being a socialist and taking certain drugs (in a fully serious spirit: as a technique for exploring one's consciousness, not as an anodyne or a crutch), that there is no incompatibility between the exploration of inner space and the rectification of social space. (201–2)

This last statement points to what has remained the most highly contested legacy of the 1960s, that of culture and the relations between "lifestyle" and politics. The more far-reaching political and historical claims of the 1960s movements were from the beginning subsumed by issues of fashion, music, drugs, and sexuality. Reagan set the tone of right-wing responses to 1960s movements in his gubernatorial campaign of 1966 by running as much against their cultural manifestations as against the political positions of his opponent, Pat Brown.[10] Reagan promised to "clean up the mess at Berkeley" and in particular the "sexual orgies so vile I cannot describe them to you" (in Cannon, *Reagan,* 148). A hippie, he said, was someone who "dresses like Tarzan, has hair like Jane, and smells like Cheetah" (in Gitlin, *The Sixties,* 217).

This reaction to the 1960s as a threatening cultural and sexual upheaval continued through the 1970s. After the overtly political energies of the 1960s had ebbed, struggles over American cultural definitions intensified, and the political targets of the Right became abortion rights and feminism, affirmative action, and drugs. Richard Viguerie, the conservative fund-raiser, said in 1981 after Reagan was elected president,

> It was the social issues that got us this far, and that's what
> will take us into the future. We never really won until we
> began stressing issues like busing, abortion, school prayer
> and gun control. We talked about the sanctity of free enter-
> prise, about the communist onslaught until we were blue in
> the face. But we didn't start winning majorities in elections
> until we got down to gut level issues. (in Davis, 171)

This emphasis from the Right on the political scope of cultural, family, and
gender issues has continued through the 1980s to the present, and its point of
reference has always been, quite explicitly, the 1960s. In the 1988 presidential
campaign, George Bush could accuse the leaders of the Democratic Party of
being "a remnant of the 1960s, the new left, those campus radicals grown old,
the peace marchers and nuclear freeze activists" (in Isserman, 990). And at a
"Second Thoughts Conference" in 1987, whose participants were for the most
part former 1960s radicals who had "recanted," Hilton Kramer, as a neoconservative elder statesmen, chided the proceedings for its failure to disavow the
1960s counterculture, as if these reformed leftists could not truly enter the
Right merely by changing their political positions on the Vietnam War, welfare, taxation, and so on. "Is it really possible," Kramer asked, "to separate the
politics of the Movement from the counterculture?" For the true catastrophe
of the 1960s, he argued, lay in

> the drug culture, the rock culture, the sexual revolution, the
> assault on the family and the middle class, the assault on high
> culture and the aggrandizement of popular culture, the devas-
> tation of the universities as centers of cultural and intellec-
> tual life.... Didn't anybody have any understanding of the
> wreckage that was left in its wake? The wreckage in family
> life and sexual life and academic and intellectual life, in the
> whole structure of Western Culture? (Collier and Horowitz,
> 176)

Of course, as many writers have observed, the extent of this reaction and
the continued durability of the 1960s as site of political and cultural struggle
testify to the successes of the 1960s social movements. As Rosalind Pollack

Petchesky writes, the New Right is largely "a movement to turn back the tide of the major social movements of the 1960s and 1970s," and the strength of the reaction "is in part a measure of the effectiveness of the women's and gay movements, the extent to which their ideas (and various commercial distortions of their ideas) have penetrated popular culture and consciousness." In fact, Petchesky insists on the central position of issues of gender and sexuality in the debates over the 1960s, arguing that "if the embodiment of absolute evil for an earlier generation of the Right was international communism, the Left, and labor movements . . . in the most recent period it is feminism and homosexuality" (450, 439).[11]

The "apocalypse," the revelatory trauma, for Reaganism, then, was not the Cold War or the presence of communists in Hollywood, though these were certainly major factors in Reagan's biography and in conservative thinking. The real apocalypse was the 1960s, both as a cultural upheaval and as a traumatic reverberation of earlier American traumas. The problem Reaganism faced was how to confront — indeed, how to account for — social and historical trauma when according to its post-apocalyptic definition of America, none should exist.

The Reaganist post-apocalypse had two main theoretical components: an outlook on American history and a development of consumerism. As a historical outlook, Reaganism's distinctive feature was a denial or disavowal of the traumas of history. Deriving from long-standing views of America as New Jerusalem or City on a Hill or promised land, Reaganism was forced to confront the critiques of American history that were articulated most powerfully in the 1960s.[12]

Reagan's speech on Martin Luther King's birthday in 1987 illustrates some of the mechanics of Reaganist history. In a crucial passage, Reagan says of King,

> What he accomplished — not just for black Americans, but
> for all Americans — he lifted a heavy burden from this country. As surely as black Americans were scarred by the yoke
> of slavery, America was scarred by injustice. Many Americans didn't fully realize how heavy America's burden was
> until it was lifted. (166)

The passage implies that the burden of racial injustice has, in fact, now been lifted. And yet the deeper implication is that this burden that he praises King for lifting really never existed at all, in that "many Americans" did not feel it as a burden. Indeed, Reagan included himself in that number. He wrote in his 1989 introduction to the speech, "I didn't appreciate what a remarkable man he was while he was living. But I suppose that's the way it is with prophets. You sometimes don't know their impact and importance until they're gone" (164). Reagan invokes the "scars" of slavery and injustice but in a way that denies them any present consequences. He denies that these scars were ever actually administered or felt as wounds.[13] The entire history of racism began and ended without his knowledge, and therefore utterly outside of his responsibility. King ended racism, and in that way "freed the white man" from any possible burden of guilt. Yet, at the same time, racism never really existed, and Reagan's own opposition to the 1964 Voting Rights Act, for example, was merely a constitutional reservation based on a devotion to states' rights. By the end of Reagan's speech, King is transformed into an eternal emblem of an imaginary racial harmony:

> Americans may have lost the comfort and courage of Dr. King's presence, but we've not really lost him. Every time a black woman casts a ballot, Martin King is there. Every time a black man is hired for a good job, Dr. King is there. Every time a black child receives a sound education, Dr. King is there. Every time a black person is elected to public office, Dr. King is there. Every time black and white Americans work side by side for a better future, Dr. King is there. (166)

Needless to say, these hopeful scenarios are at the very least counterbalanced by the discouraging realities of African American poverty, poor education, and health care and by the continuing national legacy of racial hostility. Nevertheless, Reagan cast King as a key agent in a redemptive history in which redemption has, in fact, arrived and was always assured. King, in Reagan's speech, is an American hero worthy of having his own holiday because the national traumas he addressed are disavowed. The apocalypse, or revelatory cataclysm, to which Reagan's speech obliquely refers is the racial turmoil of the 1960s. The construction of a Reaganist, American post-apocalypse consists of this series of simultaneous and contradictory moves: There was racial injustice in America once; Martin Luther King solved America's racial problems; there was never racial injustice in America. In this way, Reagan elided the ongoing struggle to achieve racial justice, for in the Reaganist post-apocalypse the battle has been won without needing to be fought.

For Reaganism, the traditional American apocalyptic prophecy — what America will be, or is meant to be, or ought to be — slides instantaneously into post-apocalyptic fulfillment. America wins because it is a "nation of champions." In his 1984 campaign for reelection, Reagan gave the Olympic Games held in Los Angeles great symbolic value. The 1984 Olympics was, of course, a somewhat empty competition that the United States dominated because of the boycott of the Eastern bloc countries — and in itself a perfect Reaganist post-apocalypse in that the chief adversary simply did not appear. But apart from the obvious element of America's effortless athletic triumphs, Reagan used the Olympics to demonstrate America's triumph over its own inner problems — and again, most critically, over the traumatic divisions of the 1960s. The climax of one of Reagan's most frequently delivered 1984 campaign speeches was a description of the passing of the Olympic torch across the continent. The torch's journey created the sense of a national harmony transcending region, age, race, and class. And at the final stage, "then, in San Francisco, a Vietnamese immigrant, his little son held on his shoulders, dodged photographers and policemen to cheer a nineteen-year-old black man pushing an eighty-eight-year-old white woman in a wheelchair as she carried the torch. My friends, that's America" (215). This passage alludes to the most traumatic events of the 1960s, the Vietnam War and racial turmoil, and eliminates all their traumatic content in an image of perfectly achieved social harmony. The Vietnamese child on his father's shoulders rewrites the My Lai massacre and American soldiers' fears of young Vietcong who could be anywhere in an urban crowd. The helpful young black man at the service of the ailing elderly white woman transforms the memories of race riots and fears of urban crime. The choice of these characters shows the persistence of the traumas of the 1960s; their transformation into figures of an actually achieved, not an imagined, social harmony shows the peculiar mechanics of the Reaganist post-apocalypse that disavows its own apocalyptic moment.

REAGAN AT BITBURG FOR THE END OF HISTORY

Never Again: In his confused, virtually incoherent press conferences before his visits to Bergen-Belsen and Bitburg, Reagan seemed to change the referent of this familiar phrase.

> And it seemed to me that this could be symbolic also of say-
> ing — what I said about the — what this day should be. And
> let's resolve, in their presence, as well as in the presence of
> our own troops that this must never happen again. (March
> 18, 1985; quoted in Hartman, *Bitburg,* 240)[14]

He used the phrase again speaking to the press on April 29:

> Well I've said to some of my friends about that, all those in
> that cemetery have long since met the Supreme Judge of right
> and wrong. And whatever punishment or justice was needed
> has been rendered by One who is above us all. And it isn't
> going there to honor anyone. It's going there simply to, in
> that surrounding, more visibly bring to the people an aware-
> ness of the great reconciliation that has taken place and, as
> I've said before — too many times, I guess — the need to re-
> member in the sense of being pledged to never letting it hap-
> pen again. (Hartman, *Bitburg,* 252)

Reagan's statements leave open the question of just *what* must never happen again. Is "it" the murder of Jews? Or the systematic genocide of any people, or brutalities and atrocities of all kinds? The statements imply, rather, that what must never happen again is war between the United States and Germany. Celebrating the "great reconciliation," after all, was the original purpose of Chancellor Helmut Kohl's invitation to Bitburg and Reagan's acceptance — be-fore the reports of the graves of SS soldiers appeared in the press. The Holocaust and its terminology entered Reagan's Bitburg statements only as a result of public and media pressure. In both press conferences just cited, Reagan said "never again" just after a reference to the dead SS soldiers in the cemetery. On April 18, he said of them, "The average age is about 18. These were those young teenagers that were conscripted, forced into military service in the close of the Third Reich, when they were short of manpower, and we're the victor and they're there." And in answering the final question of the press conference, Does that mean you're still going to Bitburg? Reagan concluded,

> I think that there's nothing wrong with visiting that cemetery where those young men are victims of Nazism also, even though they were fighting in the German uniform, drafted into service to carry out the hateful wishes of the Nazis. They were victims, just as surely as the victims in the concentration camps. (Hartman, *Bitburg,* 240)

Reagan referred to the Holocaust — "never again" — and yet the Holocaust is not what he was referring to. Rather, through a series of moral equivalences, he subsumed that central and persistent trauma of the Second World War under a Cold War narrative that relied on the American–West German alliance and assimilated Nazism and its crimes into a general notion of "totalitarianism" whose agent was the Soviet Union. Stephen Brockman has described the Cold War logic in Reagan's Bitburg speech that allowed Nazi Germany to be so easily transformed into Soviet Russia, a transformation that necessarily required de-emphasizing the Holocaust.[15] Indeed, Reagan's equating of German soldiers and concentration camp inmates as "victims" of Nazism approached the positions of the right-wing German historians involved in the *historikerstreit,* or historians' conflict, of the late 1970s and the 1980s. Andreas Hillgruber's *Two Sorts of Demise: The Shattering of the German Reich and the End of European Jewry,* for example, as its title indicates, parallels the Holocaust with the defeat of Nazi Germany and claims a tragic status for both sets of events. Hillgruber's account is especially evocative with regard to the doomed struggle of the German troops on the Eastern front against a brutal communist onslaught. Ernst Nolte, in a 1986 essay ("The Past That Will Not Pass Away"), went further, portraying the Holocaust as an "Asiatic," that is, an un-German — indeed Russian — sort of action. Nolte asks,

> Did the National Socialists carry out, did Hitler perhaps carry out an "Asiatic" deed only because they regarded themselves and their kind as the potential or real victims of an "Asiatic" deed? Wasn't the "Gulag Archipelago" more original than Auschwitz? Wasn't class murder on the part of the Bolsheviks logically and actually prior to racial murder on the part of the Nazis? (in Maier, 30)[16]

In such interpretations, the Second World War can be seen as an aberration, a detour around but finally leading back to the real struggle, which has always been the struggle against Soviet communism. Likewise, Reagan in his speech at Bitburg incredibly portrayed Americans and Germans as having always been allies against a totalitarianism wholly identified with the Soviet Union. In the emotional center of this speech, Reagan tells of how during the Battle of the Bulge, four American and four German soldiers simultaneously wander on Christmas Eve to the isolated cottage of an old German woman. As Reagan narrated the scene,

> The woman was afraid, but she quickly said with a firm voice, "... there will be no shooting here." She made all the soldiers lay down their weapons, and they all joined in the makeshift meal. Heinz and Willi, it turned out, were only 16; the corporal was the oldest at 23. Their natural suspicion dissolved in the warmth and comfort of the cottage. One of the Germans, a former medical student, tended the wounded American. But now, listen to the rest of the story through the eyes of one who was there, now a grown man, but that young man that had been her son. He said, "The Mother said grace. I noticed that there were tears in her eyes as she said the old, familiar words, 'Komm, Herr Jesus. Be our guest.' And as I looked around the table, I saw tears, too, in the eyes of the battle-weary soldiers, boys again, some from America, some from Germany, all far from home." (Hartman, *Bitburg,* 260)

In this story, there are no real differences between Germans and Americans, or between the German army and the American army. Indeed, it is almost too much to say that Reagan's speech at Bitburg celebrates a reconciliation between the United States and Germany; in the Christmas anecdote, no reconciliation is necessary. The two nations share the same Western, and Christian, culture, and this fundamental identity enables them to overcome any temporary antagonisms — as could never be the case with the atheist Soviet Union. Nazism, in this context, was a horrendous but brief misdirection of a fundamentally virtuous — and, pointedly, Christian — culture, while communism is a genuine, systemic evil. Thus, when Reagan goes on to speak of his solidar-

ity with victims of oppression, the only oppressors he can name are the Soviet
Union and their surrogates. Or rather he confuses the issue by first stating, "I
am a Jew in a world still threatened by anti-Semitism," and then continuing,

> I am an Afghan, and I am a prisoner of the Gulag, I am a
> refugee in a crowded boat foundering off of the coast of Viet-
> nam, I am a Laotian, a Cambodian, a Cuban, and a Miskito
> Indian in Nicaragua. I, too, am a potential victim of totalitar-
> ianism. (Hartman, *Bitburg,* 261).

The "Jew" in Reagan's list is without location. It can no longer be in Germany. Is it in Israel? the Soviet Union? New York? Wherever it is, it is *not*
threatened by "totalitarianism" but by an anti-Semitism that seems to have no
source or agency. The "Jew" is merely the occasion for the victims of communism that follow. Reagan's "Jew" summons the memory of the Holocaust, but
summons it as a dislocated, ahistorical atrocity, and then disperses that memory and its moral weight among the conflicts of the Cold War. Where then are
the Jews, and the Holocaust, in the Bitburg speech? They are there and not
there, everywhere and nowhere. Without the traumatic memory of the Holocaust, there would be no need for such elaborate and circuitous reconciliation.
But no sooner is it cited than it is redeemed by being assimilated to the Reaganist narrative of American perfection, now expanded to include Germany.
Reagan dedicates one paragraph early in the speech to "the survivors of the
Holocaust" and promises that "we will never forget, and we say with the victims of that Holocaust: 'Never again' " (Hartman, *Bitburg,* 258). And yet in
the very next sentence, in the most direct affront to memory possible, Reagan
characterizes the Second World War as "the war against one man's totalitarian
dictatorship" and repeats the point he had made earlier to the press regarding
the innocence and victimization of the German SS soldiers buried at Bitburg.
In Reagan's account, then, the Holocaust did occur; six million Jews died in
the Second World War—but apparently no Germans took part in killing them.

Widespread public outrage against this elision of the Holocaust as crime
forced Reagan to precede his visit to Bitburg with a visit to the Bergen-Belsen
concentration camp. His speech at the camp, however, shows in more detail
the same process of assimilating historical trauma to a narrative of redemption. As was the case with his tribute to Martin Luther King, Reagan acknowl-

edges traumatic events in the past, portrays those problems, cruelties, and injustices as definitively solved, and finally implies — in the light of the redeemed present — that the historical traumas in question were not really so traumatic after all.

Reagan accomplishes this assimilation of trauma at Bergen-Belsen by casting Anne Frank as a prophet of redemption. Having observed the natural beauty around him — "the greening farms and the emerging springtime of the lovely German countryside" — Reagan notes that the inmates of the camp "must have felt the springtime was gone forever from their lives" (Hartman, Bitburg, 254). He then quotes from Anne Frank's diary the famous passage in which she expresses her faith that " 'in spite of everything . . . people are good at heart,' " and which continues, " 'I hear the approaching thunder which will destroy us too; I can feel the suffering of millions and yet, if I looked up into the heavens I think that it will all come right, that this cruelty too will end and that peace and tranquillity will return again' " (Hartman, *Bitburg,* 255). And for Reagan, this is exactly what has come to pass. Peace and tranquillity have indeed returned in the "springtime of the lovely German countryside," and what Anne Frank saw as she looked up into the heavens has now been accomplished.

And yet, between this "prophecy" and its "fulfillment," the Holocaust itself disappears, and Reagan uses Anne Frank's diary as a way of avoiding the trauma of the concentration camps even at the moment he is speaking in one. It is not difficult to make use of Anne Frank in this optimistic way, for all of her diary that we possess was written before her imprisonment. Containing nothing about the camps, *The Diary of Anne Frank* is only in a limited sense a document of the Holocaust. Her optimism — as remarkably articulate and moving as it is — is a function of innocence. And Reagan's appropriation of this innocence as the basis of a fulfilled prophecy confirms Bruno Bettelheim's assertion in *The Informed Heart* that *The Diary of Anne Frank* "found wide acclaim because . . . it denies implicitly that Auschwitz ever existed. If all men are good, there never was an Auschwitz" (252).

"We're here," Reagan says at Bergen-Belsen, "to commemorate that life triumphed over the tragedy and death of the Holocaust — over the sickness, the testing, and yes, the gassings." A paragraph later, Reagan cites the Talmud to the effect that " 'it was only through suffering that the children of Israel obtained three priceless and coveted gifts: the Torah, the Land of Israel, and the

World to Come.' Yes, out of this sickness—as crushing and cruel as it was—there was hope for the world as well as for the World to Come. Out of the ashes—hope. And from all the pain—promise" (254). And Reagan concludes that memories of the Holocaust "take us where God intended his children to go—toward learning, toward healing, and, above all, toward redemption" (255). These passages show very clearly the Reaganist post-apocalyptic historical vision. Each term denoting the trauma of the Holocaust—"ashes," "pain," "sickness," "suffering"—Reagan immediately subordinates to a term that turns away from the trauma toward a future or, rather, toward a present, in which the trauma has already been healed and redeemed. In the same way, the speech at Bergen-Belsen itself, which was a last-minute addition to Reagan's itinerary, is subordinate to the speech at Bitburg.

As I described earlier, Reagan's suppression of the Holocaust at Bitburg and Bergen-Belsen was in part a result of the practical policies and demonic fantasies of the Cold War. At the same time, American Cold War ideologies themselves were part of older and more general Manichaean and apocalyptic tendencies in American emotional and political life. And the uniqueness of the Reaganist disavowals of trauma in the 1980s lay in its relation to the upheavals of the 1960s. But further, as the events at Bitburg make clear, even the Holocaust, for Reaganism, was invested with 1960s traumas. At Bitburg, Reagan reaffirmed the necessity and justice of the struggle against communism and claimed kinship with the recent victims of (Soviet) totalitarianism—the Afghans, Vietnamese, Nicaraguans, and others. All the instances that Reagan invoked were part of his continuous effort definitively to reinscribe the war in Vietnam as a "noble cause." Vietnam was a noble cause because it defended innocent victims against communist totalitarianism. It was thus, in these simplistic terms, a just war in the same way that the Second World War was a just war.

At Bitburg, as he did a year earlier at Normandy, Reagan again proclaimed the justice of all American military endeavors and thus rewrote and eliminated the trauma from the Vietnam War without even mentioning it.[17] As a corollary to the American perfection he insisted on, then, our German friends could not have been responsible for the Holocaust. For if the Holocaust really was perpetrated by these Christian, anticommunist allies, then Americans might have committed crimes in Vietnam, and racism might still exist in America—and the United States would not be the country that Reagan claimed it is. In this sense then, the entire Reaganist post-apocalypse of disavowal depends on disavowing the traumatic legacy of the Holocaust and assimilating it, as Reaganism assimilates all historical traumas, to a narrative of achieved redemption.[18]

The Reaganist historical view centering around redemption, the disavowal of trauma, and the achieved utopia is an "end of history" scenario. The traumatic, apocalyptic moment of American history has come, and gone, unnoticed; the wound, which was never suffered, is now healed. America has already entered its future, which was implicit in its origin. In Reaganism, the apocalypse has already happened: America is triumphant, communism is dead. This post-apocalyptic triumphalism entails the "end of history" as its corollary, and it is useful to look at Francis Fukuyama's well-known essay as Reaganist history in more intellectual form. Fukuyama's article was widely attacked for its moral complacency and the provocative absurdity of its thesis (notwithstanding his Hegelian qualifications). But it has not been sufficiently noted how directly Fukuyama's "End of History" functions as an intellectual apologetic and support for Reaganism. Fukuyama's post-apocalypticism takes the same general form as Reagan's. First, he announces an "unabashed victory" for the forces of liberal democracy. Second, he explains how this victory has been implicit nearly since the time when the principles of liberal democracy were first articulated. And finally, Fukuyama shows that all catastrophes, traumas, and injustices between the time of democracy's origin and its present fulfillment can be assimilated to his narrative of a perfect beginning and perfect ending. Citing Alexandre Kojève, his intellectual model, Fukuyama asserts that "while there was considerable work to be done after 1806 [the date of the Battle of Jena, the moment when Hegel claimed that history ended] — abolishing slavery and the slave trade, extending the franchise to workers, women, blacks, and other racial minorities, etc. — the basic *principles* of the liberal democratic state could not be improved on" (5). Likewise, while Fukuyama acknowledges economic disparities in the United States, he dismisses their importance on the grounds that they do not arise out of "the underlying legal and social structures of our society." In fact, for Fukuyama, the United States is post-apocalyptic in a Marxist sense: "But surely," he writes, "the class issue has actually been successfully resolved in the West. As Kojève (among others) noted, the egalitarianism of modern America represents the essential achievement of the classless society envisioned by Marx" (9).

For Fukuyama, as for Reagan, the world is already redeemed. The principles of liberal democracy have triumphed, and it is morning in America. Again, however, Fukuyama, like Reagan, has difficulty fitting into his redemptive narrative the most severe political and moral catastrophe of recent history—the Second World War and the Holocaust. In order that the end of the Cold War function as the end of history, Fukuyama must minimize the traumatic impact of Nazism and, even more, must positively transform the Second World War into a historical felix culpa that leads directly to a redemptive conclusion. Thus, Fukuyama writes,

> The two world wars in this century and their attendant revolutions and upheavals simply had the effect of extending those [liberal democratic] principles spatially, such that the various provinces of human civilization were brought up to the level of its most advanced outposts, and of forcing those societies in Europe and North America at the vanguard of civilization to implement their liberalism more fully. (5)

As for Nazism, Fukuyama writes that "Hitler represented a diseased bypath in the general course of European development and since his fiery defeat, the legitimacy of any kind of territorial aggrandizement has been thoroughly discredited" (16). Fukuyama's characterization of the Third Reich simply as "Hitler" and as a "diseased bypath" is in accord with Reagan's "the evil of just one man." For both, the whole phenomenon and all the deeds of Nazism can be, like a benign tumor, surgically removed from history. Indeed, the fortunate end of history is contingent on this removal.

REAGANISM AND POST-APOCALYPTIC ADVERTISING

In 1981, a group of advertising creators and executives met in New York to discuss the state and future of their industry. Of particular concern was the low regard into which business had fallen with the public. John Elliott Jr., chairman of the board of Ogilvy and Mather, cited polls showing the loss of public respect for business. Only fifteen percent of people polled believed that the chemical industry, for example, was socially responsible. Likewise, James H. Foster, senior vice president and general manager of Brouillard Communications, acknowledged that eighty-two percent believed that business was "greedy, selfish, and would make profit at the expense of the public." Foster attributed this distrust to the attacks on corporate culture they had suffered as a result of the 1960s, and he and the other participants spoke of the corporate sector's need to speak up for itself and regain public confidence.[19]

Those at the conference saw reasons for optimism, however. Foster pointed out that while the public distrusted business, they distrusted government at least as much (eighty-three percent opposed more government regulation), and eighty percent agreed that business "had the resources to provide a better quality of life." Furthermore, the 1980 presidential election had shown the business and advertising communities a new model for effective communication. As Chairman Elliott said, "Dutch Reagan seems to speak for himself better than does business." David Milenthal, executive vice president of Hameroff/Milenthal, Inc., added that "Ronald Reagan, in a sense, exemplifies the type of sincerity business needed to convey in order to win back public trust. I believe the public is into sincerity." And Pete Daley, who had helped produce ads for Reagan's 1980 campaign, spoke of Reagan as a "model for advertisers," a figure who could "change attitudes dramatically and substantively." For Daley, the key to Reagan's success as a communicator was his ability to reach an audience's emotions, and to get to the audience by the most direct route, never confusing the issue. Daley mentioned an incident from the campaign when Reagan, having listened to his aides' complex discussions of policy, summed up the *real* message: Family, Neighborhood, Peace, Freedom.

The conferees agreed that business firms and their advertising agents needed to sell not only particular products but the sense of a larger social vision, and both their vision and their means of describing it would be modeled after Reagan's campaign. Thus, the Hameroff/Milenthal television ad for an Ohio utility company stressed, "We're always there," and showed a panorama of American life: farms and cities, a black mother and her daughter on a merry-go-round, a welder, dad in his easy chair, a boy with a toy train. Through all of this, the company is "bringing you the power—to make tomorrow's dreams come true," and the ad ends with parents putting their little girl to bed and turning out the light. This vision of absolute social harmony, of an entire reconciliation of all oppositions of class, race, and gender, the repair of all families, the achievement of utopia, is at the center of the Reaganist vision as it appears in advertising, whether political or corporate.

If a vision of history that disavows trauma is the first major feature of Reaganism, the second is a social vision, expressed in advertising and in attitudes
toward commodities, which shares the disavowing logic of Reaganist history.
Consumer culture of the 1980s was, like Reaganist history, a post-apocalyptic
disavowal of social division and trauma. Not all the advertising of the 1980s
was Reaganist, but a great deal of it portrayed the Reaganist vision and gives
a clear sense of the dominant ideology of the time. Roland Barthes in the late
1950s wrote that the automobile was the gothic cathedral of capitalism, "the
supreme creation of an era, conceived with passion by unknown artists, and
consumed in image if not in usage by a whole population which appropriates
them as a purely magical object" (*Mythologies,* 88). But by the 1980s it was
clear that not the product but the ad served this function. In the 1980s advertisements reached new levels of technical skill and permeation of the social
environment. Moreover, by the 1980s the product had become inseparable from
its marketing image. Indeed its image, its ad campaign, preceded and shaped
its design and production.

The advertisement must sell more than just the product. As historians of
advertising have documented, this necessity of excess meaning has governed
advertising almost from its beginnings as small announcements in eighteenth-
century newspapers. In chronicling the rise of mass marketing in the United
States in the twentieth century, Roland Marchand shows how such ideological
factors as social ambition, social harmony, changing gender roles, patriotism,
the idea of modernity, and the consumption ethic itself were crucial elements
in mass marketing from its inception.[20] This need of advertising to portray the
product as qualitatively more than what it is, or could ever be, progressed to
the point where in the 1980s the product could even entirely disappear from
the advertisement, as in the famous Infiniti car ads of the mid-1980s. These
ads engaged in a kind of iconographic catachresis, or commercial iconoclasm,
asserting that no image of the actual car could possibly contain the car's full
character and meaning. The ads consisted instead entirely of images of nature — rain, trees, mountains, a lake, birds, the ocean. Sometimes these images
suggested sublime, uncontrollable natural power; at other times, an aestheti-
sized, humanly comprehensible natural world. Over the images, a male voice
spoke about "luxury" as a form of human relationship with beauty and power.
This relation is a mystical "Zen" sense of connection: "You don't see it, you

feel it; you're part of it, you control it; it is part of you . . ." The narrator's halting, diffident voice also contributed to this sense of the car's inexpressibility. The narrator seemed to know that nothing he said could be adequate, that, finally, he could only speak in clichés, for the car's essence would always elude him.[21]

The Infiniti ads were the extreme instance showing the irrelevance of the product in relation to its meaning, and the degree to which its meaning seemed to exceed the possibilities of expression. "Coke Is It" went another popular ad. But what is *it*? Marx called the commodity "a very queer thing, abounding in metaphysical subtleties and theological niceties" (81), and went on to describe it derisively in terms of a primitive religious fetish, a worthless physical object assuming the social position of a god. There is no need here to detail the logic of the fetish, except to point out its Marxian role as a mask covering over social relations and its Freudian role as a disavowal of trauma. For Marx, the commodity was a "social hieroglyphic" (85) that concealed exploitative social relations under the terms of divinity or nature. Freud, in theorizing individual male psychology, wrote of the fetish object as embodying a disavowal of the traumatic fear of castration by providing a substitute for the mother's missing penis. "The horror of castration sets up a sort of permanent memorial to itself" ("Fetishism," 154), pointing back toward trauma while transforming it and denying any traumatic effects.

Freud's concern is ultimately with the desire for the fetish as an emblem of restored wholeness and harmony in the wake of some trauma whose effects are still being felt. (Here as elsewhere in Freud, we do not need to retain his overemphasis on male psychology and castration fears.) Marx's stress is on the worship of the fetish (that is, of capital, the purest commodity form) and the consequent disregard for actual, oppressive social relations. To understand Reaganist advertising and consumerist ideology, we need to combine these perspectives on the fetish: to see the "social hieroglyphic" not merely as a concealment but as a disavowal of traumatic social relations, and to see the Freudian disavowal as primarily social.[22] In the characteristic Reaganist images of harmony and reconciliation—of the achieved utopia—we also see their disavowed traumas.[23]

For Reaganism, as I discussed earlier, the principal trauma was the perceived social disintegration that occurred during the 1960s and whose effects persisted through the presidency of Jimmy Carter. While much of Reagan's and the New

Right's rhetoric extolled the individual, and their policies sought to turn back the New Deal and the Great Society and to establish a more solid corporate hegemony and oligopoly, the power of Reaganist advertising lay in its powerful appeals to a sense of community, its vision of a society without divisions. In Reagan's own campaign ads, we see typically panoramic visions of a perfect nation.[24] In "Prouder, Stronger, Better" (1984) the sun rises over a montage of American scenes — over a fishing boat, a cowboy, a wedding, children playing, the American flag. The ad gives enormous weight to images of family and community, as figures of individualism (the fisherman and cowboy) are finally subordinated to strong social bonds — to images, finally, of love. Such panoramic visual effects suggesting an overarching social harmony are common to all the ads in the campaign. In "Spring of '84," a voice tells us, "This is America... and this...and this..." as we see a farmhouse, a city playground, a circus clown, a factory, the Grand Canyon. "America's Back" presents images of new houses, new cars, a factory opening, and a young African American family in front of their suburban home as the father is painting his white fence.

The imagery is utopian — it portrays a nation with no problems — and it is a utopia of the present. The social harmony we see is not an ideal we are meant to strive toward; it is already in place. But while the ads' imagery suggests no trauma at all, the ads' narration does hint at a past time of troubles, now transcended: "With a sense of pride people thought we'd never feel again. Now that our country's turning around, why would we ever turn back?" "Why would we want to return to where we were just four short years ago?" The narration refers, of course, to Jimmy Carter's presidency and its 1960s-style emphasis on moral self-criticism and national "malaise." Carter shared Reagan's traditional Christian-American view of America's apocalyptic role, but his jeremiad on national moral failings was opposed to Reagan's post-apocalyptic view of American perfection. In Reagan's ads, the apocalyptic and traumatic moment was Carter's jeremiad (which was itself a continuation of moral criticism from the 1960s). Focusing on Carter's diagnosis of "malaise," Reagan denies the content of Carter's criticism. The voice in the ad refers to trauma — as if to say, Jimmy Carter *tells you* there are fundamental problems in America — while the images deny trauma: See for yourself, this is the real America![25]

That Reagan as political commodity and as historical visionary held an extraordinarily deep appeal for many Americans is evidenced not only by his electoral successes and enduring personal popularity (even after the electorate rejected the legacy of his policies) but also by the advertisements from the 1980s that strikingly resemble Reagan's campaign ads. Advertisers took seriously the advice they gave themselves in 1981 to use Reagan's campaign techniques as models. A campaign for Bud Light beer shown at the time of the 1984 Olympics seems to have been directly inspired by Reagan's ads and by his speech at the Republican convention. One version takes place at a factory, the other at a farm. In each we see a vision of absolute social harmony. At the factory, the workers have all pitched in to help Carl's daughter train as a gymnast, and now Carl and his friends walk into the boss's office above the shop floor to watch the girl on TV, performing her balance beam routine at the Olympics in Los Angeles. And all of them — management and labor together, black workers with white workers — are united in their pride in the little girl, in themselves, and in their country. "The true measure of the Olympics," reports the narration, "is not in the winning, but in discovering the best in all of us." What this "best" consists of is the eliding of race and class distinctions — not through any changes in economic or social conditions but through uniting in a cause, or set of related causes (a young girl, a workplace, a nation) that transcend distinctions. The ad, in a way, refigures *Uncle Tom's Cabin* in that social antagonisms are reconciled for the sake of a small white girl. The difference is that in the ad, the girl is no longer a victim, she is a winner.

In the farm version of the ad, a small group of farmers, already at work in the early morning, observe the approach of a single runner along the narrow road that bisects the vast grain fields, carrying the Olympic torch in one leg of its journey from Boston to Los Angeles. The farmers stop their work to watch and, as he passes, to applaud this blond athlete who, like them, has begun his work before dawn and who is using his talents, like them, to serve his country. The scene with the torch could be part of Reagan's nomination acceptance speech: "And all along the way, that torch became a celebration of America. And we all became participants in the celebration" (215). There is another detail in the ad, realistic but also unsettling. The runner is not, in fact, alone on the country road. He is preceded and followed by several police cars with lights flashing. Of course this would have to be the case. The lone runner carrying this powerful symbol on public roads must have protection against careless or insane motorists. The parallelism of the passage just quoted from Reagan's speech links the torch being carried with ourselves as participants. The torch is everywhere ("all along the way"), and so are we ("we all"). The torch is a celebration; we are in the celebration. Therefore, the torch is us. We too are being carried by the runners. But we too must be protected. The farmers applaud the runner, but in doing so they also applaud the police. The police presence is incidental, just a necessary precaution. And yet it is also fundamental: the procession of the torch, the celebration of America, the unsullied social harmony these ads portray cannot take place without police protection. Protection from what? From the madness of the highway, from terrorists, from ordinary muggers who have overflowed their urban containment, from jealous competitors, from potholes and decaying bridges, from lack of health insurance, from performance-enhancing drugs, from costly litigation, from race riots, from teenage suicide, from unemployment. The police protection is an unintentional reminder that the achieved utopia of Reaganism relies on the denial (and, when necessary, the violent denial) of a massive weight of historical and social fact.[26]

Another direction of Reaganist advertising took a more direct approach toward the traumas of the 1960s. "Who says you can't have it all?" was the slogan of a series of Michelob beer ads in 1983. In the ads we see very hip young professional men and women enjoying their leisure time to the fullest in a bright nocturnal city flowing with sexual promise. "Who says you can't have pinstripes and rock and roll? Who says you can't have the world, without losing your soul?" These beautiful people do have it all: money and love in the midst of a city that is metonymous with their commercial and sexual ecstasy.[27] And they bring together, without pain or loss, the rock-and-roll authenticity and primal energy perceived as characteristic of the 1960s with the unchecked (either by government regulation or by moral scruple) consumerism of the 1980s. The Michelob ad is an urban, yuppie version of countless commercial portrayals of consumerist ecstasy: the parties around swimming pools (Bud Light) or on farms or at mountain resorts (Busch), the beach volleyball games selling a variety of soft drinks, the lone high-performance car on the winding mountain road. In these ecstatic ads, the participants appear to have died and gone to heaven, and heaven is contemporary America, here and now. The city, nature, technology, friendships, and sexual relations have become sites only of pleasure. The struggle to achieve happiness is over and forgotten; there is only happiness now, intense and overwhelming, like a sexual climax extended to infinity.[28] The Michelob ad contains the characteristic Reaganist posture. Gesturing toward the traumatic moment of the 1960s—toward the anarchy of rock and roll, sex, and, by implication, political rebellion—it then assimilates the trauma to a redemptive narrative of commodification.[29]

Levi's campaign for 501 Jeans (1985) invoked then defused anxieties concerning race and sex.[30] In one ad, a middle-aged or slightly older black blues singer sits by a window of a second-floor unfurnished apartment, playing the guitar and singing, and looking out the window. On the street, now observed by the blues singer, is a group of young white people dressed in tight 501 jeans enjoying themselves, kidding around and cavorting with each other, a bunch of good-looking kids on the street. There are a few girls, but most of them are white boys, and the camera's attention rests mainly on their tightly clad behinds. A few of the kids are now washing a car on the street, playfully splashing and squirting each other, and one guy flirtatiously juts out his rear end as he scrubs the car. The ad juxtaposes shots of the kids on the street and of the bluesman playing and watching from above.[31]

The black bluesman approves of, and can even be said to authorize, the white kids' activities, this intensive shaking of their booties. The ad claims to represent two complementary modes of "playing the blues." Yet surely there is also a threat, which the ad invokes and then defuses, in the black man's surveillance of the young white posteriors. As centuries of American sexual racism have emphasized, a white person—male or female—must never exhibit his ass to a big black man or he will be sure to suffer the consequences.[32] But these young, jean-clad white boys and girls do exactly that. They leave themselves open to—and perhaps even invite—the sexual attention of the old black bluesman. The bluesman, however, is now only an observer and narrator of sexuality; he is content just to strum his own guitar and enjoy the sexual abandon below him without intervening.

In this ad, then, the young white people (with the authorization of a representative of black authenticity, the bluesman) assume the gestures and attitudes of a stereotypical black street culture and black sexuality but without suffering either the threat of violence from blacks or the stigma and disadvantages of actually being black. The ad takes as its premise a traumatic history of racial difference and then, in a complex way, denies the traumatic nature of that history and preempts, through the benign presence of the bluesman, any objections to its denial. The bluesman's message is that Whites no longer need to be afraid of Blacks and no longer need to feel guilt: society is healed, is purged. The bluesman gives his blessing. He bequeaths his musically and sexually expressive culture and then removes his potentially threatening and disruptive presence. Thus, American race relations are reduced to a connection between blues and blue jeans; it is a history without trauma, a post-apocalypse without apocalypse, in either the destructive or the revelatory sense of the word.

REAGANISM AND THE TALK SHOW— AFTER THE END OF THERAPY

Reaganist history disavows historical and social traumas, claiming that all wounds have healed and were, therefore, never really wounds. Reaganist advertising portrays a society without antagonisms and implies that this wished-for, utopian world has been achieved. How then can we account for the emergence in the late 1980s of the television talk show as a major part of American popular culture?

This bizarre, excruciating form abandons the assumptions of perfect origins and ends that characterized Reaganist history and consumerism. To watch a typical episode of *Oprah, Jerry Springer, Ricki Lake, Jenny Jones, Donahue,* or *Rolanda* is a wrenchingly painful experience. It is to see that some terrible catastrophe has occurred, to view the aftermath of the destruction—perhaps of some Tower of Babel. For in spite of all the talking, the participants seem unable to communicate with each other. Each speaks his or her own language, a language of private pain. Each shouts it at the other, and at the audience. And the audience, which tries to fashion itself as a core of common opinion and morality, dissolves over the course of the program and enters the general trauma. If the dominant tendency of Reaganism is to deny the existence of trauma, the talk show's overwhelming urge is to display trauma continually: to *display,* not merely to talk about. The most painful and humiliating situations and relationships, and the problems at the center of American consciousness—the breakdown of families, betrayals of trust by figures of authority, racial hatreds (the very problems that Reaganist ideology claimed to have ended)—are acted out and repeated over and over. On talk shows these traumatic issues prove to be intractable. Discussions break down into shouting matches (often subtly, or explicitly, encouraged by the host); attempts at therapeutic closure or healing are usually comically trivial.

Who *are* these damaged, tormented, but at the same time ridiculous, people, and *why* are they telling us these awful things about themselves? What is this circus, this freak show, this convention of zombies? The talk show is the late-twentieth-century American post-apocalypse in its purest form. Its participants are "Elsies" out of William Carlos Williams: "the pure products of America/go crazy...as if the earth under our feet/were/an excrement of some sky." These are the people who live too near the river: the flood victims, the tornado victims blown out of their trailers, the victims of child abuse, the abandoned children and the parents who left them, Klan and militia weirdos and their neighbors, the haters and the hated, the victims of decaying schools, deregulation, the downsizing of industry and job growth in the "service" economy, the defeat of the labor movement, "the end of welfare as we know it." These are the living dead: the American working class.

But the talk shows present themselves not as any kind of political analysis or critique but as a form of family therapy. While class relations, as I will argue, is the catastrophe that underlies all others in the talk show, it is the least apparent. Racism, drug use, infidelity, child abuse, and homophobia are abundantly discussed but most often in the context of their effects on families. There are exceptions, of course. Oprah and Montel Williams have presented quite powerful programs on race relations in broader community and interpersonal contexts.[33] On the whole, however, on the talk show social crisis is family crisis. Jerry Springer, for example, presented an especially awful and exploitative program on the *children* of neo-Nazis. Jenny Jones presented a program on people with racists in their families.

Family therapy differs from traditional psychotherapy in that it locates illness not in the individual but in the family. Its concerns are not intrapsychic but interpersonal. Family therapy views the family as a self-perpetuating system in which each member takes on a particular role, and the system maintains its equilibrium through patterns of communication and interaction that family members invent, master, and repeat. One prominent role is that of "the sick one," the one with "the problem," but family therapy sees any problem as shared and mutually produced, a function of an entire system of interaction.

In a family therapy session, the therapist meets with the entire family. Not only does the therapist ask questions, she tries to create dramatic scenes that will allow her to see the family system reveal itself. Indeed, she herself plays a variety of roles in these scenes, allying herself with one family member and then another, often subtly urging family members into confrontations that they seem to be suppressing. Ultimately, what the family confronts is its own system. The confrontations that the therapist stages expose the system's full, systemic sickness, and so it is important that each scene unfold in its full drama. Quite astonishing is the degree to which a transcript of a family therapy session resembles a talk show, with the therapist as host:

> THERAPIST: Does she have a big temper?
> MR. SMITH: No, we've had —
> THERAPIST: No, she. She.
> MR. SMITH: No, she doesn't.
> MRS. SMITH: Oh, I scream now. I scream.
> MR. SMITH: Aw, for a minute you'll scream.
> THERAPIST: You are hiding that she has a big temper.
> MR. SMITH: No, I never thought she had a big temper.
> THERAPIST: Oh, I see it here, you know. She is like pepper. Like pepper, she is quite able to get —
> MR. SMITH: She can express herself all right.
> THERAPIST: She gets quite excited, doesn't she?
> MR. SMITH: I don't think so. You think so?
> MRS. SMITH: I think so.
> THERAPIST: Oh, yeah.
> MR. SMITH: Are we on television? (Minuchin, 179)

The camera, of course, is simply used by the therapist to record the session so that he can review it later. But given the session's dynamics, it is understandable that Mr. Smith might suddenly suspect he is a guest on *Donahue*.[34]

I am not competent to comment on family therapy's effectiveness. What I have read has impressed me. Comic resemblances to talk shows aside, it makes sense to regard individuals in the contexts of larger social structures, and patterns of interaction within families surely are crucial in how people define and misdefine themselves. At the same time, the exclusive focus on the family necessarily prevents giving attention to the family's own social contexts — the community, the workplace, the polity. The talk show and family therapy share an ideological presumption that the sources of illness and healing both reside entirely within the family. If we can cure the family, then individuals *and* society as a whole will also be cured.

This assumption regarding the central role of the family is also a key assumption of Reaganist ideology. The historian Michael Katz has written of how notions of a "culture of poverty"—the sociological predecessor of the "dysfunctional family"—having originated in liberal polemics for social reform, were ultimately adapted by neoconservatives and used to justify reductions in social programs. The pivotal document in this process was the Moynihan Report of 1965, with its remarks regarding the "pathology" of African American families. After the violent debates surrounding the Moynihan Report, political discussions of the family were increasingly severed from discussions of the economic and social circumstances of families. Social problems were seen—by thinkers like Charles Murray, Lawrence Mead, and others who influenced Reagan—as *caused by* breakdowns of the family rather than as *causes of* family problems.[35] Thus, family therapy and the talk show can be seen in the late 1980s as forms of *Reaganist* therapy. The American family, so sanctified by Reaganism, becomes, ironically, a kind of trash pit into which all social problems are thrown. And that is the real meaning of the term "trash TV."[36]

Talk shows differ from family therapy sessions, of course. In the first place, therapy sessions are private. On a talk show, the "fourth wall" of the therapy room is removed, so the session is exposed to studio and national audiences. This condition introduces the most immediately problematic issue raised in discussions of talk shows: their status as spectacle. As a public display, the therapeutic function becomes confused with exhibitionism and voyeurism, as guests strive to be more outrageous than they would be in private, and viewers watch with an increasingly gruesome sense of *schadenfreude*. This spectacular relationship between exhibitionist patient/performers and voyeurist viewers, mediated by the host-therapist, is central to the talk show's appeal. The program's therapeutic form dissolves into the fascination with mass media.

As the therapeutic setting opens up into spectacle, it brings together two apparently conflicting ideas of authority. The therapeutic ethos shares the widespread sense (discussed in chapter 2) of the authority of testimony and personal experience. Therapy involves the patient speaking of what *only* he or she knows. Even when others have had similar experiences, each person must testify him- or herself. There can be no "dittoheads" in testimony or in therapy.[37] But in an American culture so thoroughly influenced by mass media, the authority of the intensely personal runs up against an idea of authority in which *only* that which is presented to and seen by millions of people has any reality or value. There are celebrities — much of whose manifestation nowadays consists of testimony, confession, and therapy — and there are the rest of us, who are not on television, who are nobody. In celebrity culture, the authority of mass broadcast and the authority of testimony coexist. But the rest of us, who cannot broadcast our testimonies, by the logic of the spectacle have no testimonies to give. Only the private has value, but it only has value if it is massively public. The talk show bridges this gap. It allows everyone to testify publicly, and thereby to validate each private experience. Andy Warhol's prediction of the media culture bestowing on everyone fifteen minutes of fame does not capture the depth of need for this exposure. The desire to testify on a talk show is not a desire to be "famous"; it is a desire genuinely to exist, to have value at all.[38]

As therapy, opened out into spectacle, the talk show cannot succeed. Merely being on television for fifteen minutes cannot change the social relations and definitions that give value to some lives and not to others. Moreover, the personal and family problems presented and acted out on the shows cannot be solved by the platitudes generally applied to them, especially not in an hour. The pain exhibited on the talk shows is real.[39] My criticisms of the shows' form and ideology are not meant to minimize or disparage the unhappiness of so many of the participants. These families really do have terrible problems. And the appeal of hosts like Oprah, Jenny Jones, and Phil Donahue lies largely in their ability to convey a powerful empathy, and even to identify with their guests.[40] But the problems seem intractable, and part of the fascination with the talk shows' spectacles may consist in a horror at seeing such misery and humiliation that will not diminish.

And yet, the opening of the fourth wall that makes the spectacle possible also makes possible the reverse of the spectacle, namely the audience's participation in the program. If the audience, both in the studio and at home, could genuinely take part in the show, contribute to it, help to shape its direction and tone, then the talk show's failure as therapy might be salvaged as something even more valuable: perhaps a kind of democracy. Several writers have raised this possibility and discussed the talk show as a potential "public sphere" where people of different classes, backgrounds, and experiences might come together without (or with a minimum of) prejudice or selfish interest to discuss important topics.[41]

Sonia Livingstone and Peter Lunt are the most optimistic in portraying the talk show as a potential public sphere that can "act communicatively as a forum for the expression of multiple voices or subject positions, and in particular... attempt to confront established power with the lived experience of ordinary people" (160). Other commentators are more cautious. Wayne Munson regards the shows' self-reflexiveness, their "constant acknowledgment of camera and microphone," as factors that "defuse the para-sociality of the interaction, making it both a genuine social interaction *and* an electronically mediated spectacle" (76). Likewise, Robin Andersen writes of the talk show's "lost potential," a possibility for "participatory discourse" that is "wiped out by the commercial imperative" (158). For Andersen, also, the possibility of a talk-show public sphere is hampered by the show's therapeutic ethos that gives authority to the psychological "expert." Livingstone and Lunt would counter that in fact the talk show subverts expert culture. Their research consists largely of interviews with studio audience members who report frequent disagreement with the experts' prescriptions.

My sense is that Andersen's and Munson's reservations are correct. Livingstone and Lunt's empirical data are not as persuasive as they could be. The interviews they report tend to be one- or two-sentence sound bites of audience members telling whether they agree with the psychologist, whether they approve of the host's style, whether the issue was important, whether it was handled well, and so on. But Livingstone and Lunt do not question how the talk show tends to transfer political issues back onto the person and the family. In fact, they defend this move, arguing that "the personification of social issues and problems provides relevance and gives voice to the various, often marginalized groupings of the life world," and that this process "makes established power accountable to personal experience" (180).

This claim seems unlikely to me, and the extensive data they provide on audience attitudes cannot possibly support it. One might wish or believe that established power has been made accountable, but such attitudes do not make

it a fact. Nor do Livingstone and Lunt discuss the political and social contexts
in which the talk show has developed—that is, the political culture of Reaganism and the growing disparity between economic classes.[42] There have been a
few instances of a talk show functioning as something like a public sphere.
Oprah's trip to the all-white Forsythe County, Georgia, in 1987 provided a forum for expressing and debating the whole range of attitudes toward race held
by the white residents. Some opposed the county's racism, some upheld it.
Some blamed the media for blowing the situation "out of proportion—we're
just good Christian people here." Another woman said that God does not distinguish between white and black, or even homosexuals and communists! The
chairman of the "Committee to Keep Forsythe County White" used the occasion
to make all manner of outrageous statements, and Oprah asserted her authority *as* an African American:

> CHAIRMAN: Martin Luther King was a communist agent, a
> member of sixty-two communist organizations.
> A WOMAN: I think I speak for more of a consensus than you
> do. You've only been here two years.
> CHAIRMAN: But I know—
> OPRAH: Let her speak.
> CHAIRMAN: Who says so?
> OPRAH: Black me said it. (Applause).

There were attempts at a consensus that would include African Americans.
Another woman said, "It's time for change. There's nothing we can do about
it. We need to talk. Black and white together in Forsythe County. There's no
other way." But this ran up against remarks like, "These people welcoming
Blacks and niggers in, how many would want their son or daughter to marry
one? That's the question." A woman replied, "We're not talking about marriage,
we're talking about neighbors. I wouldn't want my children to marry a lot of
white people!"

   The show ended up going in circles, and it revealed most of all the traumatic
split around race at the center of American culture, and how far it is from being resolved. Oprah's lone journey into the heart of white racism certainly appeared heroic, but also painfully ineffectual. Or perhaps it did some good. We
would have to return today, ten years later, and see how people there remember

Oprah's visit and what life is like in the new, multiracial (?) Forsythe County. What one sees, looking at the program itself, is that substantial numbers of white Americans absolutely could not come to grips with the reality of the existence of black people. Oprah phrased her purpose in language poised uncertainly between that of a public forum and that of therapy. She came to Forsythe County, she said, in order "to try to understand the feelings and motivations.... That's what we do every day on this show: explore people's feelings." The result was stasis and repetition: a scene of social trauma revealed with hideous clarity.

But also not revealed—evaded. Ultimately, the talk show as public sphere fails for similar reasons that it fails as therapy. First, the problems, traumas, antagonisms it addresses are mercilessly intractable. It confronts genuine and overwhelming pain that reaches from the personal through the familial to the broadest social levels, and its status as therapeutic or as public space collapses in that confrontation. Second, the talk show fails to address the social trauma that consistently underlies all the personal, familial, and even social problems that it does address. The trauma that defines the lives of most of its audience and participants is their deteriorating economic position, their status as victims of the "class war from above" initiated in the 1970s, accelerated under Reagan, and continuing unabated today. The disenfranchisement of the talk show population is glaringly visible but never mentioned, and so participants speak with painful, or exploitative, openness about their personal and family problems but never about the social contexts that help make their lives what they are. As public sphere and therapy, the talk show becomes stuck at the level of the family, and of "family values," and so is entirely enmeshed in Reaganist thinking even as it acts out the traumas — the realities of social disharmony — that Reaganism tried to suppress.

Reaganism was not the only way of thinking in the 1980s. It won the day politically and continues to hold sway even under Bill Clinton. In terms of regressive social "reforms," Clinton has surpassed Reagan, and Clinton may be Reagan's equal in his skill with televised platitudes. Clinton, after all, campaigns like a talk-show host — all empathy and reaching out — as he engages in his bipartisan effort with the Republican Congress to complete Reagan's program and make government-sponsored social welfare inconceivable. The new memorial in Washington, D.C., to Franklin Roosevelt is a tribute to the new Reaganism; it buries the New Deal under an aura of quaintness. Those wonderful 1930s, when thin people in old clothes listened to FDR's inspiring chats on the ancient radio! Sure, the government has a role in establishing economic justice — as long as the citizens wear long tattered overcoats and fedora hats, as the George Segal sculptures show us. But today? *This* is the "information age," and all we need is Bill Gates to put Web sites in every classroom.

But traumas return; ghosts return. The country was, and remains, haunted, and some people see the ghosts and describe their returns. In this final chapter, I turn to two literary responses of the late 1980s, Thomas Pynchon's *Vineland* and Toni Morrison's *Beloved.* Both novels narrate moments of historical trauma. They present the traumas as apocalyptic, revelatory, and formative. And they recount the symptomatic and ghostly transmissions of these traumas. Pynchon and Morrison directly confront the historical work of Reaganism, in particular by placing traumatic events of the 1960s and their transmission into the 1980s at the center of their narratives. In *Vineland,* this placement is quite explicit. In *Beloved*, I will show how its setting during Reconstruction refers also to the Reaganist attempts to forget American racial traumas. *Vineland* and *Beloved* both are post-apocalyptic novels that remember the traumas of American history, acknowledge their ongoing effects, and try to imagine ways of working through them.

These are only novels, of course. I cannot claim that they have greatly affected the general course of American amnesia and disavowal. But they show at least that an accurate imagination of American history remains possible, and that seems to me the prerequisite for resuming and continuing movements for social justice.

NOSTALGIA, CULTURAL TRAUMA, AND THE "TIMELESS BURST" IN VINELAND

Nostalgia has a bad reputation. It is said to entail an addiction to falsified, idealized images of the past. Nostalgic yearning, as David Lowenthal writes, "is the search for a simple and stable past as a refuge from the turbulent and chaotic present" (21). The political uses of nostalgia are said to be inevitably reactionary, serving to link the images of an ideal past to new or recycled authoritarian structures. And it is true that nostalgia has played major roles in many of the reactionary and repressive political movements of this century—in Nazism's reverence for the "*Volk*," in socialist kitsch, and in the United States in Reaganism's obsession with idealized depictions of family life in the 1950s. Most recently, nostalgia has been described as a masculine response to feminist threats to patriarchal privilege.[1]

Nostalgia has certainly kept some bad company. And yet, it seems to me, the critiques of nostalgia have not addressed important questions concerning the mechanics of how the past is transmitted into the present and how it might best be used. Postmodern texts and readings, as Michael Berube has noted (with reference to Pynchon's *Gravity's Rainbow*), place great emphasis on problematics of "transmission and reinscription; not on overturning the hierarchy between canonical and apocryphal but on examining how the canonical and apocryphal can do various kinds of cultural work for variously positioned and constituted cultural groups" (229). In this chapter, I will reevaluate nostalgia as a form of cultural transmission that can shift in its political and historical purposes, and thus bears a more complex and, potentially, more productive relation to the past than has generally been allowed in recent discussions.

Thomas Pynchon's 1990 novel *Vineland* is a book whose low critical reputation parallels that of the term in question. In fact, *Vineland* has been criticized precisely for its nostalgia, for a politics that exhibits an overly comfortable longing for those good old days of the Movement and the attempt at revolution.[2] Indeed, *Vineland* seems, in its story's emphasis on repairing the broken family, to veer toward an almost Reaganesque nostalgia. The novel ends with a family reunion; its final word is "home."

Vineland works its way, however, to a very troubled home, and its "sickness"[3] is not a conventional nostalgia for idealized sites of origin. Its concern, rather, as it returns to the 1960s from the vantage of the Reaganist 1980s, is with how cultural memory is transmitted, and it portrays the ideological distortions, marketing strategies, and the variety of nostalgias through which Americans in the 1980s apprehended the 1960s. Central to Pynchon's conception of how the past inhabits the present is the notion of trauma. *Vineland* returns to the 1960s not as to a site of original wholeness and plenitude but, rather, as to a site of catastrophe, betrayal, and cultural trauma. Moreover, the past in *Vineland* is not simply a place to which a nostalgic text may return. Rather, it is the traumatic past that persistently leaps forward into the present.

And yet, as Pynchon presents it, along with the traumatic return of the past into the present (a return that is necessarily marked according to the prevailing Reaganist and consumerist ideologies) is another, utopian element. The utopian, or revelatory, moment is simultaneous with the traumatic moment. And so, in effect, Pynchon's nostalgia is a nostalgia for the future, for possibilities of social harmony glimpsed at crucial moments in the past but not yet realized. Pynchon's portrayal of this congruence or simultaneity of trauma and utopian possibility resembles Walter Benjamin's use of the term *jetztzeit,* the critical moment of historical, redemptive possibility that continues to erupt into the present even after many previous failures. Like Benjamin's use of *jetztzeit, Vineland*'s nostalgia possesses an ethical and political urgency, an imperative to use its glimpse of utopian potential to try to change an unjust history. And, like the *jetztzeit, Vineland*'s utopian/traumatic vision constitutes a kind of pivot or wedge by which a given historical record can be loosened, opened, made available to change. Where Pynchon's account of nostalgia chiefly dif-

fers from Benjamin's treatment of *jetztzeit* is in Pynchon's attention to the mechanics of how the traumatic/utopian cultural memory is transmitted. Through
his pervasive use of popular culture imagery and tone, Pynchon emphasizes
that historical trauma and the possibilities of working through the trauma do
not, as would seem to be the case in Benjamin's "Theses," burst unmediated
into the present. Rather, the insistent return to, and of, the past as a site both
of catastrophe and of redemptive possibility will always take particular cultural and ideological forms. In *Vineland,* these will be the forms of American
consumerism and Reaganism in the 1980s.[4]

In *Vineland*'s first sentence, Zoyd Wheeler (Frenesi's ex-husband, father of
their daughter, Prairie) wakes up in the summer of 1984[5] and prepares for an
odd ritual. Each year, in order to receive his mental disability check, Zoyd
must commit some public act that testifies to his insanity. A hippie, pot-smoking,
small-time rock-and-roll playing, long-haired freak of the '60s, Zoyd is a pic-
turesque character; he is *very* '60s. In fact, Zoyd is part of a government-funded
program designed to keep the memory of the '60s alive as a memory of insanity,
and the opening scene of the novel is a comic conflation of representations
of the '60s in the age of Reagan: a hippie wearing a dress, wielding a chain
saw, performing a self- and property-destroying act that is broadcast live on
television.

One of the greatest threats of the '60s, according to the Right, was its blurring of gender divisions. The hippie was already feminized by his long hair
and lack of aggressivity (although at the same time he was — inexplicably —
appealing to many women). Zoyd's dress heightens the gender confusion but,
through its absurdity, disarms it. This hippie, in his ridiculous K-Mart dress,
can be no threat to traditional masculinity — he is just crazy. But with his
chain saw, the '60s representative is also a physical danger. He is Charles Man-
son, the hippie as Satanic mass killer. And with the reintroduction of a physical threat, the sexual threat also returns as Zoyd, now armed as well as cross-
dressed, enters the loggers' bar.

The figure of Zoyd at the Log Jam brings together parodies of feminism,
gay activism, and senseless '80s violence all as progeny of the old '60s hippie. And, as we saw in the previous chapter, this is precisely the Reaganist
view of the '60s: a source of political and especially sexual violence and chaos.

As this opening scene of *Vineland* suggests, Reaganism had (and the New Right continues to have) an overriding interest in subsidizing and perpetuating the memory of the '60s in these terms. And so the '60s enter the '80s in *Vineland* as the Reaganist '80s would want to see them, as an aging hippie wearing a dress hurtling through a window for the local news.

But Zoyd is not the only relic from the '60s who returns. While Zoyd's return is an orchestrated, well-funded gesture of propaganda, Pynchon shows also how the traumatic memories of the '60s return involuntarily and somatically as historical symptoms that inhabit and haunt the '80s. It is in this symptomatic sense that ghosts play such important roles in *Vineland. Vineland*'s ghosts are signs pointing back to traumatic events and forcing those events back into memory.

In *Vineland,* ghosts appear in several forms. Watching the documentary footage that her mother, a radical filmmaker, shot during the '60s, Prairie becomes possessed by Frenesi, as by a ghost. Prairie

> understood that the person behind the camera most of the
> time really was her mother, and that if she kept her mind
> empty she could absorb, conditionally become, Frenesi, share
> her eyes, feel, when the frame shook with fatigue or fear or
> nausea, Frenesi's whole body there, as much as her mind
> choosing the frame, her will to go out there. . . . Prairie floated,
> ghostly light of head, as if Frenesi were dead but in a spe-
> cial way, a minimum-security arrangement, where limited vis-
> its, mediated by projector and screen were possible. (199)

Frenesi's vision of the '60s as a bodily experience inhabits Prairie, and time — and the supposed barrier in time posed by death — is porous, a "minimum-security arrangement," so that the past can actually exist, physically, in the present. History, for Pynchon, is the alien, uncanny presence that is also that which is most familiar; it is what has formed and informed the present suddenly encountered as Other, as dead. History is the living dead, buried once but come out of its grave, so that the line between living and dead (at least as they function historically) becomes blurred.[6]

The most prominent ghosts in *Vineland* are the Thanatoids. Although dead, these beings are physical and social. They eat, live in communities, watch television, and can hold conversations with living people. And the Thanatoids are, for the most part, victims of traumas of the '60s. Weed Atman, betrayed by Frenesi during the rebellion at the College of the Surf, returns as a Thanatoid. The text notes that "since the end of the war in Vietnam, the Thanatoid population had been growing steeply" (320), and Vato and Blood, the wreckers/ferrymen who convey the disoriented, traumatized dead/undead to Thanatoid Village, are themselves Vietnam veterans strangely in thrall to a Vietnamese woman who (in more ways than one) balances their accounts. The Thanatoids' traumas, as in psychoanalytic descriptions of the symptom, are not in their memories — indeed, the Thanatoids are only dimly aware that they may be dead — but on their bodies. On seeing her first Thanatoids, DL Chastain tells Takeshi Fumimota, "some of these folks don't look too good." "What do you expect?" Takeshi replies. "What was done to them — they carry it right out on their bodies — written down for — all to see!" (174).

The Thanatoids are symptoms — physical marks on the social body — of the traumatic '60s now haunting and contributing to the traumas of the '80s. And yet, the Thanatoids are also ridiculous, another absurd remnant (like Zoyd at the novel's opening) of the psychedelic '60s. And in this tension, between a serious, portentous return of historical trauma and its representation as a comic shtick enacted under the aegis of mass media, we see a crucial feature of Pynchon's literary technique in *Vineland,* his representation of history, and his version of nostalgia. A ghost of the '60s can return in the '80s only as its own simulation: a ghost playing a ghost, a "Thanatoid," a ghost expressed in technical jargon, a mediated, postmodern ghost of the Reagan era with an alarm watch that beeps out "Wachet Auf." Yet, the '60s continued to return, albeit in these ridiculous, ideologically tinted, "fetishized" forms, because of their traumatic, apocalyptic, place in American history.

Having shown, through the returns of Zoyd and the Thanatoids, how the '60s were rewritten as chaotic, infantile, and ridiculous in the Reaganist '80s, Pynchon also sets out in *Vineland* to explore why the '60s failed. The social movements of the '60s failed, in Pynchon's account — as did earlier radical movements — because of certain betrayals. And political betrayals in *Vineland* are inevitably linked to sexual betrayals, in fact, to failures of sexual purity or chastity. Both Zoyd and Frenesi describe political loyalty in sexual terms. Zoyd asks Hector Zuniga, the DEA agent, "Why this thing about popping my cherry,

Hector?" Frenesi says to Flash, her second husband, "Tell you what . . . *I'll* cross *your* picket line if *you'll* go get fucked up your *ass,* OK? 'N' *then* we can talk about busted cherries — " (352). This stress on political or sexual purity is, I will argue, ultimately intentionally misleading. As is the case with *Vineland's* language and its depiction of how the past enters and inhabits the present, purity is never in fact an option, and Pynchon derails even those myths of purity that he describes most compellingly.

Frenesi, nevertheless, does betray the Movement, her lover Weed Atman, her husband, Zoyd, and her daughter, Prairie, as a result of her sexual obsession for her worst political enemy, the federal prosecutor Brock Vond. Frenesi's failure, her "helpless turn toward images of authority," is at the center of Pynchon's portrayal of the failures of the '60s. And Frenesi fatalistically conjectures that "some Cosmic Fascist had spliced in a DNA sequence requiring this form of seduction and initiation into the dark joys of social control." Indeed, Frenesi fears "that all her oppositions, however good and just, to forms of power were really acts of denying that dangerous swoon that came creeping at the edges of her optic lobes every time the troops came marching by" (83). Reciprocally, Brock's authoritarian politics are based on a fear of women and of physicality that seems typical of right-wing politics in general. His sadistic control over Frenesi is a form of revenge against a feminine part of himself and an expression of rage against his own vulnerability — all of which we see in his recurring dreams of being raped by his feminine alter-ego, the Madwoman in the Attic (274).

The full revelation of the connection between sexuality and power comes during the "apocalypse" at Tulsa, when Frenesi joins Brock for a weekend of sex and strategy. What is unveiled, as the "weathermen" of Tulsa nervously acknowledge "the advent of an agent of rapture" (212) and the radicals at the College of the Surf feel the sense "of a clear break just ahead with everything they'd known" (244), is the gun: "Sooner or later," says Brock, "the gun comes out" (240). And the gun, as Frenesi understands it, is an extension of the penis: "Men had it so simple. When it wasn't about Sticking It In, it was about Having the Gun, a variation that allowed them to Stick It In from a distance. The details of how and when, day by working day, made up their real world" (241).

What is further revealed at Tulsa is the link between Brock's gun/phallus and Frenesi's choice of revolutionary technology, the camera. Frenesi had believed that the camera worked in opposition to the gun, that its focus made possible a form of "learning how to pay attention" that could "reveal and devastate" the sources of social injustice (195). Brock, however, persuades her that the camera is simply another way, alternate but parallel, of "sticking it in from a distance." "Can't you see," he tells her, "the two separate worlds — one always includes a camera somewhere, and the other always includes a gun, one is make-believe, one is real?" (241). The full revelation that emerges from Frenesi and Brock's relationship is that the world and all possibilities of human action and desire are circumscribed by destructive, interconnected, and all-encompassing logics of sex, power, and representation.

Frenesi can see no way out of this sexual, political, and representational impasse. The only alternative would seem to be a kind of Heideggerian withdrawal from politics, sexuality, and representation — which is, in effect, also a nostalgia for some pure, aboriginal condition of Being untainted by human imprint. Such a withdrawal and nostalgia are the effect of the parable that Sister Rochelle recites to Takeshi Fumimota, retelling the story of the Fall. Originally, in Sister Rochelle's account, " 'there were no men at all. Paradise was female.' " And the first man was not Adam, but the Serpent:

> "It was sleazy, slippery man," Rochelle continued, "who invented 'good' and 'evil,' where before women had been content to just be.... They dragged us down into this wreck they'd made of the Creation, all subdivided and labeled, handed us the keys to the church, and headed off toward the dance halls and the honkytonk saloons." (166)

Finally, drawing her moral with regard to DL, with whom Takeshi is now linked through their attempt to undo the effects of the Ninja Death Touch, Sister Rochelle solicits Takeshi not to "commit original sin. Try and let her just be" (166).

Rochelle's admonition to "let her just be" — free, that is, from impositions of notions of "good" and "evil," and from all conceptual subdivisions and labels — recalls Heidegger's dictum in the "Letter on Humanism" that "every valuing, even where it values positively, is a subjectivizing. It does not let beings: be. Rather valuing lets beings: be valid — solely as the objects of its doing" (228). From Rochelle's Heideggerian perspective, all forms of inscription —

the gun, the camera, the phallus—are equally guilty. All constitute forms of "enframing," through which the world is not encountered on its own terms but as a "standing reserve" available strictly for use.[7] And all contribute toward the construction of the "world picture," the representation whose reality replaces that of the world itself:

> Hence world picture, when understood essentially, does not mean a picture of the world but the world conceived and grasped as a picture. What is, in its entirety, is now taken in such a way that it first is in being and only is in being to the extent that it is set up by man, who represents and sets forth. ("The Age of the World Picture," 130)

What is necessary, Heidegger contends, is to create a kind of openness or clearing in which Being can become present on its own terms, which can be accomplished by humanity's maintaining combined attitudes of alert passivity and nurturing. In *Vineland,* this role is taken by Zoyd, who both nurtures his (and Frenesi's) daughter, Prairie, and is able to let her be. Zoyd is a father with the qualities of a mother, a father without the Phallus, whose penis is only a penis. He is not quite a void—some figure for feminine absence entirely outside the symbolic order; he is . . . a Zoyd: passive but capable, a laid-back fuck-up but a good parent, out of the loop but very much in the symbolic. And Prairie, as her name implies, is the clearing, the opening, that Zoyd allows to come into presence and who may become the site of a new political-sexual-symbolic order not based on the gun, the camera, and the Phallus.

This would be a straight Heideggerian reading, for which Pynchon has provided plenty of cues. But the book is too complex and excessive to allow us to stop here. In the first place, Prairie is not simply a clearing. She is also a subject, and a daughter in search of her mother—more important, as it turns out, in search of her mother's history. She is aided and guided by DL and Takeshi, who have their own history to work through, and who do not just let Prairie be. If Prairie is the opening out of the closed sadomasochistic symbolic-political system embodied by Brock and Frenesi, she achieves this status not merely through the Heideggerian presencing suggested by Sister Rochelle's injunction. She needs the help of a man and woman whose relation, like that of Frenesi and Brock, is mediated by a Death Touch.

Pynchon, then, advances Sister Rochelle's Heideggerian alternative but does not, finally, accept it. At the same time, however, Pynchon suggests the importance of Heideggerian attitudes of withdrawal in the late '60s as the New Left was falling apart. For Heidegger's opposition to all forms of "enframing" can be translated in the context of the late '60s to two instances from popular culture: to the Beatles' quietist slogan to "Let it be," and to the Rolling Stones' parodic response, to "Let it bleed." That is, the Heideggerian position in the late '60s suggests attitudes both of passive withdrawal and of terrorism.

The Beatles' song and album of 1969 spoke of a miraculous epiphany "in my hour of darkness" when "Mother Mary comes to me, speaking words of wisdom, Let it be, let it be." Like the sentiments in "Revolution" ("If you go carrying pictures of Chairman Mao / You're not gonna make it with anyone anyhow"), "Let It Be" advocates a withdrawal from a political activism that, in 1969, appeared to have utterly failed. And political activists in 1969 seemed to be faced with two alternatives: either to retire into some more private world of small community, religion, family, graduate school and let the larger world be; or to immerse themselves in the political chaos and violence, break down the barriers of their own scruples and repressions, not resist violence but become violent. To become a terrorist in that context was to "go with the flow," or as the title of the Rolling Stones' song put it, to "let it bleed."

"Let It Bleed" was released apparently in response to the vapid quietism of "Let It Be," but the tone of the song seems to belie the violence of its title. It is reassuringly melodic, without the sinister, if theatrical, edge of songs from *Beggar's Banquet* (such as "Street Fighting Man" and "Sympathy for the Devil"), which was released a year earlier. In fact, it seems in its tone and lyrics to reassert the sense of community that by 1969 had all but disappeared from the radical movements: "We all need someone we can lean on / And if you want to, you can lean on me." But there is a strange sarcastic drawl that Mick Jagger gives to the word *lean* that immediately puts the assertion of community in question. And as the song continues, it appears to be not about community but about dismemberment and the unencumbered exchange of bodily fluids. "We all need someone we can lean on" is succeeded by "dream on," "cream on," "feed on," and finally "bleed on." In the verse, a woman tells the singer that her "breasts will always be open," and Jagger responds that she can "take my arm, take my leg / Oh baby don't you take my head." And at the end of the song, having sung, "You can bleed all over me," he sings, "You can come all over me." The sarcastic emphasis on "lean" indicates that the mutual dependence and reciprocity implied by the opening line will in fact resolve into a mutual disintegration and a dissolution of both subjectivities into an undifferentiated flow of desire. The song proceeds from the mutuality of "lean" to a succession of self-shatterings: the unconscious (dream), orgasm (cream), cannibalism (feed), and bleeding (whether of a wound or of menstruation), and finally conflates the emissions of blood and semen. By the end of the song there is nothing but flow, unrestricted by any physical or social structure. To "let it bleed," then, means to eliminate all distinctions and values: to let desire desire, to let flow flow. It is, though with a shift of emphasis, really not so different from letting Being be. "Let It Bleed," I suggest, constructs a rock-and-roll version of the desiring machines of Gilles Deleuze and Félix Guattari's *Anti-Oedipus.*

Deleuze and Guattari are named in *Vineland* at the wedding of Mafioso Ralph Wayvone's daughter as authors of *The Italian Wedding Fake Book,* to which Billy Barf and the Vomitones (disguised as Gino Baglione and the Paisans) resort when it becomes clear that they do not know any appropriate songs for an Italian wedding. They are only mentioned once, without elaboration, and it may be only another Pynchonesque throwaway, but if we follow the logic from Sister Rochelle's "Let her be" to Heidegger, the Beatles, and the Rolling Stones, the reference to Deleuze and Guattari extends *Vineland*'s exploration of how to contend with the "Cosmic Fascist" that has contaminated sex, politics, and representation.

Published in 1972, *Anti-Oedipus,* like "Let It Be" and "Let It Bleed," responds to the perceived catastrophic breakdown of the '60s social movements. It is to the political, and libidinal, utopianism of Herbert Marcuse and Norman O. Brown what the Weathermen were to the earlier communitarian idealism of the SDS. That is, it is a form of theoretical terrorism conceived in the collapse of hope in effective politics. The major problem Deleuze and Guattari address, and the problem that for them invalidates conventional political action and belief, is precisely the problem raised by Frenesi and Brock's relationship, that of an inner fascism that structures sexuality, politics, and representation and that is apparently inseparable from these latter structures. As Michel Foucault wrote in his preface to *Anti-Oedipus,*

> The major enemy, the strategic adversary is fascism. . . . And
> not only historical fascism, the fascism of Hitler and Mus-
> solini — which was able to mobilize and use the desire of
> the masses so effectively — but also the fascism in us all, in
> our heads and in our everyday behavior, the fascism that
> causes us to love power, to desire the very thing that domi-
> nates and exploits us. (xiii)

For Deleuze and Guattari, there is no structure, no boundary, no form of identity that is not a blockage of the flow of desire, a flow that they posit as the
only and necessary alternative to inner fascism. Desire alone is revolutionary.
It is not governed (contra Freud) by the Oedipal conflict and its subsequent
repressions, or (contra Lacan) by some even more primal lack. Desire is no-
madic and universal, and "does not take as its object persons or things, but the
entire surroundings that it traverses, the vibrations and flows of every sort to
which it is joined, introducing therein breaks and captures"; it is only "through
a restriction, a blockage, and a reduction that the libido is made to repress its
flows in order to contain them in the narrow cells of the type 'couple,' 'family,' 'person,' 'objects' " (292–93).

This relation between structure, desire, and inner fascism seems to describe
the political sadomasochism of Brock and Frenesi and to provide a theoretical
context for the catastrophes of the New Left in the late '60s. And if the problem is structure per se, any solution, as Deleuze and Guattari elaborate, must
begin with destruction. What follows seems impossibly vague — the creation
of subject (rather than subjugated) groups that can cause "desire to penetrate
into the social field, and subordinate the socius or the form of power to desiring-
production" (348) — but the initial task is clear: "Destroy, destroy. The task of
schizoanalysis goes by way of destruction — a whole scouring of the unconscious, a complete curettage. Destroy Oedipus, the illusion of the ego, the pup-
pet of the superego, guilt, the law, castration" (311).

Anti-Oedipus marks a point in the history of theory that, both temporally
and in spirit, parallels the moment of fragmentation, catastrophe, and apocalypse when, for the New Left, all forms of reasonable politics — either of working within the system or even of resisting it — became impossible. "Let it be"
or "Let it bleed." And yet, oddly, the quietist Beatles/Heideggerian position
blurs into the revolutionary or terrorist Stones/*Anti-Oedipus* position. Both are

post-apocalyptic responses to catastrophes perceived as all-encompassing and irreversible, as coterminous with the entire existing order. Both are complete rejections of that order, and both embrace instead some incipient revelation outside of what the current, failed order is able to articulate.

It is only during times of massive cultural despair that such attitudes can appear as workable political positions, and Pynchon presents these absolute critiques of a phallic economy in the context of that late '60s moment when the counterculture tried utterly to divest itself of "Amerika" only to find those same forces of power and sexuality in itself. Yet we are not meant to see a Heideggerian or Deleuze-Guattarian position as providing the novel's moral or political or redemptive energy. These positions, rather, represent initial, immediate, post-apocalyptic spasms. Heidegger's is a voice from the grave (in Heidegger's case, the grave of the German national *dasein*) in which all human acts appear flattened in the radiant (non)perspective of Being. Deleuze and Guattari's is the voice of the revenant who has risen from the grave to devour the living. Both, in fact, are variations of Thanatoid postures, the resentful, traumatized, passive-aggressive (or aggressively passive) attitude of the living dead.

The moment of trauma, the apocalypse of the late '60s — the moment that returns and is returned to — contains the revelation that all social structures, all human acts and culturally inflected desires, are inhabited by the Cosmic Fascist. At this same traumatic-apocalyptic moment, however, *Vineland* also depicts alternatives that entail neither quietistic withdrawal nor terrorism. The first of these alternatives is Karmic Adjustment, *Vineland*'s parodic combination of psychoanalysis and Eastern religion. The second is the recurring vision of utopian possibility that in *Vineland* emerges at the same moment as does cultural trauma and inevitably returns with it as well. And these two forms of return — the working through of trauma and its symptomatic reincarnations by means of Karmic Adjustment, and the returns of utopian vision — in combination constitute *Vineland*'s revised nostalgia.

DL Chastain and Takeshi Fumimota are the first characters in the novel to attempt to "balance" their "karmic account" (163). Their whole relationship, it must be noted, doubles that of Frenesi and Brock. In fact, when they first meet, in a Tokyo brothel, Takeshi has accidentally taken Brock's place as a customer, and DL (who was to meet and assassinate Brock) is disguised as Frenesi. In this role, DL mistakenly administers to Takeshi the Ninja Death Touch, an esoteric martial arts technique that results in death up to a year after its application—acting, as doctors later tell Takeshi, "like trauma, only—much slower" (157). DL and Takeshi's relation, like that of Frenesi and Brock, is marked by trauma: the Death Touch stands in for the Cosmic Fascist.

But while Frenesi and Brock arrive at a point of apocalyptic resignation whose dual forms are quietism and terrorism—"let it be" and "let it bleed"— DL and Takeshi, with the help of Sister Rochelle, enter the business of Karmic Adjustment. Although Sister Rochelle advises Takeshi to "let her just be" (a strategy that, as we have seen, is insufficient), she also insists that DL and Takeshi remain together, and that they balance their karmic account through DL's "working off the great wrong you have done him" (163). This work involves, first, intensive therapy for Takeshi on what appears to be an enormous high-tech acupuncture machine, the "puncutron." Ultimately, however, the process of healing consists of DL and Takeshi, gradually and with great resistance, creating for themselves a sexual relationship outside the reach of the Death Touch.

While working on balancing their own karmic account, DL and Takeshi encounter the Thanatoid community and transform their personal karmic labor (as the Reaganist entrepreneurial spirit would have it) into a small, high-tech service industry based on treating unresolved Thanatoid traumas. The Thanatoids, they observe, are victims "of karmic imbalances—unanswered blows, unredeemed suffering, escapes by the guilty" (173). And in the course of their work, DL and Takeshi

> became slowly entangled in other, often impossibly complicated, tales of dispossession and betrayal. They heard of land titles and water rights, goon squads and vigilantes, landlords, lawyers, and developers always described in images of thick fluids in flexible containers, injustices not only from the past but also virulently alive in the present day. (172)

The injuries and betrayals to be healed, then, are sexual and personal but also social and historical, and Pynchon's portrayal of Karmic Adjustment suggests that similar therapies can be applied to both types. Karmic Adjustment re-sembles, though on a broader scale, the Freudian process of "working through," of learning to substitute a narrative remembering of trauma in place of a symp-tomatic repetition. As Freud wrote in *Beyond the Pleasure Principle,* a victim of trauma "is obliged to *repeat* the repressed material as a contemporary ex-perience instead of, as the physician would prefer to see, *remembering it* as something belonging to the past" (18). In *Vineland,* Frenesi and Brock, DL and Takeshi, the Thanatoids, and American culture as a whole in the '80s all are engaged in repeating traumatic conflicts of the '60s (which themselves, in Pynchon's view, repeated such earlier traumas as the suppression of the Wob-blies and the McCarthyist purges), and Karmic Adjustment provides a way to work back to those traumatic moments and retell them so as to make possible new histories and new futures.

At the same time, the whole Karmic Adjustment business is somewhat dubi-ous. It is, after all, partly a scam. As Takeshi explains to DL, "They [the Thanan-toids] don't want to do it, so we'll do it for them! Dive right down into it! Down into all that—waste-pit of time! We know it's time lost forever—but they don't!" (173). It is also, as the Thanatoid Ortho Bob Dulang reminds the two entrepreneurs, "wishful thinking" (171). Moreover, Karmic Adjustment, the Ninja Death Touch, DL's whole martial arts education, Sister Rochelle's Kunoichi sisterhood all are part of *Vineland*'s comic treatment of the Ameri-can interest in Eastern religion that took off in the '60s and reached a com-mercialized apotheosis in the '80s. Like the Thanatoids as symptoms of his-torical trauma, Karmic Adjustment as the working through of those symptoms is a joke, a bit of recycled '60s absurdity.

And yet, it is precisely as joke, as absurdity, that we can see Karmic Ad-justment as a figure for Pynchon's novelistic technique in *Vineland.* Traumas of the past return and are repeated as symptoms, but these symptoms may be outfitted in ridiculous historical costumes and take bizarre cultural forms. In-deed, *Vineland* itself is one of these ridiculous costumes and bizarre forms. *Vineland*'s structure and style, its status as comic routine, an '80s parody that approaches Fredric Jameson's notion of postmodern "pastiche"—a parody that has lost its moral axis and become indistinguishable from what it presumably had set out to satirize—enact the novel's sense that postmodern cultural memory will be linked, inevitably and inextricably, to the consumer culture in which it is formed. As a "postmodern historical novel," *Vineland* occupies a cultural position analogous to that which it creates within itself for Karmic Adjustment.

In its persistent and affectionate use of the cultural forms that it at the same time identifies as traumatic symptoms, *Vineland* verges on becoming what Michael Berube calls in his discussion of *Gravity's Rainbow* a Pynchonian "pornography." Berube describes this "pornography" in political and historical, rather than in sexual, terms as a "regressive anamnesia that re-creates illusory, prelapsarian (or prelinguistic) unities through a complex mechanism of dismemberment and reconfiguration; and since," Berube continues, "nostalgia itself works by much the same dynamic, Pynchon's 'pornography' gives us fresh purchase on the cultural critique of nostalgia as well" (248). If *Vineland* did nothing more than show the inescapability of postmodern cultural forms, then it would be a "pornography" in Berube's sense. Hanjo Berressem comes close to making this claim when he argues that *"Vineland's* main theme is the *complicity* of the subject with power" (237) and that in its inscriptions of popular and media culture, the novel "acknowledges thematically as well as structurally that literature (as well as criticism) is never innocent" (236). While the latter statement is certainly true, what needs to be added to Berressem's Lacanian examination of Pynchon's aesthetic strategies in *Vineland,* and what removes the novel from the status of nostalgic "pornography," is the decisive role of historical trauma in helping both to create and to destabilize the postmodern cultural forms that the novel employs. The novel cannot help but be complicit, nostalgic, "pornographic" — a part of the symbolic order — and yet it consistently returns to those historical moments that disrupt its "regressive anamnesias." It continually stumbles on what Slavoj Zizek calls the "rock" of the Lacanian Real: "that which resists symbolization: the traumatic point which is always missed but none the less always returns, although we try...to neutralize it, to integrate it into the symbolic order" (*Sublime Object,* 69).

Vineland's stylistic and thematic insistence on its whimsical deflections through American consumer culture, its role as shtick or pastiche, should not blind us to its historical seriousness and accuracy. Consider that DL is an American military brat who puts the Death Touch on an Asian man through a displacement of American domestic concerns and then is linked to him by guilt. This sounds historically familiar. And the novel's depictions of betrayals and repressions of and within the old and new Lefts are essentially accurate: The IWW in the Northwest really was brutally repressed by local and federal authorities during the First World War. The FBI really did infiltrate and subvert leftist movements in the '60s. Hanging the "snitch jacket" on radical leaders (as Frenesi did to Weed) really was a common tactic. Lenient regulations regarding federal grand juries in the early '70s really did allow federal prosecutors (like Brock) to conduct open-ended investigations of people and organizations who had not been accused of any crime.[8] And, most generally, as historians such as Sara Evans have pointed out, much of the New Left's failure was, in fact, due to its inability to conceive of an egalitarian sexual politics.[9]

Part of *Vineland*'s project, then, is to represent the transmission of the social traumas of the '60s into the '80s, and to suggest a method — which in the '80s can only be parodic — of coming to terms with these traumas. But trauma is not all that returns in *Vineland* from the '60s. Pynchon also describes a utopian, communitarian vision and energy as having provided the basis for '60s radicalism and then returning to indicate a moral and political axis for confronting neoconservative and Reaganist politics of the '80s. Frenesi, in the mid-'60s, "dreamed of a mysterious people's oneness, drawing together toward the best chances of light, achieved once or twice that she'd seen in the street, in short, timeless, bursts" (117). The model for such a community is Frenesi's radical film collective, 24fps, and it is important to note that this group explicitly dedicates itself to a kind of visual-political revelation:

> They went looking for trouble, they found it, they filmed it,
> and then quickly got the record of their witness someplace
> safe. They particularly believed in the ability of close-ups to
> reveal and devastate. When power corrupts, it keeps a log of
> its progress, written into that most sensitive memory device,
> the human face. Who could withstand the light? (195)

Frenesi's vision is a form of witnessing and is meant to be transmitted — as it is, twenty years later, to her daughter, Prairie, who, seeing her mother's films, "could feel the liberation in the place that night, the faith that anything was possible, that nothing could stand in the way of such joyous certainty" (210).

These utopian moments, "timeless bursts" of light, liberation, and possibility, are the sites of Pynchon's revised nostalgia. Along with the disasters and failures of the '60s, whose traumatic residues continue to haunt the landscapes of the '80s, Pynchon also locates moments of vision that leap outside their traumatic histories. These moments, in the first place, oppose the social injustices of their time. In the second place, they indicate alternative, communitarian, nondomineering, nonacquisitive forms of social life. We see these forms partly embodied in the social fabric of 24fps and in the early days of the "People's Republic of Rock and Roll" at the College of the Surf. These forms of idealistic, politically committed communal life resemble the ideal Sara Evans describes in *Personal Politics* as the "beloved community."[10] And, finally, the "timeless bursts" of utopian feeling are unsuccessful; they are never achieved but exist and are transmitted primarily as vision — and so it is fitting that Pynchon portrays this utopian *vision* as the work of radical filmmakers.

Pynchon's revised nostalgia, then, is for sites of unrealized possibility, and it is a nostalgia that, as if akin to the social traumas that surround it, returns of its own accord, together with those traumas, and opposing them. In this revised nostalgia, it is not so much that we seek to return to a site of original wholeness; rather, the unrealized possibility of social harmony and justice itself compulsively returns, providing an alternative to existing conditions and a motive for changing them. *Vineland* describes a post-apocalyptic, post-traumatic, and utopian nostalgia whose longing, amid the traumatic effects of historical crisis and disaster, is for yet unrealized forms of community. This nostalgia shoots into the present as a "timeless burst," but it entails the effort to work through historical trauma and to construct the social relations that it has imagined.

Vineland's revised nostalgia, then, is quite distinct from the nostalgias attributed to it by its critics — the "60s nostalgic quietism" attributed to it by Alec McHoul. Pynchon does describe in *Vineland* these more conventional processes of nostalgia, the ways in which specific traumatic and political memories are obscured by memories of fashion and by universal laments about "the world," "the business," and human nature. And Pynchon shows how the nostalgic machinery that has already obscured the Wobblies, the Second World War, and McCarthyism had begun in the '80s to reimagine the '60s.[11] Pynchon's nostalgia for the "timeless bursts" of the '60s is, rather, more akin to Walter Benjamin's idea of "*jetztzeit,*" that urgent "time of the now," the pivotal moment in which the history of oppression can be rewritten. And we should note that Benjamin, anticipating the fate of the Thanatoids, writes that "*even the dead* will not be safe from the enemy if he wins" (255, Benjamin's emphasis).

Pynchon, like Benjamin, gives a new political meaning to the pain of the returning past, and demonstrates that nostalgia need not have only a negative or reactionary value. Pynchon's revised nostalgia does not constitute (as, for instance, does Reaganist nostalgia) a leapfrogging back past historical trauma to some imagined age of solid family values. It emerges, rather, directly out of the moment of greatest trauma, out of the moment of apocalypse itself. Thus, the family reunion with which the novel ends is not, despite superficial resemblances, a paean either to the "family values" of the New Right or to a middle-aged New Leftist's yearning for vanished youth. Even Prairie's eventual reunion with her mother, Frenesi, turns out to be, ultimately, beside the point. Her more important encounter, and reconciliation, is with the Thanatoid Weed Atman, the former revolutionary whom Frenesi had caused, or allowed, to be murdered back at the College of the Surf. Weed, in turn, "still a cell of memory, of refusal to forgive," can only work through his "case," his obsession "with those who've wronged [him], with their continuing exemption from punishment" (365) by means of this relationship with the daughter of the woman who betrayed him. Prairie, touching Weed's hand, is "surprised not at the coldness... but at how light it was, nearly weightless" (366). It is this relationship that gives his existence weight and allows him, like the tails of the Thanatoid dogs, to "gesture meaningfully in the present" (367).

The physical presences and meaningful gestures of these ghosts of history in *Vineland* allow us finally to distinguish Pynchon's revised nostalgia from the genuinely regressive nostalgia of a work like *Forrest Gump*. *Gump,* of course, brings the '60s back to the present through its extraordinary "documentary" special-effects scenes that show us Forrest shaking hands with Lyndon Johnson, as well as Forrest participating both in the Vietnam War and in antiwar protests. Forrest redeems the traumas of the '60s, but the redemptive formula in that film lies in being oblivious to politics — and to adult sexuality — altogether: in simply (that is, *very* simply) being "human." This vision of an apolitical, virtually infantile "humanity" that can redeem a damaged national history is probably, unfortunately, the source of the movie's enormous appeal. This vision is also a large part of the appeal of Reaganism and of the current neo-Reaganist Republican ascendancy. In *Vineland,* however, every human feeling and relation springs from political-historical premises and is laden with political consequences. While *Forrest Gump* firmly separates the traumatic from the redemptive, in *Vineland* the two are always fused. The real reunion at the end of *Vineland* is of the living with the dead: a reunion with the traumatic past (now at least partially "karmically adjusted") and with the utopian sense of possibility that flashed into being at the same apocalyptic moment.

GHOSTS OF LIBERALISM: *BELOVED* AND THE MOYNIHAN REPORT

HISTORY AND APOCALYPSE: LOCATING THE SITE OF TRAUMA

Beloved is, first of all, a historical novel. It is based on a documented event — an act of infanticide by the fugitive slave Margaret Garner, who murdered her daughter to prevent the child from being sent back into slavery. Described in a newspaper report Morrison discovered while working on *The Black Book* for Random House, Garner's action becomes the model for Sethe's infanticide, and Sethe's act stands at the center of *Beloved.* The accounts in the novel of life at Sweet Home and of Sethe's and Paul D's escapes from slavery lead unswervingly toward Beloved's death; likewise, the events that follow the murder remain charged with its horror and cannot be interpreted apart from it. *Beloved*'s narrative spirals around, is ordered by, a central, traumatic event whose model is historical.[12]

Morrison frames this event, however, in the language of apocalypse. "When the four horsemen came," the beginning of the chapter in which the infanticide occurs, signals the approach of a world-ending catastrophe. The reference to the Book of Revelation makes the slave hunters' entrance into Baby Suggs's yard a sign and portent that transcends history, rends it apart, utterly restructures its movement, and perhaps brings it to an end. Morrison's apocalyptic language constructs a pivotal moment that separates what came before from what comes after. The apocalypse determines the form and direction of everything that follows, and it rewrites all previous history as premonitory.[13]

The apocalyptic event, then, generates new meanings and new historical narratives, as it obliterates old ones. Thus, as its etymology suggests, the apocalypse is a revelation, an unveiling. Struggling to kill her children, Sethe "collected every bit of life she had made, all the parts of her that were precious and fine and beautiful, and carried, pushed, dragged them through the veil, out away, over there where no one could hurt them. Over there" (163). The apocalyptic scene, as Morrison presents it, is both catastrophic and revelatory.

In the context of African American intellectual history, reference to "the veil" invokes W. E. B. Du Bois's *The Souls of Black Folk,* in which the veil is a figure for both American racial separation and for African American double-consciousness. Du Bois maintains the etymological link between the veil and "revelation," as he writes that the American Negro, "born with a veil, and gifted with second-sight in this American world" can achieve "no true self-consciousness" but can only "see himself through the revelation of the other [i.e., the white] world" (3). Morrison's characterization of Beloved's death as a forced journey through the veil parallels Du Bois's account of the death of his infant son as an escape from the veil: "All that day and all that night there sat an awful gladness in my heart, — nay, blame me not if I see the world thus darkly through the Veil, — and my soul whispers ever to me, saying, 'Not dead, not dead, but escaped; not bond, but free' " (213). For Du Bois, as for Morrison, release from the veil has apocalyptic significance. "Surely," he writes, "there shall yet dawn some mighty morning to lift the Veil and set the prisoned free" (213). In *Beloved,* however, the apocalyptic unveiling is not deferred to an uncertain future but has taken place and continues to take place within history.

But if this scene of maternal violence is apocalyptic, what exactly does the scene reveal? Four horsemen enter; Sethe pushes Beloved through the veil: a sign, a catastrophe, a revelation. What is revealed? First, that these horsemen are not the cosmic forces of War, Drought, Pestilence, and Famine; they represent, rather, an alliance of political forces, who commit acts of political and racial violence. In a perfect Foucauldian constellation, the Schoolteacher joins with the Sheriff—knowledge with power, legal ownership with legal coercion—to enter the property of a free black woman in a free state. For Baby Suggs, the revelation unveiled by this scene is, as she repeats to Stamp Paid, the fact that "they came in my yard" (179). This trespass means that no African American, slave or free, can genuinely own property or live as a subject in a society that gives overriding value to property rights. Even in a free state and after slavery, the former owners, under the auspices of law and science, can still regard the African American as object, property, and specimen. Morrison reinforces this point in many ways throughout *Beloved.* The first revelation

coming under the sign of the four horsemen is of a continuing series of trans-
gressions, violations, and dispossessions. The scene reveals a political and social history whose entire duration — which has not ended — is traumatic and
apocalyptic.

The second revelation — Sethe's pushing Beloved through the veil — occurs at the moment when Schoolteacher and the others come into the yard. In
the context of white societal, institutional violence against blacks, Morrison
describes an act of unspeakable violence between blacks, within an African
American family. The first unveiling is of the continuing and repeated catastrophe of white racism; the second is of African American self-destruction.
These apocalyptic concerns are, in fact, the twin themes of all of Morrison's
work. Racial violence shapes the social and political space of her novels, while
in the foreground — in *The Bluest Eye,* in *Sula,* in *Song of Solomon,* in *Jazz,*
and in *Beloved* — are forms of individual and collective suicide.

THE MOYNIHAN REPORT, THE CRITIQUE OF LIBERALISM, AND THE DENIAL OF HISTORICAL TRAUMA

Because of *Beloved*'s concern with violence committed both against and within
African American communities, the novel can be read as an intervention in
two distinct but related debates on American histories of race. Morrison emphasizes in *Beloved* the systemic, structural effects of racism during slavery
and reconstruction, and — since *Beloved* is above all a novel concerned with
historical transmission — continuing into the present. This emphasis opposes
the neoconservative and Reaganist polemics of the 1980s that attributed the
poverty and violence of urban ghettos, the problem of the "underclass," to intrinsic and individual moral deficiencies, as well as to the liberal policies of
the War on Poverty.[14] The few negative reviews of *Beloved* emerged from this
conservative position and condemned the novel for setting Sethe's infanticide
in the context of general social injustice. Martha Bayles, in *The New Criterion,*
wrote,

> A slave commits a crime, but it's not really a crime because
> it was committed by a slave. The system, and not the slave,
> stands unjustly condemned for a deed that would possess an-
> other meaning if committed in freedom.... In Morrison's

mind there seems to be only one crime, that of slavery itself, and no person who lives under it has to answer for anything. (36)

Likewise, Stanley Crouch, in *The New Republic,* declared that Morrison

explains black behavior in terms of social conditioning, as if listing atrocities solves the mystery of human motive and behavior. It is designed to placate sentimental feminist ideology and to make sure that the vision of black woman as the most scorned and rebuked of the victims doesn't weaken. (39)

These views of the novel follow from the widespread attacks on the remnants of the Great Society programs launched by such writers as George Gilder, Charles Murray, and Lawrence Mead — attacks that formed much of the intellectual and moral foundation for Reaganist social policies in the 1980s. These writers share the view that since the elimination of legal discrimination in the mid-1960s, racial injustice has ceased to have any role in social problems.[15]

The common factor in these conservative arguments, as Michael Katz writes, is "the attempt to classify poor people by moral worth" (140), an attempt that culminated in a variety of theories of the Underclass, a group virtually without socialization and composed of single (i.e., welfare) mothers, drug addicts, and gang members. Morrison, writing in the mid-1980s when these views had achieved their greatest influence, insists on the continuing and structural effects of race. The political and psychological links between the good slave owner (Garner), the bad slave owner (Schoolteacher), and the abolitionist (Bodwin) indicate a pervasive racism that mere legislation cannot eradicate. The repeated returns of the ghost of the murdered child geographically into the North and temporally into Reconstruction suggest the inevitable return, or reincarnation, of racial violence at any time or place as long as the systemic nature of racism is not addressed. And in the apocalyptic presentation of the slave hunters, Morrison responds to the conservative polemics of the Reaganist 1980s by insisting that the violence within the African American community can only be understood in a context in which law and science, power and official knowledge continue to violate African American lives.

At the same time, however, by depicting the most alarming cases of violence within African American communities, *Beloved* joins another debate, about the status and representation of the black family. Sethe is a single mother working at a low-paying job. She suffers a mental breakdown, loses her job, and must be supported by the community. Her sons leave the home never to be seen again. One of her daughters is incapable of leaving home, and Sethe murders the other one. Sethe's family is certainly dysfunctional, if not (to use a loaded term from the Moynihan Report) "pathological." Since in ongoing discussions of race from the 1960s to the present, the family has occupied a central and problematic place, reading *Beloved* in the context of the Moynihan Report and the debates that followed its publication can help historicize this novel and Morrison's work, which address African American families so powerfully and painfully.[16]

In June 1965 at Howard University, in a speech cowritten by Daniel Patrick Moynihan (then an assistant secretary of labor), Lyndon Johnson described changes he envisioned in civil rights policies. Congress had passed legislation in 1964 effectively ending legal discrimination, but Johnson argued that legal equality was not enough. "You do not wipe away the scars of centuries by saying: Now you are free to go where you want, do as you desire, and choose the leaders you please." Emphasizing employment, housing, and health care, Johnson sought, rather, "not just equality as a right and a theory but equality as a fact and as a result" (Rainwater and Yancey, 126). He announced a conference to be held in the fall of 1965 to discuss the economic problems of black Americans and to frame policies to address them. In the context of the 1980s, when Toni Morrison wrote *Beloved,* Johnson's speech at Howard is an extraordinary document. Johnson spoke of scars, the continuing effects of historical wounds; he acknowledged the history of race as a glaring, traumatic failure in American history. And he spoke of the need for major economic reform, for an equality of result with regard to race.

Needless to say, the massive reforms that Johnson called for did not take place. Nor did the idea of American racial history as traumatic remain on the surface of American political discourse; rather, American racial trauma became submerged, appearing in disguised forms in discussions of crime, welfare, and the underclass. This suppression of the dialogue and agenda on race was due partly to the Vietnam War, which diverted Johnson's attention and the country's resources, and to the white backlash that followed urban racial violence, most immediately the Watts riots, which occurred just months after Johnson's speech at Howard. And the diminishing of the dialogue on race was due also to major shifts in the thinking and practices of civil rights activists, who in the middle and late 1960s came to reject the policies of white liberals.[17]

Johnson's speech at Howard relied largely on the then unreleased report Moynihan had prepared for the Department of Labor's Office of Policy Planning and Research. A subsidiary but important point of the speech came to be the major topic of contention in the Moynihan Report: the view that a breakdown in African American family structures was a major factor in continuing black poverty. Borrowing a phrase from Kenneth Clark, Moynihan described black urban life as a "tangle of pathology" at the center of which was "the weakness of the family structure" (Moynihan, 76). Moynihan was particularly critical of what he saw as a matriarchal structure in black families. His implication that black women were usurpers and black men emasculated aroused enormous resentment among African American readers.[18] Bayard Rustin, for example, criticized the report for concentrating "almost solely upon what is negative in Negro life" and for neglecting "the degree to which the 'abnormality' of some of the ghetto mores . . . represents a desperate, but intelligent attempt on the part of a jobless Negro to adapt to a social pathology" (Rainwater and Yancey, 422). James Farmer, director of the Congress of Racial Equality, blamed the report for providing "a massive academic cop-out for the white conscience" (Rainwater and Yancey, 410). Responding to the report's particular animus against "matriarchy," Dorothy Height, president of the National Council of Negro Women, wrote, "You need recognition of the fact that women have saved the family in the crises of three hundred years, and there would be no family at all without what they have done. There are strengths in the family which should have been brought out by Moynihan" (Rainwater and Yancey, 186).

Moynihan's strong endorsement of major investments in employment, housing, and health care programs was forgotten in the controversies surrounding his perceived attacks on black manhood and womanhood, indeed on black culture as a whole. The report, then, furthered the severing of ties between liberal policymakers and African American activists and thinkers, who increasingly turned in the late 1960s toward black nationalism and separatism. As a missed opportunity for changing social policy, as a symptom of liberal insensitivities and black feelings of militance and vulnerability, and as a register of shifts in

attitudes regarding race, the debate over the Moynihan Report represents a pivotal moment in American racial discourse.

The Moynihan Report is also, however, the culmination of a line of liberal
thinking — a "liberal orthodoxy," as historian Walter Jackson calls it — on race
and on the black family that goes back to radical black social scientists like E.
Franklin Frazier and Ralph Bunche in the 1930s. They were important sources
for Gunnar Myrdal's widely influential book *An American Dilemma: The Negro Problem and Modern Democracy* and for subsequent liberal thinkers and
policymakers, including Moynihan. This tradition focuses on the traumatization of African American culture under slavery and on the continuing racial
oppression that followed. Frazier, in *The Negro Family in the United States*
(1939), described the history of black family life as a series of wrenching dislocations, the first of which was the nearly total removal from African culture:
"Probably never before in history has a people been so nearly completely
stripped of its social heritage as the Negroes who were brought to America"
(15). Lacking a culture of their own, the slaves were forced to adopt, or at
least adapt to, the culture imposed by their masters. After this adjustment, however, emancipation arrived as a second apocalyptic cultural break — "a crisis
in the life of the Negro that tended to destroy all his traditional ways of thinking and acting. To some slaves who saw the old order collapse and heard the
announcement that they were free men, emancipation appeared 'like notin'
but de judgement day' " (73). The third major disruption in black cultural life
came with the great migrations from southern rural areas to northern cities, in
which rural blacks, "uprooted from the soil," lost their "roots in a communal
life and [broke] all social ties" (224). For Frazier, these overarching cultural
traumas had specific and destructive effects on black family life — illegiti-
mate births, the abandonment of families by men, households headed by
women, and thus a family structure Frazier classified as matriarchy.

Frazier's book today appears naive in its confident assessments of social
and sexual mores. Nevertheless, it argued against the powerful current of "scientific" racism characterized by Morrison in *Beloved* in the figure of Schoolteacher. Frazier focused his attention always on historical and social determinants of African American family life, and he denied the possibility of intrinsic
racial "characteristics" of the sort that Schoolteacher sought in order to bol-
ster his racial contempt. Frazier helped shift the locus of racial debate in Amer-

ica from biological discussions of race to discussions of economic and political structures. A striking weakness in his account, however, is the absence of any sense of agency on the part of African Americans. The African American community, for Frazier, was the community traumatized beyond culture.

In *An American Dilemma* (1944), a book that became the major intellectual reference for liberal policymakers from the Roosevelt through the early Johnson years, the Swedish sociologist Gunnar Myrdal and his colleagues[19] drew largely on Frazier's description of African Americans as a radically traumatized, virtually deculturated group. Yet, in relying on the work of Frazier, Bunche, and St. Clair Drake, Myrdal chose to ignore other directions of research being pursued by Melville Herskovits, Carter Woodson, and W. E. B. Du Bois, all of whom stressed in different ways the autonomy of African American culture, its continuities with African cultures, and its influences on American culture at large. According to Walter Jackson, Myrdal regarded black history, the discipline being pioneered by Carter Woodson, "as a 'waste field' . . . and he failed to investigate carefully the growing literature that examined black institutions and portrayed Afro-Americans as historical actors rather than as the objects of white action" (112). In an important and symptomatic passage from *An American Dilemma,* Myrdal wrote, "In practically all its divergences, American Negro culture is not something independent of general American culture. It is a distorted development, or a pathological condition, of the general American culture" (in Jackson, 225). Like Frazier before him and Moynihan after, Myrdal recommended massive political and economic reforms to create an environment for black social equality. The "American dilemma" he referred to, however, was at all points a dilemma to be resolved by white Americans. African Americans, as he depicted it, were too severely damaged by oppression to take an active role in their own redemption.[20]

By the end of 1965, in the wake of the Watts riots and the Moynihan controversy, this line of liberal thinking and its implied practices and policies had been largely discredited. Activists in the civil rights movement stressed the need for African American communities to organize and mobilize themselves rather than rely on policymakers in Washington, and scholarship on African American social structures spoke more of strengths and adaptiveness and less of deficiencies or "pathologies."[21] In *Black Power: The Politics of Liberation in America* (1967), Stokely Carmichael and Charles Hamilton rejected Myrdal's thesis of an "American dilemma" opposing democratic ideals against racist traditions. "There is no 'American dilemma,' " they wrote, "no moral hang-up, and black people should not base decisions on the assumption that a dilemma exists" (77). They rejected the premise shared by Frazier, Myrdal, and Moynihan that African American culture was merely a shattered distortion of a homogeneous white American culture, and attacked racial integration as a policy "based on the assumption that there is nothing of value in the black community and that little of value could be created among black people" (53). Carmichael and Hamilton called for African Americans to "win [their] freedom while preserving [their] cultural integrity" (55).[22]

Paralleling these shifts in civil rights theory and strategy were changes in the writing of history and social science. Eugene Genovese and Herbert Gutman challenged liberal assumptions that slavery and racism had overwhelmingly traumatic effects on African American social and family structures. In *Roll, Jordan, Roll: The World the Slaves Made* (1976), Genovese, a Marxist historian, acknowledged that slavery exerted "extraordinary" pressures on black families and "took a terrible toll," but he wrote that nevertheless "the slaves created impressive norms of family life, including as much of a nuclear family norm as conditions permitted, and that they entered the postwar social system with a remarkably stable base" (451–52). Considering family life, work, religion, and the open and subtle resistance to slavery, Genovese rejected in particular Stanley Elkins's view that slaves were passive and infantilized. Gutman's *The Black Family in Slavery and Freedom, 1750–1925* (1976) aimed to show how blacks "adapted to enslavement by developing distinctive domestic arrangements and kin networks that nurtured a new Afro-American culture, and how these, in turn, formed the social basis of developing Afro-American communities" (3). Genovese and Gutman viewed their work as direct responses to Frazier, Myrdal, and Moynihan. Genovese began his chapter "The Myth of the Absent Family" with a reference to the "the ill-fated Moynihan Report" and its reliance on Frazier's work that inaugurated "the conventional wisdom according to which slavery had emasculated black men, created a matriarchy, and prevented the emergence of a strong sense of family" (450). Gutman criticized Frazier for underestimating "the adaptive capacities of slaves and exslaves" (10), and devoted much of his afterword to a critical review of the Moynihan Report.

The sociologist Carole Stack set out to demonstrate the effectiveness of African American kinship systems in a housing project in Chicago in the early 1970s. Her *All Our Kin: Strategies for Survival in a Black Community* (1974) was highly influential as contemporary confirmation of Genovese's and Gutman's historical arguments for African American adaptiveness and as a powerful alternative to Moynihan's view. Stack concluded that

> highly adaptive structural features of urban black families comprise a resilient response to the social-economic conditions of poverty.... [T]he distinctively negative features attributed to poor families, that they are fatherless, matrifocal, unstable, and disorganized, are not general characteristics of black families living substantially below economic subsistence in urban America. The black urban family, embedded in cooperative domestic exchange, proves to be an organized tenacious, active, lifelong network. (124)

Thus, by the mid-1970s, in the emerging New Left and black nationalist analyses, African American culture in general and its family structures in particular were no longer regarded as sites of radical dislocation and trauma but as functioning, adaptive, and resistant entities, fundamentally healthy. At the same time, since national economic growth declined through the 1970s and early 1980s and the massive economic and social reforms promised by Johnson were never accomplished, conditions for urban blacks deteriorated. In response, the New Left and black nationalist analysts, who denied that there were social problems intrinsic to black urban communities, could only offer generalized descriptions of racism. The American electorate, in embracing Reagan, chose a set of conservative positions that revived the old liberal notions of ghetto pathology while ignoring the liberal social policies intended to cure the problems. These parameters defined the debate on poverty in the 1980s, in which the Right used the term *underclass* to describe a range of cultural and family pathologies and behaviors, while the Left tended to reject the term and its implications altogether. William Julius Wilson has framed this debate explicitly in relation to the Moynihan Report: "The controversy surrounding the Moynihan Report had the effect of curtailing serious research on minority problems in the inner city for over a decade, as liberal scholars shied away from researching behavior construed as unflattering or stigmatizing to particular racial minorities" (4). The discourse of race by the 1980s, then, was constrained by a double denial: Reaganist conservatives denied American racism, and descendants of the New Left denied any dysfunction within African American communities.

Morrison's novels oppose both forms of denials.[23] *Beloved* is a challenge to all American racial discourse of the 1980s—to Reaganist conservatism and to the New Left and black nationalism. *Beloved* revives the liberal position of Frazier, Myrdal, and Moynihan, placing historical trauma—the continuing apocalypse within history—at the center of American race relations. But *Beloved* revises traditional liberalism by insisting on African American personal and cultural agency and on a powerful role for women.

HISTORICAL TRAUMA, SOCIAL SYMPTOMS, AND THE EMBODIED GHOST

Whereas the Right and the Left deny trauma in history, *Beloved* insists that a traumatic presence in excess of any discourse is a key factor in historical transmission. The novel attempts to describe the "passing on" of "unspeakable thoughts"—and unspeakable actions—"unspoken" (199), and Morrison introduces historical trauma into the narrative primarily through the figure of the returning and embodied ghost. Beloved's persistent returns, her existence in a physical body, her ambivalent, often destructive relations to symbolic and social structures mark her as a conflation of all the social, personal, and familial traumas of American race relations that continue to persist and return to this day.[24]

This emphasis on trauma as extratextual brings us back to our discussion of *Beloved* as apocalyptic, as catastrophic and revelatory. To the question, what is revealed in the novel's central, apocalyptically laden scene, we answered that the entry of the four horsemen into Baby Suggs's yard and Sethe's pushing her daughter "through the veil" represented two types of violence: an institutional, transgressive, and racist violence and an internal, self-destructive violence. These two types of violence correspond exactly to the two denials of historical or social trauma we located in the discourses on race from the political Right and Left. We can say now that revelation in *Beloved* is the revelation of historical trauma. Indeed, since another chief feature of the apocalypse in *Beloved* is its relentless propensity to *return*—as the scar of a wound, as a physical body, or as repeated behavior — it is not too much to say that in *Beloved* apocalypse *is* trauma, that historical trauma is the revelatory catastrophe that returns as symptoms on the social body and that Morrison represents at the moment of its occurrence through figures of religious apocalypse.

While the biblical apocalypse is the unique world-transforming event, in *Beloved* nothing happens only once. Baby Suggs and Sethe must repeat over and over a single phrase that recalls their respective catastrophes. When Baby Suggs leaves the social world to live the remainder of her life in a private world of colors, she resists Stamp Paid's explanatory paraphrases — "You blaming God," "You saying the whitefolks won?" "You saying nothing counts," "You saying God give up?" — and repeats her apocalyptic encapsulation, "I'm saying they came into my yard" (179). And Baby Suggs's repetition repeats Sethe's repeated response to Paul D regarding the memory of her most traumatic violation: not that, as Paul D tries to understand, "they used cowhide on you," or "they beat you and you was pregnant," but that "they took my milk" (16–17). What returns, for both Sethe and Baby Suggs, is not a contextualizing or explanatory narrative of the event but, rather, as nearly as language can approximate, the direct, gripping memory of the event itself. In these repeated phrases, the events themselves return, occur again, possess Sethe and Baby Suggs and compel them to continue the process of traumatic repetition. This process is part of what Sethe means by "rememory": "If you go there and stand in the place where it was, it will happen again" (36). Neither Sethe nor Baby Suggs is able to leave "the place where it was."

The principal site of return in *Beloved* is the embodied ghost, Beloved herself. Beloved is the site not just of one traumatic return — of Sethe's murdered daughter — but is a conflation of traumatic returns. She is the murdered daughter; she seems also to be, as Deborah Horvitz argues, Sethe's mother during the Middle Passage.[25] Indeed, Sethe's act of infanticide is not the only such act in the novel. Sethe's mother also killed some of her children — those of white fathers; and Ella killed her mixed-race children. The apocalyptic scene in Baby Suggs's yard is already a repetition of previous violations of black women's bodies and property, and of previous self-destruction of African American families. And the scene will be repeated again when Sethe tries to kill Bodwin. In the broadest sense, Beloved brings together all the unresolved traumas of slavery. The two-year-old daughter's legal status as slave is the reason the four horsemen come into Baby Suggs's yard, and the milk stolen from Sethe was intended for her daughter. Beloved is the murdered child and the mother's guilt, but she returns also to mark as traumatic the whole set of social relations that produced, and whose descendants continue to produce, such apocalyptic disruptions in families.

After her death, Sethe's unnamed daughter actually returns three times. First, she appears as the inscription on her tombstone, an appearance that is itself traumatic in that Sethe must barter her own body in order to pay the stonecutter. The tomb's function is to lay the dead to rest, to preserve only certain "beloved," that is, nontraumatic, memories and to bury all others. But this culturally legitimized form of memorial cannot contain the traumatic impact of the infant's death. Sethe's inscription of "Beloved," while an act of love (as even her killing of her daughter was evidence of the "thickness" of her love), is also an act of repression, a premature burial under a single name that given the circumstances of the death and burial, must be seen as in some sense a misnomer: as the novel's second epigraph says, "I will call . . . her beloved which was not beloved."

The murdered child, repressed under the denial of trauma inscribed on her tombstone, then returns as the baby ghost who haunts 124. This disembodied poltergeist imposes greater demands and produces physical effects. It drives Sethe's sons from the house and becomes an invisible companion to Denver. And it seems to provide a form of painful but acceptable penance for Sethe, who can acknowledge the ghost's sadness but not its venom. The ghost's intentions seem scattered; it is there and not there, real and not real. Sethe does not have to face her traumatic past in this disembodied ghost. Indeed, her life during this time consists largely of "keeping the past at bay" (42), of the "serious work of beating back the past" (73). The baby ghost is more difficult to accommodate than the mute tombstone, but even this accommodation is disrupted by Paul D's exorcism. Paul D takes from the murdered infant, as it were, the "responsibility for [Sethe's] breasts" (18)—that is, at least in part, her responsibility as mother. He wants Sethe to be able to let go of the past and live in the present. "She got enough without you. She got enough!" Paul D shouts at the ghost, meaning both that she has enough problems and, now that he has entered her life, she has enough solace. The exorcism, however, is another premature burial, an act of repression that repeats the repression of the tombstone.

Sethe, of course, is far from being the only character in *Beloved* who represses traumatic memories. Paul D regards his heart as a tobacco tin whose function is to contain traumatic memories and never release them:

> It was some time before he could put Alfred, Georgia, Sixo, schoolteacher, Halle, his brothers, Sethe, Mister, the taste of iron, the sight of butter, the smell of hickory, notebook paper, one by one, into the tobacco tin lodged in his chest. By the time he reached 124 nothing in this world could pry it open. (115)

And Ella, who, like Sethe, felt obligated to kill her children, repeats Sethe's and Paul D's attitude and behavior with regard to the past as something "to leave behind. And if it didn't stay behind, well, you might have to stomp it out" (256).

The final incarnation of Beloved is a conflation of all these traumas and repressions. She is the sign of a society — both white and black — that cannot narrate its past and thus is trapped in an ever escalating circle of trauma and symptom. And, equally important, she is *incarnated,* a ghost who does not merely inhabit or possess but who *exists as* a physical body. Although in somewhat strange and significantly limited ways, Beloved lives in the world. She eats, sleeps, speaks, makes love, ice skates. This physicality, this presence both biological and social, is crucial to Morrison's portrayal of historical transmission. The past — and not only but markedly the traumatic past — lives among us, apparently ordinary, almost indistinguishable, entirely alive: not a narrative but a living organism.[26] Historical trauma returns as somatic-social symptom. Thus "rememory" — of which Beloved herself is the novel's principal instance — is not a narrative "working through," is not the undoing of repetition as Freud describes in "Repeating, Remembering, and Working Through." It is, rather, that repetition that cannot yet be worked through.[27]

The symptom marks a place of pain and, therefore, as Elaine Scarry writes, of incoherence. Scarry argues that

> [p]hysical pain is not only itself resistant to language but also actively destroys language, deconstructing it into the pre-language of cries and groans. To hear those cries is to witness the shattering of language. Conversely, to be present

> when the person in pain rediscovers speech and so regains
> the powers of self-objectification is almost to be present at
> the birth, or rebirth, of language. (172)

The site of trauma exists outside of language, or trauma shatters the linguistic frame in which it would otherwise be embedded. It is unrepresentable. As Slavoj Zizek puts it, the trauma (or the Lacanian "impossible Real") is "the rock upon which all formalization stumbles." And yet, he continues,

> it is precisely through this failure that we can in a way en-
> circle, locate the empty place of the Real. In other words,
> the Real cannot be inscribed, but we can inscribe this im-
> possibility itself, we can locate its place: a traumatic place
> which causes a series of failures. (*Sublime Object,* 172–73)

Language, if it cannot *inscribe* trauma, can *circumscribe* it. Thus, trauma, even while resisting and shattering language nevertheless continues to generate a variety of discourses that spiral around it. Indeed, such a circumlocution characterized racial discourse in the post-Moynihan 1980s, as debates over teenage sexuality, unwed mothers, welfare queens, drugs, and crime served as signifiers in orbit around the unspeakable topic of race.

This circling of language around a central, generative, but unrepresentable event is also what Kierkegaard referred to, in *Repetition,* as "circumnavigation." In Kierkegaard's text, as in *Beloved,* the fact of repetition can only be revealed through a movement of circling:

> For hope is an alluring fruit which does not satisfy, recollec-
> tion is a miserable pittance which does not satisfy, but repeti-
> tion is the daily bread which satisfies with benediction. When
> one has circumnavigated existence, it will appear whether
> one has courage to understand that life is a repetition, and to
> delight in that very fact. He who has not circumnavigated
> life before beginning to live will never come to the point of
> living. (34)

Kierkegaard reverses the psychoanalytic goal of ending repetition through narrative, replacing this goal with a more "existential" goal of embracing the symptomatic, and thus repetitive, structures that have come to define the subject. Kierkegaard's is, in effect, a Nietzschean call to "become who you are," an entreaty that Zizek repeats when he identifies the subject with his symptom. For Kierkegaard's pseudonymous narrator, the moment of repetition in which he locates delight and self-definition is at the same time a moment of agony and self-dissolution. The delight in repetition is an embrace of an experience of horror seen to be authenticating and redemptive.

And yet this experience, this moment, cannot be addressed directly. It must be circled. The figure of circling appears also in *Either/Or:*

> If I imagined two kingdoms adjoining one another, with one of which I was fairly well acquainted, and altogether unfamiliar with the other, and I was not allowed to enter the unknown realm . . . I should still be able to form some conception of its nature. I could go to the limits of the [known] kingdom . . . and follow its boundaries, and as I did so, I should in this way describe the boundaries of this unknown country. (52–53)

Finally, and most crucially for a discussion of *Beloved,* in *Fear and Trembling* Kierkegaard's narrator writes that his various analogies to Abraham are intended "not to make Abraham more intelligible thereby, but in order that his unintelligibility might be seen more in the round." The analogies "indicate, from the point of view of their own sphere, the boundary of the unknown land by the points of discrepancy" (136). Abraham's faith and attempted sacrifice of Isaac remain throughout the book radically incommensurable with the varied textual means Johannes de Silentio employs to represent them. The text continually reenacts its inability to represent this faith and this sacrifice, and does so through the repetitive figure of circling verbally around a central, unknowable event — Abraham's willingness to murder his son.

Sethe's murder of her daughter has already been represented in a text, in the newspaper account that Stamp Paid shows Paul D. This document, of course, does not adequately represent the event. Stamp Paid tries to fill in the gaps but is unable to do so, primarily because the infanticide was partly facilitated by a shameful lapse of moral attention on the part of the whole community. Furthermore, Paul D cannot read; he can only look at the newspaper sketch of Sethe's face, and even this he misreads. And yet, Paul D's illiteracy and misreading are not so much personal deficiencies or blindnesses as they are indications of the fundamental insufficiency of the textual document. Paul D cannot read the newspaper account because it cannot be read. What it claims to represent shatters its representation, and so knowledge of the event must be transmitted by other means.

Paul D denies the veracity of the written document, repeating to Stamp Paid, "That's not her mouth." Or, he might say, that mouth in the newspaper posited as the origin of part of this written text is not the mouth that will tell the true story. That is not *her* mouth. He will go home and hear the story from her mouth. The oral narrative will supersede the written document. Paul D's hope for a true oral account, however, is not fulfilled, for if the written, official document of the event is so distorted as to be unreadable, Sethe's account can only accomplish a Kierkegaardian circling. As Sethe tells the story, she physically "was spinning. Round and round the room. . . . Paul D sat at the table watching her drift into view then disappear behind his back, turning like a slow but steady wheel" (159). Paul D recognizes the link between the physical and the discursive circumnavigation, that Sethe was "circling him the way she was circling the subject" (161). And Sethe, as she walks and speaks in circles, understands that, like Kierkegaard's narrator, she will never close her verbal circle and touch the event with language: "she could never close in, pin it down for anybody who had to ask . . . Because the truth was simple. And if she thought anything, it was No. No. Nono. Nonono" (163). And at that point the encircling narrative reaches the apocalyptic veil that Sethe's action penetrates.

Abraham's faith, for Kierkegaard, manifested itself in an act of sacrificial violence that remained incomprehensible except in the context of that same faith, which is at the same time incommensurable with any discursive categories. For Morrison, Sethe's maternal love manifests itself as infanticide, a traumatic event that, again, cannot be situated in language. "If she thought anything," Sethe recalls, it was a multiplying exclamation of negation, a repeated syllable of pain that "unmakes," in Scarry's term, the linguistic world. While for Kierkegaard the incommensurable center of discursive orbits is a religious event, a phenomenon in the realm of negative theology, Sethe's and Morrison's event is a conflation of social and familial trauma. And yet the similarity of these two discursive encirclings, their meeting at a point of family violence, reinforces the value Morrison gives to the incommensurable, traumatic, social, and familial violence as apocalypse — an apocalypse that must continually exceed and shatter any linguistic accounts, including, perhaps especially, the texts that constitute historical knowledge.

The traumatic fact and memory and transmission of the daughter's murder have the power throughout *Beloved* to jar characters outside of the symbolic order. A schoolmate asks Denver, "Didn't your mother get locked away for murder? Wasn't you in there with her when she went?" And Denver "went deaf rather than hear the answer" (104–5). She stops going to school and withdraws into a silent world devoted to the company of the baby ghost. Even after her hearing returns—she hears the baby ghost trying to climb the stairs—Denver still will not leave the house until finally, and significantly, she goes to Lady Jones, her former teacher, who had taught her to read. Denver's immersion in the world of the ghost coincides precisely with her self-exclusion from school, the purveyor of language.

The most dramatic instances of traumatic disruption of the symbolic order are the chapters of merger and possession (pages 200–217). These monologues and final trio in a single voice of Sethe, Denver, and Beloved, Stamp Paid overhears and cannot understand. "The speech," for Stamp, "wasn't nonsensical, exactly, nor was it tongues. But something was wrong with the order of the words and he couldn't describe or decipher it to save his life." He at first interprets the incomprehensible speech as "just that eternal, private conversation that takes place between women and their tasks" (172). When he listens again, however, the speech has become "a roaring," and he now interprets it in the context of historical trauma. "This time, although he couldn't cipher but one word, he believed he knew who spoke them. The people of the broken necks, of fire-cooked blood and black girls who had lost their ribbons" (181). Finally, Stamp Paid senses "mixed in with the voices . . . recognizable but undecipherable . . . the thoughts of the women of 124, unspeakable thoughts, unspoken" (199).

These unspeakable thoughts, unspoken but overheard, unspoken but enacted and repeated, are the litanies of the mother and the child she has killed, reverberations of the catastrophic breakdown of an African American family, in a northern city, after slavery. Morrison does not allow the reader to forget or to mitigate the fact that Sethe murdered her child, installing this "pathology" at the center of her text as the "unspeakable," about which, especially in these crucial chapters of semantic breakdown, the characters cannot stop speaking. At the same time, Stamp Paid's characterization of the voices as "unspeakable thoughts, unspoken" follows directly on his analysis of the internal jungle, which was not "the jungle blacks brought with them to this place . . . [i]t was the jungle whitefolks planted in them" (198). And "the secret spread of this new kind of whitefolks' jungle was hidden, silent, except once in a while when you could hear its mumbling in places like 124" (199).[28]

The chapters of unspeakable thoughts trace a movement back away from language to a linguistic approximation of pure trauma, both familial and historical, that ends in a complete merger of personalities and withdrawal from the social world.[29] Sethe and Denver lose themselves entirely in the mazes of trauma and symptom embodied in Beloved. The repetitions of possession and loss, presence and absence resemble an endless round of Freud's "fort-da" game, but played with no trace of playfulness and no possibility of mastery over the fact of loss:

> I loved you
> You hurt me
> You came back to me
> you left me
> I waited for you
> You are mine
> You are mine
> You are mine (217)

In being possessed by Beloved, and thus by the whole conflation of personal, familial, and historical events she embodies, Sethe leaves the symbolic order to be locked permanently into the unspeakable, now incarnated, repeated, symptomatic moment of trauma.[30]

Historical trauma, then, enters the present not only through textual representations but through physical repetitions, the repetitions of woundings. The document is not enough. It is unreadable. And first-person testimony or witnessing can only circle the event it seeks to describe. Speaking in her mind to Beloved, who by this time increasingly possesses her, Sethe says, "[T]here is no world outside my door. I only need to know one thing. How bad is the scar?" (184). The scar is an indexical sign that points toward a wound, and the severity of the scar indicates its proximity to the wound.[31] Beloved, we recall, is physically entirely normal except in one striking respect. She is—again with one exception—utterly unmarked. Her skin has no lines, no variations in pigmentation, no fingerprints. The only mark on her skin is the scar on her neck. Without any other marking, the scar defines her. Beloved assumes a synecdochic relation to the scar, becoming, in effect, a living scar who points toward the social and familial wounds that she tenuously sutures. At the beginning of part 3, shortly after the litany of merger, it is Sethe's attention to Beloved's scar that finally separates Sethe from the world entirely and brings her wholly into the language-shattering hold of trauma and symptom.

And yet, Sethe already has this traumatic index inscribed on her own body through the figure of the chokecherry tree on her back. When the wounds from her last beating before her escape are still open, they overwhelm language. The loquacious Amy sees Sethe's lacerated back and can only say, "Come here, Jesus." She addresses Sethe's wound with her hands, and when she speaks again, speaks figuratively, transforming Sethe's wound into the beautiful but poisonous chokecherry tree. Sethe subsequently continues to define herself by the scar of this wound, and by the wound that will soon reappear as Beloved: that is to say, by wounds that are simultaneously personal and social. "I got a tree on my back and a haint in my house," she tells Paul D (15). Sethe's assimilation of the scar, however, has, as we saw earlier in Sethe's burial of Beloved, a strong component of repression. Sethe entirely identifies her scar with Amy's recuperative metaphor, an identification that Paul D gradually disputes.

Paul D first feels the tree through Sethe's dress: "He rubbed his cheek on her back and learned that way her sorrow, the roots of it; its wide trunk and intricate branches." When he sees her back, however, he does not see it as a tree but as "the decorative work of an ironsmith too passionate for display." And when he touches every (now metallic, not organic) "ridge and leaf of it with his mouth," Sethe cannot feel, "because the skin had been dead for years" (17–18). The scar, translated to tree and then to art, has not healed the wound but only covered it over and ossified it. Shortly afterward, Paul D further erodes Amy's metaphor by reidentifying the scar with the original wound. He decides that "the wrought-iron maze he had explored in the kitchen like a gold miner pawing through pay dirt was in fact a revolting clump of scars" (21). The scar as "revolting clump" reverts to the condition of wound.[32]

In a world structured by "rememory," in which terrible events can "happen again," there is only a thin and permeable boundary between scar and wound, symptom and trauma. As Zizek describes it, the wound is, in effect, always open, as Sethe's scar is opened when Paul D unmakes the "tree" and the "iron-work" to reveal the "revolting clump." The wound, for Zizek, continually re-embodies the traumatic act that produced it, and so remains an unspeakable, bodily sign that structures the subjectivity of its bearer. Wound and scar, symptom and trauma, in Zizek's account, become interchangeable, for all mark the place of the Lacanian Real, which is the place of the breakdown of meaning in any symbolic order. The wounded body is such a place. So is a body politic marked by the pressures of repressed social antagonisms.[33]

There is another, more puzzling aspect to Zizek's reading of symptom and trauma. Zizek writes several times of a *jouissance* experienced in relation to the symptom, defining the symptom as "a certain signifying formation pene-trated with enjoyment: it is a signifier as a bearer of *jouis-sense,* enjoyment in sense." And, two paragraphs later, "This, then, is a symptom: a particular, 'patho-logical,' signifying formation, a binding of enjoyment, a stain which cannot be included in the circuit of discourse, of social bond network, but is at the same time a positive condition of it" (*Sublime Object,* 75).

Zizek then refers to the symptomatic wounds in Kafka's "A Country Doc-tor" and Wagner's (and Syberberg's) *Parsifal* as signifiers "not enchained in a network but immediately filled, penetrated with enjoyment, [their] status by definition 'psychosomatic,' that of a terrifying bodily mark which is merely a mute attestation bearing witness to a disgusting enjoyment." Amfortas's wound, as symptom, "embodies his filthy, nauseous enjoyment, it is his thickened con-densed life-substance which does not let him die" (76–77).

If we have correctly described Beloved as the somatic, extratextual symp-tom of historical and familial traumas, the wound of inter- and intraracial vio-lence that continues to return open and alive to the American social body, how can we explain Zizek's insistence on the importance of *jouissance* with regard to the symptom? Or, conversely, does Morrison's treatment of trauma and symp-tom in *Beloved* put Zizek's emphasis in question?

Baby Suggs's sermon in the clearing urges the freed slaves to love and take pleasure in their own flesh: "This is flesh I'm talking about here," she tells them, "Flesh that needs to be loved." And she anatomizes the body in an almost

Whitmanesque listing (cf. "Not an inch, nor a particle of an inch is vile"), seeking to free psychologically and spiritually the legally freed body. And yet, the sermon is filled with tension because the African American body is still a site of conflict, or antagonism. The black congregation *must* love their eyes, hands, mouths, feet, backs, necks, livers, genitals, and hearts because their white compatriots do not love this flesh and continue to injure and humiliate it. The African American bodies whom Baby Suggs addresses have entered the clearing already psychically and ideologically constructed as sites of trauma, as wounded bodies. Thus, in order to love their bodies as Baby Suggs instructs them, they must also, in Zizek's phrase, love their symptoms—and this is the point that Baby Suggs fatally misses.

Her ritual of laughing, dancing, and crying goes a long way toward working through these wounds and traumas, but finally her congregation is *not* yet ready to love and enjoy their bodies. Her feast to celebrate the liberation of her daughter-in-law and grandchildren constitutes a premature closure to the story of racial oppression. Its "excess"—the quality that turns the community against her and permits the catastrophe in the yard—consists in its forgetfulness of the still-open wounds of slavery. Her resentful neighbors compare her to Jesus in her ability to multiply food for the feast, but at the feast, unlike in the ritual in the forest, there is no memory of suffering. The magic reproduction of the feast makes a claim for a complete remaking of flesh, rather than for a renewed love for a wounded, slowly healing flesh. And the neighbors note that Baby Suggs's own flesh is not scarred: she "had never been lashed by a ten-year-old whiteboy as God knows they had" (137).

Baby Suggs's sermon implies but does not state, and her feast forgets entirely, that love and enjoyment of flesh can only be ambivalent, for they must include a relation—call it love—to the damage the flesh has suffered, a relation that then also involves hatred, horror, disgust. And we see this complex, ambivalent love of wounded flesh embodied in Paul D's sexual relation with Beloved. She is the synecdochic wound or symptom that haunts and disrupts the social and symbolic order, and he makes love with her involuntarily. "She moved him," both out of the house and into her body, and Paul D experiences this compelled pleasure as humiliating, indeed as a confirmation of Schoolteacher's "scientific," behavioralist racism ("If schoolteacher was right it explained how he had come to be a rag doll—picked up and put back down anywhere any time by a girl young enough to be his daughter. Fucking her when he was convinced he didn't want to" 126). And yet, as they engage in sex, Paul D must also call her by her name, must say "Beloved," even as, he later recalls,

> coupling with her wasn't even fun. It was more like a brainless urge to stay alive. Each time she came, pulled up her skirts, a life hunger overwhelmed him and he had no more control over it than over his lungs. And afterward, beached and gobbling air, in the midst of repulsion and personal shame, he was thankful too for having been escorted to some ocean-deep place he once belonged to. (264)

Recall again Zizek's comment on Kafka's "A Country Doctor": "The open wound growing luxuriantly on the child's body, this nauseous, verminous aperture—what is it it if not the embodiment of vitality as such, of the life-substance in its most radical dimension of meaningless enjoyment" (*Sublime Object,* 76).

But Paul D's enjoyment is not meaningless, and this divergence from Zizek points out the most crucial blurring in Zizek's thinking. Paul D's "enjoyment" of Beloved—his *jouissance,* or, in Kristeva's useful term, his "abjection"—is not just an engagement with "vitality" or "life-hunger" "*as such.*" Rather, this enjoyment is historically situated. Paul D's "life-hunger" directs itself toward a symptomatic embodiment of a specific traumatic past that he must, and will, relive with the most extreme ambivalence. The past is hateful and humiliating, and has marked and damaged him. And yet it is the only past he has; it has also formed him and shaped his desires.

Sethe experiences a similar ambivalence in her rememory of Sweet Home: "and although there was not a leaf on that farm that did not make her want to scream, it rolled itself out before her in shameless beauty. It never looked as terrible as it was and it made her wonder if hell was a pretty place too" (6). Sethe and Paul D acknowledge their ambivalent "love of the symptom" that underlies their nostalgia for Sweet Home, the site of trauma that repeatedly rematerializes for them in pleasing forms. As Paul D says, "It wasn't sweet and it sure wasn't home." "But it's where we were," Sethe replies, "All together. Comes back whether we want it to or not" (14). Their conflicts over the ambivalently marked "rememories" of Sweet Home, then, repeat their ambivalence toward their own flesh and toward the personal and social histories embodied in Beloved.

Beloved must be read not only as a critique of a tradition of racism that extends from the pseudobiological racism of schoolteacher to the pseudosociology of contemporary neoconservatives; it must also be read as an anatomy of African American self-hatred and self-destructiveness as manifested—indeed, as I have been stressing, *embodied*—in individuals, families, and communities. Thus, *Beloved* first revives the historiographical tradition of Frazier and his liberal successors who stressed above all the traumatic nature and effects of slavery, and at the same time *Beloved* revises this line of thinking, wresting it conclusively away from its neoconservative misappropriations. In *Beloved*, Morrison stakes out a complex political position that blends, critiques, and surpasses the positions of conservatives, leftists, and liberals. Morrison represents the symptoms of historical trauma and institutional violence (contra the conservatives) and the symptoms of personal trauma and familial violence (contra the leftists), while portraying the victims of trauma as still possessing culture and agency (contra the liberals).

BODWIN AND MOYNIHAN: THE ABOLITIONIST AS LIBERAL?

At the end of *Beloved*, the symptomatic ghost disappears, exorcised by the community, at the same moment when Sethe attacks Bodwin, mistaking his appearance for the return of Schoolteacher. Beloved's exorcism and the subsequent dispersal of her memory mark the novel's final repressions of her traumatic signature, after the tombstone's inscription that Sethe purchases with her own body and Paul D's initial exorcism of the baby ghost. Denver, Sethe's living daughter, is often rightly viewed as a locus of optimism at the novel's conclusion. But we should also recall her participation in repressing Beloved's memory when she cuts off her conversation with Paul D. Discussing who or what Beloved was, Paul D begins, "Well, if you want my opinion—"; "I don't," replies Denver, "I have my own" (267). While this response is evidence of Denver's new maturity and independence, Denver's maturity also has the effect of ending the discussion. Presumably, as the novel's enigmatic final chapter suggests, Denver and Paul D will never mention Beloved again:

> They forgot her like a bad dream. After they made up their
> tales, shaped and decorated them, those that saw her that day
> on the porch quickly and deliberately forgot her. It took longer
> for those who had spoken to her, lived with her, fallen in
> love with her. . . . So, in the end, they forgot her too. Remem-
> bering seemed unwise. . . . [B]y and by all trace is gone. (274)

Thus Beloved is gone, deliberately forgotten, utterly effaced. And yet, the logic
of trauma and symptom that seems to inform this novel insists that nothing is
forgotten. Only if traumas are remembered can they lose, gradually but never
entirely, their traumatic effects. The narrator of the final chapter can claim
that the world at last contains "just weather," that the wind is simply wind and
"not the breath of the disremembered and unaccounted for" (275) — that the
world is no longer a landscape of symptoms, no longer haunted. But the final
word of the novel, "Beloved," shatters this claim. Even if the story is not passed
on, the ghost will return to inhabit each succeeding present until the crimes
that repeat themselves are faced and worked through in every organ of the body
politic. The ending of *Beloved* reminds us of Theodor Adorno's judgment: "We
will not have come to terms with the past until the causes of what happened
then are no longer active. Only because these causes live on does the spell of
the past remain, to this very day, unbroken" ("What Does Coming to Terms
with the Past Mean?" 129).

Events in the United States today and in the recent past make it difficult to
agree with readers who claim that the exorcism of Beloved represents a successful working through of America's racial traumas. Indeed, in my view,
such optimistic interpretations of *Beloved* participate in the repressions and denials of trauma that the novel opposes.[34] For instance, Ashraf Rushdy holds as
exemplary Sethe's friend Ella's repressive attitude toward the past, arguing
that by "exorcising Beloved, by not allowing the past to consume the present,
[Ella] offers Sethe the opportunity to reclaim herself" (584). Rushdy's statement that "the novel both remembers the victimization of the ex-slaves who
are its protagonists and asserts the healing and wholeness that those protagonists carry with them in their communal lives" (575) seems particularly suspect in view of the destructive divisions Morrison portrays in the African American community after Baby Suggs's feast. The community comes together
under Ella's leadership to expel the naked, pregnant, and beautiful figure of

Beloved, who has perhaps finally become the "flesh" that Baby Suggs urged her congregation to love. While the community, led by Ella, does overcome its divisions and readmits Sethe and Denver, the absent space where Beloved stood is another scar in the symbolic order, sutured by an act of repression. The ritual that can put Beloved to rest must instead resemble Baby Suggs's ceremony in the forest, involving laughing, dancing, and crying. Beloved must, first of all, be mourned.

Some readings render not only the exorcism but even the act of infanticide unproblematic. Bernard Bell describes *Beloved* as a "retelling of the chilling historical account of a compassionate yet resolute self-emancipated mother's tough love" (9). This bizarre formulation places Sethe's act in the context of "the historical rape of black American women and of the resilient spirit of blacks in surviving as a people"; both connections are correct, but Bell's interpretation evades what Morrison takes pains not to evade: the traumatic violence within African American communities and the damage to the resilient spirit Bell speaks of.

Bell and Rushdy would agree with Mae Henderson that "the story of oppression becomes a story of liberation; a story of inhumanity has been overwritten as a story of higher humanity" (79). What these and similar interpretations miss, in my view, is that Beloved's story is not over, that she will return — indeed, has returned.[35] Henderson rightly regards Sethe's attack on Bodwin as a repetition of the apocalyptic (or, as she puts it, "primal") scene of infanticide. However, Henderson sees Sethe's violence against the white abolitionist as part of a successful working through of the trauma of the infanticide, since Sethe, taking Bodwin for Schoolteacher, believes that she attacks the slave owner and not her daughter. "Thus, by revising her actions," Henderson writes, "Sethe is able to preserve the community, and the community, in turn, is able to protect one of its own" (61).

Bodwin, however, contrary to Henderson's suggestion, is not Schoolteacher. Bodwin is a lifelong and active abolitionist, not an owner of slaves. Sethe, in a state of delusion, mistakes him for Schoolteacher. She sees Bodwin's entrance as portending a reenactment of the apocalyptic scene — that condensation of a multitude of historical traumas — in which her borders were violated by white institutional power and she pushed her daughter through the veil. Henderson's argument raises the question whether there is in fact a hidden connection, recognized by Sethe, between the white abolitionist and the white slave owner. Placing *Beloved* in the context of racial discourses of the 1980s extends the question. Is Sethe's attack on Bodwin an attack also on white liberals? Does Morrison in her presentation of Bodwin suggest that, as Kenneth Clark argued in 1964, the white-liberal position on race is a "more insidious" form of racism?

The most prominent evidence for regarding Bodwin as racist is a statuette near the back door of his house of a kneeling black boy, who has an enormous mouth filled with coins for tradesmen and rests on a pedestal bearing the words "At Yo Service" (255). While Bodwin despises slavery, he still regards blacks as subservient and has, apparently, no comprehension of African American culture apart from stereotypes. Moreover, during his ride toward his unexpected encounter with Sethe, Morrison shows Bodwin as a vain and self-absorbed man whose chief interest in abolition may have been in the feelings of moral elevation and political excitement he derived from the movement personally. And Morrison, I believe, links Bodwin here with a view of 1960s liberalism seen from the 1980s. As Bodwin looks back *twenty years later* to the time of his greatest political and moral achievements, he muses, "Nothing since was as stimulating as the old days of letters, petitions, meetings, debates, recruitment, quarrels, rescue and downright sedition" (260). For Bodwin, as for liberals and leftists in the age of Reaganism, "those heady days were gone now; what remained was the sludge of ill will; dashed hopes and difficulties beyond repair. A tranquil republic? Well, not in his lifetime" (260). Bodwin (like the liberals) now senses that what he regarded as his greatest victory, the abolitionist movement (like the civil rights movement), was only a minor triumph in a larger story of defeat. And in both his self-congratulation and his despair, he remains blind to the interests and culture of African Americans, as his facile memory of the murder of Beloved suggests. He recalls "a runaway slavewoman who lived in his homestead with her mother-in-law and got herself into a world of trouble. The Society managed to turn infanticide and the cry of savagery around, and build a further case for abolishing slavery. Good years, they were, full of spit and conviction" (260). Good years, that is, for feelings of moral rectitude; terrible years in their content of racial injustice and suffering.

Bodwin shares with twentieth-century liberals the features that led the civil rights movement of the late 1960s to reject the Moynihan Report and the liberal tradition of Frazier and Myrdal. Sethe's attack, like Henderson's interpretation, rejects white liberalism as hypocritical, blind to African American culture, and implicitly critical of (or at least condescending to) the victims of racial oppression. For Morrison, however, these aspects of Bodwin, and of liberalism, are not the whole story. Bodwin is a man with his own history and concerns, which are not congruent with those of African Americans. At the same time, he provides jobs and housing for the African American community, exactly what civil rights activists have demanded since they repudiated the Moynihan Report. For all the liberals' spiritual failings, jobs and housing have always been at the center of their agenda—including its embodiment in the Moynihan Report and in Johnson's original prescriptions for the War on Poverty. Morrison insists that we recognize Bodwin's contribution and therefore realize that Sethe's attack on him is delusional; immersed in the symptom of trauma, she has mistaken him for someone else. Sethe is not the only one to make this mistake, as we see in the history of attacks on liberalism from the Left and in Henderson's interpretation of Sethe's attack as a successful therapy. Stamp Paid's judgment of Bodwin seems accurate: "He's somebody never turned us down. Steady as a rock. I tell you something, if she had got to him, it'd be the worst thing in the world for us" (265).[36]

This analysis has suggested a kind of detachment for Bodwin. He helps with jobs and housing but remains absorbed in his own concerns. Morrison's portrayal does not allow us to grant Bodwin this detachment. Although the fact barely enters his consciousness, Morrison presents Bodwin as intimately and irrevocably connected to the black community. With his white hair and black mustache, he is a kind of hybrid—a "bleached nigger" to the racists (260). Moreover, the house he is visiting—where Baby Suggs, Sethe, and Beloved lived, the site of apocalyptic and historical trauma—is also the house where he was born. Going to his violent meeting with Sethe, where Beloved was murdered, Bodwin goes to the place of his own origin. Neither he nor Sethe knows it, but their histories are entwined.

Bodwin's self-absorption, his privacy, is as delusional in its way as Sethe's attack on him. These qualities, further, define the American—and, in particular, Reaganist—delusions of the 1980s: beliefs that the private, unregulated pursuit of wealth could eliminate poverty, that the poor and the rich, and whites and blacks lived in separate nations. Like the African American characters in the novel, and like most Americans in the 1980s, Bodwin lives under the weight of an enormous repression of personal and historical memory. After all, he re-turns to 124 not only to pick up Denver for her new job but also to locate things he had buried there as a child. Among these things is a box of tin sol-diers, a box perhaps like the box of tobacco that Paul D uses to hold his un-wanted memories. Bodwin wants to "recall exactly where his treasure lay" (261), a recollection that would also reveal, as Jesus says in Matthew, the lo-cation of his heart. Bodwin, like Sethe and Paul D, is trying to uncover his own heart, which, again like theirs, like ours, is buried at a site of historical trauma.

The world has not ended, though certain things are gone, "ingenious lovely things" among them — as well as people, cultures, possibilities whose destructions have rendered even William Butler Yeats's violent elegy inadequate: "We pieced our thoughts into philosophy / And planned to bring the world under a rule, / Who are but weasels fighting in a hole."[1] Everything is *not* all right. The Bomb has not exterminated us, nor has the Virus; aliens have not landed and blown up the White House. And yet, unspeakable and portentous events have occurred, are occurring, as we were looking the other way, or even watching directly. And, as this book has argued, American culture over the past twenty years has, both directly and symptomatically, tried to represent (and disguise) the unspeakable in its disaster films, its talk shows, its fictions, and its politics. Everything is changed, yet everything is the same — that is the representational puzzle. Like the new-old city of Freiburg that Josef Pesch showed me, American post-apocalyptic culture continually rebuilds itself over its traumatic, apocalyptic sites: "the end of thinking and the task of marketing." At the same time, there are still thinkers and writers, like Toni Morrison and Thomas Pynchon, who identify the culture's symptoms and allow its ghosts to speak. Let our commerce also include those we have murdered or allowed to be murdered! Let the dead into the system, and not just to be sequestered into a "Memorial Day." Give them ATM cards and interest on their accounts.

But now I am flying off the handle, intoxicated by some "after-the-end" frenzy. The apocalypse happened, and nothing changed; the apocalypse did not happen, but so much real damage was inflicted and suffered. The sense of absolute newness merges with a sense that everything has happened already.

William Carlos Williams wrote in 1923, "THE WORLD IS NEW"—having, in his imagination, destroyed the old one. And if it were new, would the sufferings and crimes of the old world be canceled and redeemed? Williams looked at that NEW world and STILL saw "the contagious hospital," the old sick woman dying, the "pure products of America" going crazy, "the crowd . . . beautiful . . . alive, venomous."[2] The traumas and the revelations of the traumas were transmitted from old to new. The apocalypse served only to show them more clearly. And yet Williams's apocalypse truly was beneficial, for it burned away layers of habits of perception that made both beauty and suffering imperceptible. Williams followed William Blake in making the apocalypse an explosion of perception, of sensual and empathic and intellectual responses—from which new political possibilities would not necessarily follow. But they might, and they could not follow without the new, post-apocalyptic perceptions.[3] If the world were made anew, then all suffering could and must be addressed and relieved. Having no history, all injustice would be our responsibility, as contemporaries. And there would be no histories of justification, rationalization, property, and succession. There would be only the injustice, there immediately in the present. See it this way—that is to say, SEE it—and you have no choice but to act on it.

SEE it, yes. The world is new, therefore unconstrained. But the moral vision has, and should have, bifocals. Make the perception new, but recognize that the damage is long-standing, symptomatic, haunting, and historical. The damaged, post-apocalyptic world is sustained by powerful institutions that benefit from the world as it is. "Even the dead are not safe." The Holocaust's dead are enshrined in Washington—not in Berlin. And the dead of the Middle Passage and of slavery . . . unmourned, not beloved,[4] haunt America in living forms.

And so, that representational impasse with which this book began—"after the end" as oxymoron, as straddling both sides of an impossible conceptual limit—turns out to have real ethical and historical consequences. What cannot be said, what the apocalyptic event obliterates, is a consequence of particular political needs and relations of power. In the cases I have discussed—the Shoah, American racism, Reaganism, the 1960s—the semantically unsayable is translated into politically somatic forms, into symptoms on the body politic, into ideological-narrative fetishes. Events have consequences, there are remainders to every catastrophe, and "obliteration" is always a relative term, for a cultural memory has many storage areas and modes of expression. To see a world as post-apocalyptic is to recognize its formative catastrophes and their symptoms, and to identify the ideological sutures that hide the damages and repetitions. It is also, finally, to recognize and create narratives that work through these symptoms and return to the apocalyptic moments that traumatize and reveal. At that point, new — more healthy and more truthful — histories and futures may be possible.

1. Josef Pesch, "Frank Gehry's 'Ginger and Fred' in Prague: Playfully Postmodern or Seriously Post-Apocalyptic?"; "Post-Apocalyptic War Histories: Michael Ondaatje's *The English Patient*"; "Beyond Dystopia: Post-Apocalyptic Writing"; "End in Ruin — Ruined Ends? Some Remarks on Conspicuous Absences in Recent Publications on Ends and Ruins."

2. There is not room here to say anything in detail about this extensive scholarship on apocalypse. I will only mention some of the work that has most helped my thinking. For discussions of ancient and biblical apocalyptic thinking, see David Hellholm, ed., *Apocalypticism in the Mediterranean World and the Near East,* a massive collection of articles treating apocalyptic writings ranging from Egyptian through early Christian. John J. Collins, *The Apocalyptic Imagination: An Introduction to the Jewish Matrix of Christianity,* Adela Yarbro Collins, *Crisis and Catharsis: The Power of the Apocalypse,* and Paul Hanson, "Old Testament Apocalyptic Reexamined," are especially important in describing and theorizing the historical conditions of biblical apocalyptic writings. Norman Cohn's classic *Pursuit of the Millennium* analyzes medieval Christian apocalyptic movements. Alan Mintz, *Hurban: Responses to Catastrophe in Hebrew Literature,* and David G. Roskies, *Against the Apocalypse: Responses to Catastrophe in Modern Jewish Culture,* are enormously valuable books showing what I would call the post-apocalyptic character of much Jewish literature. For collections of essays discussing apocalyptics from a variety of periods and cultures, see Sylvia L. Thrupp, ed., *Millennial Dreams in Action: Studies in Revolutionary Religious Movements*; Frank E. Manuel, ed., *Utopias and Utopian Thought*; Saul Friedlander et al., eds., *Visions of Apocalypse: End or Rebirth?*; and Malcolm Bull, ed., *Apocalypse Theory and the Ends of the World.* For histories of American apocalypticism, see Ernest Tuveson, *Redeemer Nation: The Idea of America's Millennial Role*; Timothy Weber, *Living in the Shadow of the Second Coming: American Premillennialism, 1875–1925,* and especially Paul

Boyer, *When Time Shall Be No More: Prophecy Belief in Modern American Culture.* For an interesting account of American apocalyptic rhetoric, see Stephen O'Leary, *Arguing the Apocalypse: A Theory of Millennial Rhetoric.* For an excellent discussion of the psychology of American millennialists, see Charles Strozier, *Apocalypse: On the Psychology of Fundamentalism in America.* Steven Goldsmith's *Unbuilding Jerusalem: Apocalypse and Romantic Representation* is an excellent study of the relations between English romanticism and apocalyptic thought that sets the standard for work in this area and illuminates apocalyptic issues in other periods as well. For discussions of modern and postmodern apocalyptic literature and culture, Frank Kermode's *The Sense of an Ending* remains the starting point. Two recent books, *Apocalyptic Overtures: Sexual Politics and the Sense of an Ending* by Richard Dellamora, and *Anti-Apocalypse: Exercises in Genealogical Criticism* by Lee Quinby, have done a great deal to add to and critique Kermode's analyses. Quinby's Foucauldian analyses locate apocalyptic sensibilities at the center of ideologies that help sustain American corporate and military power. Dellamora describes the constructions of male homosexual identities in the wakes of the catastrophes of the Oscar Wilde trial and the AIDS epidemic, and the uncanny appropriations and suppressions of gay discourses by liberal theorists, including Kermode. In its stress on the immediate and continuing effects of historical traumas refigured as apocalypses, Dellamora's work is an important contribution to thinking on post-apocalypse. See also the volume edited by Dellamora, *Postmodern Apocalypse: Theory and Cultural Practice at the End.*

3. Saul Friedlander, address, University of Virginia, March 1992.

1. POST-APOCALYPTIC RHETORICS

1. "For a hundred years or more the world, *our* world, has been dying. And not one man, in these last hundred years or so, has been crazy enough to put a bomb in the asshole of creation and set it off. The world is rotting away, dying piecemeal. But it needs the *coup de grace,* it needs to be blown to smithereens" (*Tropic of Cancer,* 26).

2. There seems no question that Foucault desires the fulfillment of the apocalyptic prophecy he utters at the end of *The Order of Things:* "If those arrangements were to disappear as they appeared, if some event of which we can at the moment do no more than sense the possibility — without knowing either what its form will be or what it promises — were to cause them to crumble, as the ground of Classical thought did, at the end of the eighteenth century, then one can certainly wager that man would be erased, like a face drawn in sand at the edge of the sea" (387).

3. "Babylon," for Lindsey, symbolizes "the whole Satanic world system, including all the Godless commercialism and hedonistic worship of luxury and pleasure which economic success permits" (quoted in Boyer, 290). Doug Clark, another Christian fundamentalist apocalyptic writer, adds that Babylon is "all governments and businesses . . . and God can't wait to destroy it all in one hour" (quoted in Boyer, 289).

4. Marshall Berman took this phrase as the title of his excellent book on the experience of modernity. Michael Phillipson summed up very well the apocalyptic perception of the modern when he wrote, "The modern experience...cannot be comprehended in the languages of the past, of Tradition, and yet we do not find ourselves except in this present—hence the need for...a language without history, without memory...a language against representation" (28).

5. Quinby's critique of ironic apocalypse is weakened by her insistence that apocalyptic thinking in general serves the interests of existing power relations. For Quinby, "absolute monarchy and the Vatican, for example, are structured in accordance with principles of apocalypse" (63), insofar as they rely on "self-justifying categories of fixed hierarchy, absolute truth, and universal morality" (55). Quinby does not recognize how profoundly hostile most apocalyptic imagination is to the versions of hierarchy, truth, and morality currently in power. Dostoyevsky's story of the Grand Inquisitor still illustrates the probable response of any institutional authority to the Second Coming.

6. Cf. Leo Bersani's brilliant and provocative discussions of the masochistic, traumatic, and apocalyptic character of sexuality in *The Freudian Body* and "Is the Rectum a Grave?" Bersani, in effect, takes the position of the punk wastelanders of *Road Warrior* in arguing (in the latter essay) that the apocalyptic terror of the AIDS virus, particularly among heterosexual men, derives in large part from a fear of the shattering of identity that Bersani claims is central to sexuality, though often denied. "Phallocentrism," Bersani writes, "is...not primarily the denial of power to women (although it has obviously led to that, everywhere and at all times), but above all the denial of the *value* of powerlessness in both men and women. I don't mean the value of gentleness, or nonaggressiveness, or even of passivity, but rather of a more radical disintegration and humiliation of the self" ("Rectum," 217). In homosexuality—and especially in its linkage since the 1980s with AIDS—heterosexual men perceive a threat to the integrity of their bodies and senses of selfhood, the same threat perceived by the human/humanist enclave in *Road Warrior.*

7. There is another side to this—the apocalyptic removal of male sexuality. Cf. Angela Carter's *The Passion of New Eve,* Anne Rice's *The Queen of the Damned,* and Spencer Holst's "The Santa Claus Murderer." In these works, the violent elimination of masculine sexuality, seen as a will to domination and aggression, leads to utopia. We should also note, however, that Rice's novel condemns this project as insane and that Carter's and Holst's texts are parodic. Apocalypse as denial of the sexual other, then, appears primarily as a masculine problem.

8. See also Jacques Derrida's response to Emmanuel Lévinas's descriptions of the "other" as irreducible to any previous concept. It still is necessary, Derrida wrote, "to state infinity's *excess* over totality *in* the language of totality; that it is necessary to state the other in the language of the Same; that it is necessary to think *true* exteriority as non-*exteriority,* that is, still by means of the Inside-Outside structure and by spatial metaphor; and that it is necessary still to inhabit the metaphor in ruins, to dress oneself

in tradition's shreds and the devil's patches" ("Violence and Metaphysics," 112). From his position in the metaphor in ruins, Derrida's is a post-apocalyptic response to Lévinas's apocalyptic invocation.

9. Feminist thinking has had an ambivalent attitude toward apocalyptic imagery. Quinby argues powerfully for an explicitly anti-apocalyptic, or "genealogical," feminism, but she acknowledges that "feminist apocalypse is rhetorically powerful and has moved women to social action" (33). An even more marked ambivalence can be found in Donna Haraway's "A Cyborg Manifesto." The cyborg is "outside salvation history" (150), "would not recognize the Garden of Eden; it is not made of mud and cannot dream of returning to dust. Perhaps that is why I want to see if cyborgs can subvert the apocalypse of returning to nuclear dust in the manic compulsion to name the Enemy" (151). At the same time, the cyborg is post-apocalyptic in being "a creature in a post-gender world" and standing, in general, after the conceptual end of all dominant contemporary modes of thought. The cyborg is compelling because it seems to border on the unthinkable, even the obscene. Its strategic role is to shatter the sense of the inevitability and naturalness of dominant discourses, and it does so by posing as a seductive figure sent back from after their end.

10. For the best account of gay apocalyptic writing, and one of the best books on apocalyptic writing in general, see Richard Dellamora's *Apocalyptic Overtures: Sexual Politics and the Sense of an Ending.* Dellamora analyzes how particular historical crises — the Oscar Wilde trial and the onset of AIDS — have been central to the formations and disintegrations of certain constructions of homosexual male identity, and argues that "the most notable feature of the history of the formation of male sexual minorities has been the repeated catastrophes that have conditioned their emergence and continued existence" (1). Dellamora studies the vicissitudes of gay identity in fictions by Wilde, Pater, Alan Hollinghurst, and Neil Bartlett. He also studies another set of blocked transmissions of homosexual discourses, in which liberal or left-wing literary intellectuals have appropriated important features of gay culture while suppressing their specifically sexual contexts and implications. Analyzing J. Hillis Miller's use of Pater as a precursor of deconstruction, Frank Kermode's dismissal of William Burroughs's apocalyptic writing as insufficiently skeptical, David Cronenberg's cinematic transformation of *Naked Lunch,* and Fredric Jameson's criticisms of Andy Warhol, Dellamora demonstrates that these liberal or leftist heterosexual writers emphasize the "difference" or "dissidence" of these texts in the abstract but cannot or will not discuss their specifically gay differences and oppositions.

11. The plays' politics, however, are confusing. Kushner's portrayal of Louis, the gay Jewish liberal, seems inexplicably cruel. Why should the Jewish liberal be a kind of villain, while Prior, the descendent of Puritans, functions as the enlightened hero-victim? Furthermore, Roy Cohn, like Milton's Satan, is *Angels'* most vivid, brilliant creation. In a play whose deepest value is life and the will to live, Cohn is the most in-

tensely living character. There may be an important lesson in this paradox concerning progressive politics and personal vitality, but I do not believe Kushner is sufficiently conscious of what it is.

12. Norman O. Brown, in *Life against Death: The Psychoanalytic Meaning of History,* analyzes instances in literature, theology, psychoanalysis, and economics of "the conflict between our animal body, appropriately epitomized in the anal function, and our pretentious sublimations" (186). His goal is a bodily mysticism that "takes seriously, as traditional psychoanalysis does not, the possibility of human perfectibility and the hope of finding a way out of the human neurosis into that simple health that animals enjoy, but not man" (311). Georges Bataille, less optimistically, describes the concepts of "expenditure" and the "heterogenous" as including whatever lies outside the realm of "production," zones of pure, excessive waste that are, however, the true bases of civilization. Expenditure consists of "luxury, mourning, war, cults, the construction of sumptuary monuments, games, spectacles, arts, perverse sexual activity" (118). The heterogenous consists both of the sacred and the desecrated, of "waste or [of] superior transcendent value" (142).

13. See also Martin Amis's *Time's Arrow* for a brilliant use of images of excrement in marking apocalyptic inexpressibility. Amis suggests the Holocaust's incomprehensibility by making time in his novel run backward. One principal consequence of this temporal reversal is that excrement becomes nourishment, the source of life. Auschwitz, the *"anus mundi,"* becomes a factory to *create* the Jews of Europe. "Our preternatural purpose? To dream a race. To make a people from the weather. From thunder and from lightning. With gas, with electricity, with shit, with fire" (120). Only in the context of such absolute contradictions of the natural order, the novel implies, can genocide possibly be represented.

14. Cf. Herbert Marks's essay on the "prophetic stammer" as a representation of a "central moment of blockage" that is intrinsic in prophetic utterance: "the 'slow tongue' of Moses and its variations, the 'unclean lips of Isaiah,' the demur of Jeremiah, the mutism of Ezekiel. The topos has had a full career in secular literature, invariably marking the subject's resistance to an overwhelming influx" (4–5).

2. Trauma and the End of the World

1. My thanks to my friend and host in Freiburg, Josef Pesch, another researcher into post-apocalyptic phenomena, who gave me a tour of Freiburg block by block, showing me which buildings had been destroyed and which survived and how to tell them apart, and thus introduced me to Freiburg as a post-apocalyptic city. Baudrillard did not need to go to California to theorize the simulacrum, Josef told me, he could have found it here in Germany.

2. We see this attitude most pointedly at the end of *Civilization and Its Discontents:* "And now it is to be expected that the other of the two 'Heavenly Powers,' eter-

nal Eros, will make an effort to assert himself in the stubble with his equally immortal adversary. But who can foresee with what success and with what result?" (92).

3. See Freud's "Remembering, Repeating, and Working Through," *Beyond the Pleasure Principle,* and "Mourning and Melancholia."

4. See Freud's "Fetishism," "Negation," and "The Splitting of the Ego in the Process of Defense."

5. See also Cathy Caruth's view of traumatic reference as "falling," in which, paradoxically, figurative language is best able to register "the impact of an event" (74), the friction of the physical world as it drags against language, the process by which a wound becomes voice. Geoffrey Hartman also links trauma to literature, arguing that a theory of trauma discloses "an unconscious or not-knowing knowledge—a potentially literary way of knowing. . . . In literature, as in life, the simplest event can resonate mysteriously, be invested with aura, and tend toward the symbolic. The symbolic, in this sense, is not a denial of literal or referential but its uncanny intensification" ("On Traumatic Knowledge and Literary Studies," 544, 547).

6. There is, of course, another major direction in postmodern theory, which is, broadly, pluralist, multicultural, postcolonial, and feminist. It sees the postmodern as characterized by increasing openness, diversity, and emancipatory possibilities for marginalized populations. We should note, however, that this trend in postmodern theory still retains a post-apocalyptic tone with respect to masculine, Eurocentric master narratives. Kaja Silverman, for instance, defines "historical trauma" specifically as a problem for men deprived of their phallogocentric certainties. But it seems to me that these directions of postmodern theory, with their post-apocalyptic and post-traumatic implications, cannot be so easily separated in terms of who suffers the catastrophe. I agree with Houston Baker that "if there is a whitemale 'crisis,' " it is nevertheless "a 'crisis' that implicates us all" (271).

7. Today, June 17, 1997, the Dow-Jones average stands at 7772.09, just under its all-time high. Unemployment is below five percent. Can anyone still talk about problems in the American economy? I think so. The gap between rich and not-rich is still expanding. Inner cities are still in ruins. The future of health care and pensions is very much in question. People are working longer and harder than ever but not really getting ahead. The economic picture for corporations is rosy—but the rest of us are working for their benefit.

8. Mary Shelley's *The Last Man* is one; another is Gore Vidal's *Kalki.* Both these novels are first-person accounts in which the end of all human life will coincide with the extinguishing of the narrator's consciousness.

9. As Adela Yarbro Collins points out, the persecution of Christians at the time the Apocalypse of John was composed was not, in fact, terribly severe. Nevertheless, given the instability in both the Christian and Jewish communities, the enduring cultural aftermath of the destruction of the temple in 70 C.E., and the persecution that did

take place, the author indeed felt an acute sense of historical crisis. Obviously, there can be no firm criteria to determine how much social crisis is sufficient to initiate apocalyptic thinking. The devastation of the First World War was sufficient, but so were the far less destructive crises of the 1960s.

10. I mean *ecstasy* in something like Baudrillard's sense, not as bliss but as a terrifying immersion in something resembling the sublime, the dissolving of the boundaries of selfhood, the opening of the self to absolute alterity. See also Leo Bersani's analyses of eroticism in *The Freudian Body*. For Bersani, a self-shattering, or fundamental masochism, is central to sexual experience. Thus, traumatic repetition—and the death drive—is a primary component of sexuality. In Bersani's analysis, the apocalypse is sex.

11. Dominick LaCapra makes this point as well, drawing attention to the unhistoricized "near fixation on the sublime... [and] almost obsessive preoccupation with loss, aporia, dispossession, and deferred meaning" that he sees in much postmodern theory (xi), and suggesting that "the post-modern and the post-Holocaust... [are] mutually intertwined issues that are best addressed in relation to each other" (189).

12. *Time* magazine, November 29, 1993, asked on its cover, "Is Freud Dead?" showing Freud's head as a three-dimensional jigsaw puzzle that was losing its pieces. The article, in characteristic *Time* fashion, presents both sides. Freud may have "managed to create an intellectual edifice that *feels* closer to the experience of living, and therefore hurting, than any other system currently in play," but at the same time, "[i]n the ultimate accounting, psychoanalysis... may turn out to be no more reliable than phrenology or mesmerism." Interestingly, the article ends on a nostalgically apocalyptic note, imagining that a world without psychoanalytic theory—and with nothing to replace it—would empty our "inner lives" of the "drama and hidden meanings" that psychoanalysis provides. This ending, which conjures the end of psychoanalysis, however, is also the transition to *Time*'s topic of more immediate concern, the controversial clinical "recovery" of repressed memories of childhood abuses—a controversy that, as the article fails to mention, invokes the beginnings of psychoanalysis: Freud's discovery and rejection of "seduction."

13. We should note the ways in which Wenders's depiction of the apocalyptic dream and the technology that makes it available to consciousness is a fundamental revision of psychoanalytic dream theory. In *The Interpretation of Dreams,* the dream is never, not even in its original occurrence, a direct presentation of primary process. "So far as we know," Freud writes, "a psychic apparatus possessing only the primary process does not exist, and is to that extent a theoretical fiction" (536). The dream is at all stages subject to processes of repression. The primary process would be some form of pure desire, "filled with the uninhibited energy which flows from the unconscious and strives for discharge" (538). The Farbers' technology reaches back, then, to a kind of ur-dream, to a stage of primal dreaming that, for Freud, does not actually occur.

14. From this ontological primacy of the survivor, we tend to assume a transparency in his testimony. I will discuss in the next chapter the problematics of testimonial representation.

15. See Kalí Tal's *Worlds of Hurt* for discussions of the testimonies of survivors of child abuse, incest, and rape. The strength of Tal's book lies in its detailed and empathetic accounts of survivor testimonies and in her discussions of their publishing histories and critical reception. The book's principal weakness is its lack of a theoretical grasp of trauma and its historical transmissions.

16. For several interesting, and alarmist, works that portray the elimination of boundaries between internal and external horrors, see Brian Massumi, ed., *The Politics of Everyday Fear*; Arthur and Marilouise Kroker and David Cook, eds., *Panic Encyclopedia*; Adam Parfrey, ed., *Apocalypse Culture*; and O. K. Werckmeister, *Citadel Culture*.

17. The Republican Congress's determination two years later to shut down the federal government during the budget impasse was a kind of repetition of the Oklahoma City bombing. The Republicans did, of course, first evacuate the children from any day care centers before they bombed their funding. The bombing, the militia movement, and the government shutdown point to prevalent American apocalyptic impulses that I will discuss in chapter 5 with regard to the 1980s ascendancy of Reaganism.

18. For this reason, it seems to me that Nicolas Abraham and Maria Torok's view of the phantom as the secret of a previous generation taking possession of an unknowing successor is useful but not wholly adequate. Abraham and Torok see this haunting only in terms of the family, rather than in broader social settings. And they overstate the aspect of "ventriloquism" (that the parental phantom speaks through the haunted descendant) in stressing the ignorance, and thus innocence, of the one who is possessed. This individual is not isolated from the familial or social landscape of symptoms and repressions; he grows up among them, and they help create his personality. The traumas of history that haunt the present are usually not secrets. They may be denied, but they are not unknown.

19. Cf. the work of the early-twentieth-century anthropologist Robert Hertz on the custom of the double burial. Hertz notes in many cultures the practice of two separate funeral rites, sometimes separated by many years. The second is delayed until the corpse has completely decomposed, for the physical corruption of the corpse is seen as indicating a highly volatile and dangerous spiritual condition that could affect the whole community. Hertz writes, "It is unthinkable to give the deceased his final burial while he is still immersed in infection" (45), and "Death is fully consummated only when decomposition has ended" (46). The period between the two burials is, in effect, an extended time of mourning in which the dead is gradually integrated into its new symbolic status *as* dead. For the dead to be prematurely given "final" burial would ensure its malevolent return.

20. According to a *Life* magazine cover story on the angel phenomenon (December 1995), sixty-nine percent of Americans believe in angels, and thirty-two percent report that they have felt an angel's presence.

21. These examples come from a television program, *Angel Stories,* broadcast June 29, 1996, on the Learning Channel.

22. The friendly American angels are outside a sizable tradition of angelic alterity that moves from the biblical angels with swords expelling Adam and Eve from paradise to Walter Benjamin's angel of history hurled in horror by the storm of progress. See Harold Bloom's *Omens of Millennium: The Gnosis of Angels, Dreams, and Resurrection* for a fascinating account of the history of angels in relation to gnostic thinking. Bloom regards the current infatuation with angels as a debased form of gnosticism. Bloom, however, treats the gnostic search for a knowledge of transcendence as a historical constant and does not investigate why it erupts with more or less force at different times. In contemporary culture, there are several instances of angels who are not here simply to help us, notably the sympathetic but distant angels in Wenders's *Wings of Desire,* the warring angels in the film *Prophecy* (starring Christopher Walken as a malevolent angel Gabriel), and the ponderously sublime angels of stasis in Tony Kushner's *Angels in America.*

3. Representing the Holocaust after the End of Testimony

1. This, for example, is part of Lyotard's project in *The Differend* and *Heidegger and the Jews,* in which he presents the difficulties in representing the Shoah as paradigmatic instances of the problematics of all postmodern representation.

2. For an account of film representations of the Holocaust in the 1960s, see Judith Doneson, who shows especially how these representations were made to correspond "to American problems, concerns, or needs. That means even that the 'Jewishness' of the Holocaust must be muted if the event is to have meaning in an American context" (97). See also Alvin Rosenfeld, "Popularization and Memory: The Case of Anne Frank," an analysis of the reception of Anne Frank's diary and its crucial role as a central symbol of the Holocaust during the 1950s and 1960s.

3. See in this regard T. W. Adorno and his colleagues' psychological study *The Authoritarian Personality,* Erich Fromm's *Escape from Freedom,* and Hannah Arendt's *Eichmann in Jerusalem.* In "Fascinating Fascism," Susan Sontag investigated the aestheticization of Nazi imagery and its uses in pornography. In the 1960s, as the Vietnam War intensified, opponents of the war asked to what degree American use of power resembled that of the Nazis. A film like *The Dirty Dozen,* in its portrayal of the rigidity and brutality of the American military hierarchy (in contrast to the "real" Americans,

the criminal rebels of the film's title), implicitly links the American military in Vietnam with Nazism.

4. Michael André Bernstein also uses the term *third generation* to describe recent Holocaust representation. "Since the generation of survivors will soon die out," Bernstein writes, we need to keep alive the "tribal story" as "part of communal memory" that "needs regularly to be retold and reinterpreted" (45). For me, Bernstein gives too much weight to conscious motives and not enough, as I will argue later, to the traumatic compulsion to retell the events.

5. Walter Reich, the director of the Holocaust Museum in Washington, D.C., demonstrated the ways that religious and traumatic language could merge in describing responses to testimony. In an account of a group of psychologists watching video testimony of Holocaust survivors, Reich said, "reality...drove out theory" as the psychologists watched "interviews of survivors talking not about Freud but about the black and lifeless sun of Auschwitz. That talk was about memory, its life and its death, and it stunned the group into reverent submission"; "A Psychiatrist and the Holocaust: Encountering the Past and Facing the Future," speech presented at George Washington University, Department of Psychiatry and Behavioral Sciences, Washington, D.C., Nov. 14, 1995.

6. Langer's *Holocaust Testimonies,* while discarding literary representation, nevertheless continues, I believe, the line of thinking he began in his 1975 book on Holocaust literature. *The Holocaust and the Literary Imagination* also relies on a theory of radical, nonrepresentational "mimesis" in which shattered and grotesque aesthetic forms stand as models for unimaginably horrific events. *The Holocaust and the Literary Imagination* makes claims for the dislocating power of avant-garde art techniques. But, surprisingly, so does *Holocaust Testimonies,* in proposing oral testimony as an anti-art. In both books, Langer assumes that a particular aesthetic form (or anti-form) is capable of revealing the essence of an inconceivable event.

7. Young would add, contra Brinkley and Youra, that the testimonial text is, like any text, open to interpretation. As Young concludes, "Our aim here then is to sustain both the privileged status of these testimonies and their invitation to critical interpretation" (*Writing and Rewriting the Holocaust,* 170). Michael André Bernstein is the only theorist I have read who has unequivocally rejected the privileged position of testimony, calling this privilege "one of the most pervasive myths of our era" (47). There is, he argues, "no single order of memorable testimony, no transparent paradigm of representation, that can address the different narrative needs of all those gripped by the subject" (50). I agree with his conclusion, but in this essay I try to explain, as Bernstein does not, the persistent recurrence of testimonial texts within fictional texts that would seem to have, as Bernstein puts it, "different narrative needs."

8. See Alvin Rosenfeld, *Imagining Hitler,* and "Another Revisionism: Popular Culture and the Changing Image of the Holocaust"; Saul Friedlander, *Reflections of Nazism: An Essay on Kitsch and Death.* For a view closer to mine, see Norma Rosen's "The

Second Life of Holocaust Imagery," in which she argues that changing contemporary uses of terms and images derived from the Shoah are inevitable and indicate the continuing grip those terms have on the present, and that "for a mind engraven with the Holocaust, gas is always that gas. Shower means their shower. Ovens are those ovens" (58).

9. The influence of video testimony can be seen in the endings of the films *Europa Europa* and *Schindler's List,* when the survivors who have been the subjects (played by actors) of these highly stylized narratives appear as themselves, in effect, to verify, validate, authorize the films that have used their stories.

10. See the more detailed account in chapter 2 of the relations between trauma and language.

11. See Geoffrey Hartman's recent work on the position of the bystander—"what others suffer, we behold" (*The Longest Shadow,* 88)—and on the "kakangelic" impulse of contemporary mass media. Hartman is less optimistic about the effects of what he calls "secondary trauma" than is either Cathy Caruth or Dominick LaCapra in their theorizing on acting out and the belated narrativizing of trauma. In *The Longest Shadow,* Hartman consistently cites oral testimony as the most legitimate form of Holocaust representation. See also in this regard Marianne Hirsch and her idea of "post-memory." Post-memory, for Hirsch, is the memory of someone else's memories, of the other's stories, and of physical memorabilia. It is "distinguished from memory by generational distance and from history by deep personal connection" (8). For Hirsch, the photograph is the most representative object of post-memory, as, in my thinking, the testimonial text forms the basis for writing after the end of testimony. There is, however, a closer connection between post-memory and memory than I find between post-testimony and testimony. Hirsch bases her thinking largely around an analysis of Spiegelman's *Maus* and transmission of memory from father to son.

12. See Marianne Hirsch's comments on the silencing of women in *Maus* ("Family Pictures"). See also Joan Ringelheim, "Thoughts about Women and the Holocaust"; and Myrna Goldenberg, "Different Horrors, Same Hell," on women's experiences in the Shoah.

13. Since Prager is Jewish, Sander Gilman's *Jewish Self-Hatred,* Jonathan Boyarin's *Storm from Paradise,* and Alain Finkielkraut's *The Imaginary Jew* provide valuable corollary texts that can comment on Prager's use of anti-Semitic imagery.

14. At last, in one of the most inspiring moments in psychoanalytic literature, Dora breaks off the analysis. "Dora had listened to me without any of her usual contradictions. She seemed to be moved; she said good-bye to me very warmly, with the heartiest wishes for the New Year—and came no more" (Freud, *Fragment of an Analysis of a Case of Hysteria,* 130).

15. See Elisabeth Rose, "Cynthia Ozick's Liturgical Postmodernism," for an intelligent reading of *Messiah* that follows from Ozick's iconoclasm in *Art and Ardor.* Rose

describes the novel as an instance of "liturgical postmodernism," a kind of textual idol "which self-destructs and in so doing, strives beyond itself toward God" (99).

4. The Absent Referent

1. There is an ironic, Sidneyan quality to Doctorow's essay, as he acknowledges that his "is a novelist's proposition. I can see that very well. It is in my interest to claim that there is no difference between what I do and what everyone else does" (26). Cf. Sidney's more witty apology: "If I had not been a piece of a logician before I came to him, I think he would have persuaded me to have wished myself a horse. But thus much at least with his no few words he drave into me, that self-love is better than any gilding to make that seem gorgeous, wherein ourselves are parties" (215).

2. For American and British contexts, see Tony Kushner, *The Holocaust and the Liberal Imagination: A Social and Cultural History*; and Judith Doneson, *The Holocaust in American Film*. For French postwar responses, see Henry Rousso, *The Vichy Syndrome: History and Memory in France since 1944*; Judith Friedlander, *Vilna on the Seine: Jewish Intellectuals in France since 1968*; Alain Finkeilkraut, *Remembering in Vain: The Klaus Barbie Trial and Crimes against Humanity*; Marcel Tetel, "Whither the Holocaust?"; and Lawrence Kritzman, ed., *Auschwitz and After: Race, Culture, and "the Jewish Question" in France*.

3. For a variety of perspectives on the apocalyptic rhetorics of poststructuralism, see Matei Calinescu, "The End of Man in Twentieth-Century Thought: Reflections on a Philosophical Metaphor"; Fredric Jameson, *Postmodernism, or, The Cultural Logic of Late Capitalism* (chapter 1); Christopher Norris, "Versions of Apocalypse: Kant, Derrida, Foucault"; Steven Goldsmith, *Unbuilding Jerusalem: Apocalypse and Romantic Representation*; Richard Dellamora, *Apocalyptic Overtures: Sexual Politics and the Sense of an Ending*; and Martin Jay, *Force Fields: Between Intellectual History and Cultural Critique* (chapter 7).

4. It is puzzling that New Historicist critics did not turn their attention to the Holocaust at this moment when poststructuralist thinkers, responding in part to New Historicist critiques, did so. My sense is that possible interest in the Shoah was blunted by the overriding anticolonialist politics of New Historicism. Attitudes toward Nazism intersected with attitudes toward Zionism and Middle East politics. Contemporary postcolonial politics and theory seem to have difficulty accounting for the intra-European racism and genocide of the Second World War. The Klaus Barbie trial in France in 1987 made these tensions very apparent. See Finkielkraut's account in *Remembering in Vain*.

5. Hayden White is unusual in making a major shift in his thinking. From maintaining that no forms of representation are either privileged or forbidden with respect to any historical event (see especially the essays in *The Content of the Form*), White moved to asserting that representing an event like the Holocaust calls for certain

modes and not others. White argues that modernist forms are more suitable than realist
or documentary forms, and he outlines an idea of a "middle voice," neither active nor
passive, that might best portray an event of such "unrepresentable" horror. White's
courage in reversing such a well-established position is commendable, but I believe his
theory of the modernist middle voice is deeply muddled. White is arguing against Berel
Lang's position that only documentary and testimonial forms are appropriate, but having
made the case against Lang's modified iconoclasm, it does not follow that a Joycean
or Barthesian modernism is the answer. White's argument resembles Erich Auerbach's
analyses of *Ulysses* and *To the Lighthouse* in *Mimesis,* and Auerbach's implied suggestion that each era's particular worldview generates a particular mimetic form appropriate to it. I remain in awe of Auerbach's readings, but the corollary implication does not
hold, either for him or for White. The previous chapter's discussions of Holocaust testimony and fiction indicate a wide range of possible forms for Holocaust representation. White seems to share the fears of his former conservative critics that the choice is
between all or nothing, between absolute relativism and firm mimetic prescription. I
do not believe this fear or this choice is necessary. There is obviously not space here
for extended theorizing on aesthetic-moral judgments. I can only say that it is possible
to make such judgments without relying on a standard (*only* documentary, *only* modernism) that will apply to every case.

   6. "Closure," as I take it, means for Derrida the conceptual end of a logocentric
signification that presumes to substitute the sign for some form of presence. Even though
people may continue to use language in the old, unconscious way, it will have been revealed to be no longer viable, to be an illusion. This distinction between "end" and
"closure" resembles Hegel's, Kojève's, and Fukuyama's formulations of the "end of
history," in which while everyday life goes on, the historical dialectic has reached its
final point. See Lutz Niethammer, *Posthistoire: Has History Come to an End?* for useful summaries and analyses of various versions of the "end of history."

   7. Derrida makes this point about "apocalypse" itself in "Of an Apocalyptic Tone
Recently Adopted in Philosophy." "Apocalypse," in that essay, becomes a structural
component of language, as language is continually in the process of unveiling and obliterating. "Wouldn't the apocalypse be a transcendental condition of all discourse, of all
experience itself, of every mark or every trace?" Thus, the particular genre of apocalyptic writing is merely, "in the strict sense . . . [the] exemplary revelation of this transcendental structure" (87).

   8. Derrida states in a later interview that he regarded the 1968 revolt as a "seismic
shock" that indicated the complete inadequacy of French political institutions, but that
his personality did not permit him to be caught up in any "cult of spontaneity." "I was
not against it, but I have always had trouble vibrating in unison" (*Points,* 347–48).

   9. See James F. McMillan for an account of the political and social contexts of
the 1968 revolts. Bernard E. Brown, in *Protest in Paris: Anatomy of a Revolt,* gives a

thorough chronology of the events and summaries of the responses of Raymond Aron, Michael Crozier, and Alain Touraine. Kritzman, *Auschwitz and After*; Judith Friedlander, *Vilna on the Seine*; and Rousso, *The Vichy Syndrome,* provide accounts of the cultural aftermaths of '68 as they relate to the Holocaust. See also the special issue of *Contemporary French Civilization* (vol. 6, 1981–82).

10. Derridean deconstruction in the late 1960s can be seen as providing a link between what Leon S. Roudiez described as the two major, and opposing, positions within the 1968 uprising: the "lyrical illusion" of the romantic revolutionary and the "advanced theoretical stance" called for by the Marxists of the *Tel Quel* group ("Lyrical Illusions and Their Succession," 2). Derrida's writings of this time are nothing if not rigorous and theoretically "advanced," but their politics still are "lyrical."

11. This is so unless we consider "after Plato" or "after the Enlightenment" to be a particular moment. I believe this is true of Foucault as well, in spite of his historical specificity regarding the genealogies of prisons, asylums, and hospitals. Each particular circumstance he describes is always, finally, an instance of a logic that applies throughout all post-Enlightenment society.

12. Luc Ferry and Alain Renaut are, I believe, overly tendentious in critiquing poststructuralism's "antihumanism." It seems to me that Bernard Yack's analyses of ideas of "total revolution" from Rousseau to Nietzsche as frustrated humanisms, or humanisms that have painted themselves into corners, apply equally well to poststructuralism in the late 1960s and 1970s. All these sets of ideas, in Yack's terms, involve radically liberatory impulses based on social critiques that deny the possibility of liberation. Heidegger, however, would not be included in this analysis, in spite of his affinities both with Nietzsche and with later poststructuralists. The late Heidegger, in my reading, is completely indifferent to human life, agency, and liberation. Derrida, however obscurely, does wish for human liberation. Nevertheless, Ferry and Renaut, I believe, are right that Derrida's strategy in "Differance" is "to be fundamentally more Heideggerian than Heidegger himself" (130).

13. Derrida used a similar formula to define *trace* in *Of Grammatology:* "not more *natural* (it is not the mark, the natural sign, or the index in the Hussurlian sense) than *cultural,* not more physical than psychic, biological than spiritual. It is that starting from which a becoming-unmotivated of the sign, and with it all the ulterior oppositions between *physis* and its other, is possible" (47).

14. "Unconcealment" is Heidegger's customary translation of the Greek word for truth, *aletheia,* which does etymologically imply the negation or reversal of a forgetting.

15. This "other side of nostalgia" idea marks the end of the essay "Differance." Having utterly punctured the notion of a "unique word, a master-name" that would provide an origin or foundation for the infinite play of language, Derrida tries to speak from beyond any longing for the "transcendental signified." And there, somewhat

paradoxically as he acknowledges, his thinking rejoins Heidegger's, though with a different emphasis. "Being" still speaks, as Heidegger wrote, " 'always and everywhere throughout language,' " but Derrida has vastly problematized the idea of how language works. In doing so, and in imagining a move to the "other side of nostalgia," Derrida also shifts the site of apocalypse from an "unconcealing" yet to come to a linguistic process always-already taking place.

16. The question I am asking is not whether the Holocaust was an event uniquely beyond any manner of historicization—I would argue that it is not. Rather, I am questioning the benefits and consequences of positing a universal process of historical occurrence. The Holocaust is not necessarily diminished by viewing it in a context with other genocides. It is diminished, I believe, when viewed from a perspective that levels *all* events and discards the significance of the event as such.

17. See Fritz Stern, *The Politics of Cultural Despair: A Study in the Rise of the Germanic Ideology,* for a brilliant description of this political and cultural context.

18. The opposition of a "vulgar" to a more sophisticated anti-Semitism reappears in Derrida's defense of de Man in "Like the Sound of the Sea Deep within a Shell: Paul de Man's War," with even more dubious results.

19. See Allan Stoekl's excellent analysis of *Of Spirit* in *Agonies of the Intellectual: Commitment, Subjectivity, and the Performative in the Twentieth-Century French Tradition.* Stoekl also sees a continuity in Derrida's use of Heidegger from the 1960s through the 1980s, and concludes that in the later work, "the only method that Derrida has at his disposal to analyze Heidegger's complicity is a Heideggerian one that prevents him from recognizing the importance of crucial oppositions....Nowhere in *De l'esprit* is there a serious recognition that the humanism so closely identified with the spirit, subjectivity, the 'sacredness of the human person' may be in any way preferable to nazism" (227).

5. "Achieved Utopias"

1. Ernest Tuveson, Sacvan Bercovitch, Richard Slotkin, and Paul Boyer have written on the decisive importance of apocalyptic thinking in the formation and development of American ideologies. Bercovitch focuses primarily on Puritan society and the role of the jeremiad. Tuveson studies the nineteenth century and "Manifest Destiny" as an apocalyptic trope. Slotkin has written extensively on the apocalyptic ideologies of Western expansion. Boyer's more comprehensive study reviews American apocalyptic thinking from colonial times but pays particular attention to developments since the Second World War. For more specific studies of American apocalyptic movements, see Timothy Weber, *Living in the Shadow of the Second Coming,* and Stephen O'Leary, *Arguing the Apocalypse.*

2. Ronald Reagan, *Speaking My Mind: Selected Speeches,* 227. Unless otherwise indicated, all quotations from Reagan's speeches are from this book, and subsequent page numbers will be given in the text.

3. See, for example, John Judis's judgment in *Grand Illusion: Critics and Champions of the American Century* that "the dominant political theme of the 1980s" was "the attempt by Americans to redeem the present by regression — to preserve the American Century by returning to those ideas they happily remembered from its emergence" (225). Robert Dallek and Sydney Blumenthal also describe Reaganism as fundamentally nostalgic. Gary Wills observes a temporal confusion in Reaganism that "gives our history the continuity of a celluloid Mobius strip.... We are carried forward under the impression that we are going *back* to our cherished dreams, taking a shorter route there" (371, 373). Stephanie Coontz's *The Way We Never Were: American Families and the Nostalgia Trap* provides a useful corrective to nostalgic portrayals of family life invoked by Reagan and the New Right. Coontz shows how contradictory elements from *different* nostalgic portraits were combined in the creation of the archetypal family of the 1950s that has played such a key role in Reaganist and New Right polemics.

4. Dallek makes the point that Reagan's Cold War rhetoric often refers primarily to anxieties over domestic concerns. Dallek writes, "When Reagan speaks of Soviet statism, of Communist indifference to personal freedom and the dignity of the individual, he is referring as much to conservative perceptions of recent trends in America as to the state of Russian affairs" (132).

5. *Premillennialist* refers to the belief that Christ will return to Earth before the world's final millennial transformation and will personally lead the final battle against the forces of evil. Postmillennialists postpone Christ's second coming until after the final days. The apocalypticism of premillennialists places more emphasis on struggle and cataclysm in the existing world as necessary preconditions for the millennium. See Boyer and Weber for detailed accounts of premillennialist thinking.

6. The phrase "achieved utopia" is Baudrillard's, from his parodic travelogue *America.* Although I do not share Baudrillard's sense of the United States as a realm of pure simulation and hyperreality, his description of America as the achieved utopia comes eerily close to Reaganist America's self-description. I take Baudrillard's voice to be, in large measure, a Swiftian persona spinning out modest proposals whose absurdities point toward truths that are equally, if more gradually, disturbing. Of course Baudrillard's "America" is a European fantasy. At the same time, the Reaganist would wholeheartedly answer yes to Baudrillard's question: "But is this really what an achieved utopia looks like? Is this a successful revolution? Yes indeed! What do you expect a 'successful' revolution to look like? It is paradise. Santa Barbara is a paradise; Disneyland is a paradise; the U.S. is a paradise. Paradise is just paradise." The critic in Baudrillard still continues, "Mournful, monotonous, and superficial though it may be, it is paradise. There is no other" (98). But the point of convergence has been reached. Baudrillard's

deadpan parody expresses Reagan's true conviction. For a specifically Baudrillardian analysis of Reaganism, see Diane Rubenstein, "The Mirror of Reproduction: Baudrillard and Reagan's America." For other accounts that stress an essential fictionality in Reaganism, see Michael Rogin, *"Ronald Reagan," The Movie: and Other Episodes in Political Demonology*; and Richard Schickel, "No Method to His Madness."

7. Harvey Kaye calls this process a "class war from above" and traces it back to efforts by corporate leaders and conservative activists in the early 1970s.

8. Jonathan Rieder argues that the "outlines of Reagan's popular victory may be glimpsed in shadowy form in the Goldwater debacle" and that the final shape of Reagan's coalition resulted from a combination of Goldwater's Cold War anticommunism and free-market economics and George Wallace's populist racism. "The reborn right," writes Rieder, "was a populist right, at least in its oratory" (243–44). "To budding New Right theorists, the Wallace voters were the key to a transformed Republicanism centered on populist themes and lower-middle-class resentment" (252). Mike Davis also writes that Goldwater's campaign, although a huge failure, set in place many of the strategies used successfully by Reagan, for example, the rejection of an Eastern "establishment" in favor of the demographics of the Sunbelt and a belief in the power of social issues. See also Dan T. Carter's study of the role of race in conservative politics from George Wallace to Newt Gingrich.

9. Both Gitlin and Hayden, in fact, refer to the traumas of the Second World War and the Holocaust as shaping political thinking on both the Left and the Right. Hayden remarks that "Auschwitz, Hiroshima, and Nuremberg were the 'birth pangs' of our generation, and middle class apathy our inheritance" (77). Gitlin describes how the memory of the Holocaust influenced both sides of the debates over Vietnam, in that "the Jewish Cold Warriors of the Fifties and early Sixties were dead set on stopping Communism precisely because they had failed to stop the Nazis — whereas to me and people I knew, it was American bombs which were the closest thing to an immoral equivalent of Auschwitz in our lifetimes. When the time came, we jumped at the chance to purge ourselves of the nearest thing to the original trauma" (*The Sixties,* 25).

10. Gitlin attributes Reagan's victory to an "antiblack, antiobscenity, and antistudent backlash" (*The Sixties,* 217). Likewise, Davis writes, "Ronald Reagan was catapulted into the governor's mansion in Sacramento by a wave of anti student, anti Black reaction" (160). For Judis, "Reagan invented the tactic, which became a hallmark of the new right, of targeting the white working class by campaigning against the civil rights, antiwar, and countercultural movements of the 1960s" (236). Also, Wills suggests that for the right, "the 'lifestyle' revolution was the more serious [threat] because it was the more lasting phenomenon: it changed attitudes toward sex, parents, authority, the police, the military" (340).

11. For further theoretical and historical perspectives on antifeminism on the Right, see Neil Hertz, *The End of the Line*; and Klaus Theweleit, *Male Fantasies.* Hertz dis-

cusses the conflation of sexual and political responses of right-wing writers to the French Revolution and the uprisings of 1848. Theweleit studies in great detail the writings of members of the protofascist German Freicorps after the First World War.

12. Rogin writes, "The 1960s, by recovering imperial history in the civil rights struggle in Vietnam, challenged the racial constitution of American national identity. The Reagan doctrine had to forget, therefore, the moment in which American history was remembered" ("Make My Day," 118). Judis and Joel Krieger discuss Reaganism as a response to a loss of American political and economic hegemony. Krieger writes, "Reagan's agenda, precisely because it flies in the face of the realities of the post-hegemonic international order, demonstrates the extent of the U.S. decline.... Above all else, Reagan is the electoral expression of a culture of defeat — Vietnam and Iran, the dollar, stagflation and unemployment — and fear — of reduced life chances, fear by men of women, fear by middle-aged middle Americans of the fragmentations of society, and the lingering *Weltanschauung* of the 1960s" (131). See also Tom Engelhardt's highly perceptive discussion of what he calls American "victory culture," its erosion during the 1960s and its revival in the 1980s under Reagan.

13. Contrast Reagan's attitude with that of Lyndon Johnson. In 1965, speaking at the commencement ceremony at Howard University, Johnson directly addressed present inequality and injustice, both political and economic. "You do not wipe away the scars of centuries," said Johnson, "by saying: Now you are free to go where you want, do as you desire, and choose the leaders you please" (in Rainwater and Yancey, 126). This speech was written by Daniel Patrick Moynihan, then assistant secretary of labor, and formed the basis for his report *The Negro Family: The Case for National Action,* a document that triggered debates shaping the discourse on race continuing into the present. See chapter 6 for a discussion of how the Moynihan Report controversy enters into Toni Morrison's response in *Beloved* to the racial climate of the 1980s.

14. *Bitburg in Moral and Political Perspective,* ed. Geoffrey H. Hartman, contains the speeches by Reagan and German politicians at Bitburg and Bergen-Belsen, as well as extensive excerpts from press coverage of these events and commentaries by journalists and Holocaust scholars.

15. Stephen Brockman, applying methods of deconstruction to political analysis, posits a binary structure in American foreign policy in which the previous enemy (Nazi Germany) is replaced immediately after the Second World War by the new enemy (the USSR). "This magical transformation," Brockman writes, "is possible only if Nazism is ignored, falling wholly under the category of 'totalitarianism,' which is in turn transferred wholly to the Soviet Union." Brockman continues, "In the binary oppositions created by contemporary ideology, third terms are necessarily dangerous since they threaten to unbalance the equation, and so they are destroyed by fusion with one of the terms of the governing equation" (163, 165). While I agree with Brockman with regard to the fact of Reagan's de-emphasis of Nazism in favor of totalitarianism, I would argue

that this substitution has less to do with the ideological geometries of binary opposition and depends more on the dynamics of historical trauma and on Reagan's incapacity to accept any traumatic event in which the United States might be in any way implicated.

16. For a thorough account of the *historikerstreit,* see Charles S. Maier, *The Unmasterable Past: History, Holocaust, and German National Identity.* Dominick LaCapra provides a useful commentary in *Representing the Holocaust.*

17. For an excellent discussion of how the 1984 commemoration at Normandy served as a rewriting of Vietnam, transforming Vietnam in both moral and technical terms, see Timothy W. Luke, *Screens of Power: Ideology, Domination, and Resistance in Informational Society.* D-Day, in Reagan's re-creation, was a "clean, quick strike of well-trained experts" rather than an "anonymous annihilation" of soldiers, allowing the Second World War to be invoked as a war which was just, winnable, and nearly painless (175, 174).

18. Cf. Wills's observation that "Ronald Reagan...is so energetic a believer in the counter-myth to the Fall that, when he was asked to discuss his religious experiences as President, every instance he could think of was a matter of seeing the bright side to death or disaster" (385).

19. The videotapes of this conference on "The Future of Issue Advertising" are available at the Wisconsin Center for Film and Theater Research, State Historical Society of Wisconsin, Madison (VHA 306, 309, 312).

20. The detachment of the product from any actual attributes has been a gradual process. The early- and mid-twentieth-century print ads described by Roland Marchand, while linking products to emerging ideologies of modernity, still often retain the form of an argument, that the product is effective. Television clearly accelerated the transition to advertising whose meaning is entirely in excess of its product. Television advertising into the early 1960s exhibited the ambivalent relation to information and argument of earlier print ads. It was perhaps the witty Alka-Seltzer ads of the mid-1960s ("No matter what shape your stomach is in") that showed the way toward a predominantly visual style of advertising whose appeal lay primarily in imagination and fantasy. A study in 1984 by Gail Tom et al. (using as its criteria statements regarding price, quality or performance, content, availability, nutrition, packaging, warranties, and safety) concluded that fifty percent of television ads conveyed no information at all about their products.

21. The logic of the ad for the dematerialized product culminates in a bizarre commercial form of negative theology, a marketing of the ineffable. Richard Goldman discusses this discourse of ineffability with regard to print ads for perfume, a product that is, in reality, dematerialized and whose use is inevitably linked with fantasy (15–36). In such ads, there are no words to describe the product because the product has become the sign (perhaps the icon) representing a conflation of the culture's most sacred values — of sexual attractiveness, independence, youth, individuality — while still, in its ultimate je ne sais quoi elusiveness, exceeding even these values. An interesting de-

velopment in perfume advertising that works against this iconoclastic tendency is the inclusion of the fragrance in the ad itself. Since no actual fragrance can ever equal the ideological qualities placed under its sign, the presence of the smell in the magazine may indicate a commonsense resistance on the part of consumers to ideological fantasy invocations. The advertiser recognizes the consumer's need to determine whether she actually likes how the perfume smells. Yet, at the same time, this practical, physical appeal to the smell itself also reveals its own inadequacy. First, the consumer knows that the perfume's true fragrance only reveals itself on her own body. Second, a magazine contains so many perfume samples that it is impossible to tell them apart; they blend together into a strange artificial atmosphere of perfume and paper. Thus, it may be that this gesture away from fantasy leads back toward fantasy, toward the sense of lack and the desire for completion that ideology and fantasy invoke and promise.

22. Freud does point briefly to wider social and political implications. The process of fetishization "reminds one," he writes, "of the stopping of memory in traumatic amnesias" ("Fetishism," 155), a statement that seems clearly to refer to Freud's work on war traumas that led to his writing *Beyond the Pleasure Principle.* Freud translates the boy's fear of castration directly into political terms when he writes that "[i]n later life grown men may perhaps experience a similar panic, when the cry goes up that Throne and Altar are in danger" (153).

23. The relation between commodity fetishism and utopian longings has been theorized in several ways. Fredric Jameson, following the work of the Frankfurt School, argues that a utopian element is contained even in the most ideologically inflected works of mass culture, that these works, "even if their function lies in the legitimation of the existing order — or some worse one — cannot do their job without deflecting in the latter's service the deepest and most fundamental hopes and fantasies of the collectivity, to which they can therefore, no matter in how distorted a fashion, be found to have given voice" ("Reification and Utopia in Mass Culture," 144). Out of Jameson's insight has come one of the central debates in cultural studies of the 1980s and 1990s, that is, the degree to which these utopian elements can be appropriated and used in ways oppositional to the existing order. My analysis of Reaganist advertising suggests only limited oppositional potential in these ads, for their utopias, while often ecstatic, are utopias of pure cliché. Many Reaganist ads portray an ideal of American community, for example — which all viewers desire in some vague sense. This common desire, however, remains so vague that its presumed consensus must dissolve as soon as each viewer begins to imagine the ideal community in more specific terms. See also Susan Willis, "Earthquake Kits: The Politics of the Trivial," for an excellent discussion of some of the complex ways in which commodities invoke and then deflect utopian social aspirations. Another important direction in theorizing commodities, advertising, and utopia is broadly Lacanian. Judith Williamson accounts for the appeal of advertising in terms

of the consumer's desire for wholeness, a desire that "is directed both at the symbol and at the unity with the symbol," thus blurring "the boundary between Imaginary and Symbolic." For Williamson, the ad re-creates an almost Keatsian paradise, whose figures are "like characters on a Grecian urn, trapped in their expectation of enjoyment. We are led to desire an imaginary unity with the subject who *will enjoy* and this also creates an imaginary unity between our time and the projected future time of the ad" (65, 161). Using different aspects of Lacanian theory, Slavoj Zizek's analysis in *The Sublime Object of Ideology* of the "quilting point" describes how ideological fantasy (such as advertising) enters the symbolic order and creates a utopian edifice at precisely the place of traumatic lack or rupture. Finally, T. J. Jackson Lears and Raymond Williams, in different ways, discuss advertising as an extension of religion and thus a purveyor of, in some sense, ultimate values.

24. Lou Cannon notes that Reagan loved his own campaign ads: "Reagan took advertising far more seriously than he ever took himself. Though he skimmed or ignored many a briefing paper, he rarely missed a showing of a new campaign commercial." Cannon also reports that Reagan wept at a screening of the ad "Morning in America" (*President Reagan,* 513).

25. Joanne Morreale discusses ways in which negative elements are excluded in the documentary "New Beginning," which was shown on the evening of Reagan's nomination at the 1984 Republican convention. In its depiction of Reagan's foreign policy, the film manages to avoid "any direct reference to the Soviet Union, Central America, or the Middle East," and likewise "the deleterious effects of urbanization and technology [do] not impinge on the film's representation of the myths of the individual and community." "The past," writes Morreale, "is selectively recalled but only to confirm that it has been transcended by the 'new beginning' made possible by the Reagan administration" (64, 53).

26. Other notable examples of panoramic social-harmony advertisements from the 1980s are AT&T's "Reach Out and Touch Someone," Chevrolet's "Heartbeat of America," ABC's self-promotion campaigns, and campaigns by Kodak.

27. Barbara B. Stern and Katherine Gallagher discuss the utopian content in print advertisements for Tanqueray gin ("It's worth the price to have at least one thing in your life that's simply perfect"), Perrier water ("... everything happened just right"), and Spanish tourism ("The day's not over yet but already it seems perfect") as evocations of a "terminal state," a condition of absolute plenitude purged of any negative features. While Stern and Gallagher's discussion of these ads in terms of literary genres is unconvincing, the article is valuable in so clearly emphasizing the importance of the representation of perfection in advertising of the 1980s. The distinctively Reaganist quality of this insistence on *complete* perfection becomes evident in Stern and Gallagher's description of an ad for Drano from the 1940s whose emphasis is on the threat

of biological contamination of the kitchen and bathroom. In the 1980s, ads for Drano do not portray the product as a protection against dangerous germs; even Drano takes its place in a perfect world.

28. Mark Crispin Miller describes very well the post-apocalyptic advertising sensibility: "We are meant to look back at that impassive face with a longing that s/he has long since transcended, now that s/he has found a place in the refrigerated heaven of commodities. Beyond desire, and with a perfect body, s/he must view us hungering viewers with irony, seeing how ludicrous it is to be mortal and a person, and therefore having something left to lose" (15–16).

29. Cf. Gitlin's 1987 discussion of a Dodge car ad from the early 1980s ("Car Commercials and *Miami Vice*"). A young man is lured by and pursues the car through a science-fiction urban wasteland setting. As, at last, he enters the car, "instantly, dystopia segues into utopia." The car, writes Gitlin, is a "carrier of adrenal energies, a sort of syringe on wheels." As Gitlin describes, the Dodge ad "shares an emotional and ideological territory" with other phenomena of the Reagan years. The ad addresses the anxieties that enabled Reaganism to succeed, but in the context of an immediate, definitive end to those anxieties. Or in other words, an anxious response to social trauma refigures that trauma as an apocalypse, a total transformation. Gitlin writes of the Reaganist "desire to take flight, and a fear that everyone around us has taken flight too; about the giddiness we feel at having outlasted the old traditions, and an insecurity at finding ourselves dangling in free fall beyond tradition; about the longing for open space, innocence, the sense of infinite possibility, and the distance one has to go to recapture the plenitude of the wild frontier" (140). These are indeed the Reaganist desires and fears; the final Reaganist twist, which the Dodge ad clearly conveys, is to portray the fears as ended and the desires as fulfilled.

30. For discussions of the cultural roles of blue jeans, see Stewart Ewen and Elizabeth Ewen, *Channel's of Desire: Mass Images and the Shaping of American Consciousness*; and Lee Quinby, *Anti-Apocalypse: Exercises in Genealogical Criticism*. The Ewens describe the process by which jeans were transformed from mere work clothes to signifiers of political, cultural, and sexual rebellion (in the 1950s and 1960s) to a highly marketed "designer" product that tried to maintain its connections with cultural opposition and working-class status. Quinby argues that the images of blank perfection in many jeans ads represent a postmodern consumerist analogy to the eugenics movement of the early twentieth century. I do not entirely accept her analogy, but I agree with her placing blue jean imagery in an apocalyptic context, as when she describes a series of "Guess" ads as a "post-Edenic celebration of simulated sexual coercion" (12).

31. See chapter 1 for a discussion of the significance of anality and excrement in post-apocalyptic imagery.

32. The prison scenario repeats this fantasy most tirelessly. Thomas Pynchon in *Vineland* invokes the stereotype of the black homosexual rapist when evil Federal Mar-

shall Brock Vond tells his prisoner Zoyd Wheeler that the "question pending is do you want to go inside forever, because there's a bed open on the top tier in cellblock D, waiting just for you, your cellmate's name is Leroy, he is a convicted murderer, and next to eating watermelon, his favorite pastime is attempting to insert his oversized member into the anus of the nearest white male, in this case, you. Are you getting any clearer sense of your options here?" (301). In another instance, a public service ad from 1985 sells a message against drunk driving by appealing to the white male fear of prison rape. In this ad, the white man (a professional in a clean white shirt) has been arrested for DWI and now is locked in a cell with eight or ten big, mean guys, most of them black or Hispanic. If you drive drunk, you are going to be gang-banged.

33. In 1987 (her show's first year as a national program), Oprah broadcast a show from Forsyth County, Georgia, the county that had permitted no blacks to live in it since early in the century. The studio audience was entirely composed of Forsyth County residents — that is, it was all white; Oprah was the only African American — and Oprah very skillfully brought out and orchestrated the tensions and conflicts within the white community. Meanwhile, outside the auditorium, Oprah informed the audience several times, African Americans were demonstrating, protesting their exclusion from the county, and from the program. During the show, a number of the demonstrators were arrested. In a Montel Williams episode from 1995, individual racists were sent offstage to talk with small groups of people of the race they hated. Significantly, off camera, where no posturing was necessary, a bit of progress apparently was made. After their contacts with the "other," all the racists reported at least slightly changed attitudes — a very unusual event on talk shows, and probably in life in general.

34. The therapist, Salvador Minuchin, comments, "Confronted by an alliance of his wife and the therapist, which is working toward a spouse subsystem confrontation, Mr. Smith jumps outside the context and becomes preoccupied with the TV cameras, which were explained to him before the session. This is an indication that the threshold of pressure which Mr. Smith can tolerate is being reached" (179).

35. See Michael B. Katz, *The Undeserving Poor: From the War on Poverty to the War on Welfare.* In chapter 6, I discuss the Moynihan Report and debates concerning the African American family in relation to Toni Morrison's *Beloved.* For the text and a collection of responses to the Moynihan Report, see Rainwater and Yancey.

36. For an eloquent and effective discussion of the talk show as failed therapy, see Robin Andersen, *Consumer Culture and TV Programming.* Talk shows, she writes, "like advertising and entertainment programming, address real needs but do not fulfill those needs. . . . Talk shows speak with a therapeutic language that examines only a privatized landscape of human experience, further rupturing individual needs from collective solutions" (172). I agree completely with Andersen's conclusions and admire her book very much. My analysis tries to be more specific about the therapeutic basis and ideological contexts of talk shows.

37. As listeners of Rush Limbaugh know, the dittoheads are those who no longer need to try to articulate opinions of their own because Rush has already done it for them. Thus, they phone Rush and say, for instance, "Mega-dittos, Rush, on what you said last week about the Femi-nazis."

38. A very sad experience: A few years ago I was at Shea Stadium in New York, watching a Mets game. I was way up in the upper deck. Beside me, with his parents, was a small boy, about seven years old. He held a small cardboard sign he had made that read, "Go Mets." Mets fans are famous for their imaginative signs, and TV broadcasts always look into the stands and show the more interesting ones. This little boy spent the early innings holding up his sign and calling out for a camera to notice him. His desire to be seen by, and on, TV consumed him. He was desperate to be on television and distraught that no camera found him. But we were way up in the middle of nowhere, and his sign was tiny and completely undistinctive. I had my camera with me, so in about the fifth inning I took his picture, and that cheered him up considerably. He wanted to be part of real life, part of media life. Luckily, he was too young to understand how far my camera was from that reality. I still have the photo: a little kid with a Mets cap and a dumpy little sign, grinning as if he were on TV.

39. Most of the time. Sometimes, of course, it is fake. Gina Graham Scott cites instances of people appearing on Ricki Lake with made-up stories—most notoriously, a woman who claimed to have AIDS and to be having unprotected sex with as many people as she could, apparently out of spite. Her story was false in its entirety (261). But this form of weird exhibitionism would indicate another form of pain and desperation.

40. It is well known by now that Oprah suffered sexual abuse as a child, and testified to this experience on her show. The most moving moment I have seen on a Jenny Jones program came near the end of an otherwise ordinary show about mothers' and daughters' not getting along. Jenny Jones began speaking about her difficult relationship with her own mother, and broke into tears. The guest psychologist came to her and gave her a hug. It sounds very hokey, but I believed it and almost cried myself.

41. The term *public sphere* was given currency by Jürgen Habermas in *The Structural Transformation of the Public Sphere: An Inquiry into a Category of Bourgeois Society* (1962). Habermas argued that the public sphere as a realm of free inquiry and expression that *partly* crossed social classes began in the eighteenth century in coffeehouses and letters to the editor in periodicals. In the public sphere, at least ideally, social status became irrelevant. Only the discussion mattered, not the speakers. And any topic could freely be discussed. The public sphere, for Habermas, represented a formal, social basis for the "life-world" that stood opposed to the ever encroaching administered world of industrial modernity. Habermas took the view that in late-twentieth-century corporate and media society, the public sphere was in danger of being absorbed by mass media forms—disagreeing diametrically with Marshall McLuhan's vision that mass media would make the world a village. Nevertheless, Habermas never aban-

doned belief in the politically liberating potential of the type of discussion to be found in a public sphere. His later work on "communicative reason" (in *The Theory of Communicative Action*) in effect spells out the structure and goals of that discussion.

42. And in England, Thatcherism. Livingstone and Lunt are British scholars, and most (though not all) of the programs they discuss are British. It may be that the British talk shows really do function more as public spheres. As Livingstone and Lunt describe them, they appear to choose social issues as topics more often than do American talk shows.

6. NOT THE LAST WORD

1. "In the imaginative past of nostalgic writers," write Janice Doane and Devon Hodges, "men were men, women were women, and reality was real. To retrieve 'reality,' an authentic language, and 'natural' sexual identity, these writers fight the false, seductive images of a decadent culture that they believe are promoted by feminist writing" (3).

2. See, for example, Brad Leithauser's ridicule: "How delightful it is as one's joint-passing youth is now revealed to be no mere idyll but—Wow! Neat!—the stuff of great art" (10). Alec McHoul criticizes *Vineland*'s politics as "60s nostalgic quietism" (98), and Alan Wilde writes that "by locating the ideal in the lifetime of his characters, Pynchon betrays again his nostalgia for the regretted time before the eclipse of 'the analog arts...by digital technology'" (171). See also Ellen Friedman's more sweeping critique of *Vineland* as an example of an American male nostalgia for the vanishing privileges of patriarchy, in which "even the most radical expressions of rebellion and discontent...are suffused with nostalgia for a past order, for older texts, for the familiar sustaining myths" (250).

3. Recall that "nostalgia" was originally a medical term designating a physical illness experienced by travelers far from home.

4. Pynchon's fiction has continually returned to historical trauma and has presented historical trauma in terms that are both catastrophic and revelatory—that is, in apocalyptic terms. The German colonial genocide in Southwest Africa (treated both in its own right and as a precursor to the Nazi genocide of European Jews), the slaughters of the First World War relived by Brigadier Pudding in his masochistic, coprophagous encounters with Katje at the White Visitation, the ongoing bureaucratic-scientific control procedures practiced by "the Firm" in *Gravity's Rainbow,* and the implicit emptiness and oppression of the Tupperware America presented in *The Crying of Lot 49* all stand as portents for some potentially all-encompassing and definitive disaster. Further, they are revelations that this disaster has, in reality, been present all along, that we live, as *Gravity's Rainbow* would have it, always along the trajectory of the rocket. *Vineland*'s complex response to the apocalyptic question that ends *The Crying of Lot 49*—"either there was some Tristero...or there was just America"—goes beyond the

binarism of that question and, I believe, beyond the curative potential contained in the vague countercultural "Counterforce" of *Gravity's Rainbow.* In *Vineland,* there is "only America," but there is a great deal to be retrieved and reworked in that traumatic legacy.

5. It is hard to remember now, over a decade later, all the cultural weight attached to that Orwellian year. For forty years, *1984* served as the measure of our social fears. Especially during the crises of the 1960s, 1984 loomed ahead as a prophecy. People could say in 1968, either there will be a revolution or it will be 1984 — either way, the apocalypse. 1984, in effect, replaced the millennium. In *Vineland,* 1984 marks an ironic conflation of the anticlimax of Orwellian prophecy and the high-water mark of Reaganism. For a discussion of the millennial significance taken on by Orwell's novel, see Hillel Schwartz, *Century's End: A Cultural History of the Fin de Siècle from the 990s through the 1990s.* Particularly useful is the bibliographic note 75 on page 356.

6. In a similar way, the Becker and Traverse families, in Eula Becker's narrative, become living memorials to the labor movement: "Be here to remind everybody — any time they see a Traverse, or Becker for that matter, they'll remember that one tree, and who did it, and why. Hell of a lot better 'n a statue in the park" (76). And for Frenesi, of course, "the past was on her case forever, the zombie at her back" (71).

7. See especially Heidegger's "The Question Concerning Technology": Enframing "banishes man into that kind of revealing which is an ordering. Where this ordering holds sway, it drives out every other possibility of revealing.... Where Enframing holds sway, regulating and securing of the standing-reserve mark all revealing. They no longer even let their own fundamental characteristics appear, namely, this revealing as such" (27).

8. See Frank J. Donner's *The Age of Surveillance: The Aims and Methods of America's Politcal Intelligence System,* as well as Todd Gitlin's and Tom Hayden's accounts of the 1960s.

9. Pynchon is historically accurate in pointing to sexuality and gender relations as particular problems for New Left politics. As Stokely Carmichael commented in 1965, "The only position for women in SNCC is prone." Sara Evans, Barbara Epstein, Barbara Ehrenreich, and Alice Echols have written compellingly of the sexual turmoil and contradictions in the New Left as rebellion against the restrictive gender roles of the 1950s had very different implications for men as for women. As Echols writes, "By advancing an untamed masculinity — one that took risks and dared to gamble — the New Left was in some sense promoting a counterhegemonic... understanding of masculinity," but one at odds with any feminist sense of gender roles (16). A very interesting text from the 1960s that treats this problem is Eldridge Cleaver's *Soul on Ice,* in which Cleaver, a convicted rapist, argues that sexuality is always incompatible with political action, that the political activist must be a kind of eunuch in order to be effective and uncorrupted — an extreme position taken by a man with his own extreme problems. But its implications are still part of current debates, as when Andrea Dworkin in her

discussion of pornography writes, "The Left cannot have its whores and its politics too" (217).

10. The vision of a "beloved" or "redemptive" community that informed the early civil rights movement, Evans writes, "constituted both a vision of the future to be obtained through nonviolent action and a conception of the nature of the movement itself" (37). In showing how this sense of community was taken up by the New Left in the early 1960s, and then adopted by feminists in the late 1960s and early 1970s after the New Left's fragmentation, Evans, much like Pynchon, tells the story of the historical transmission of a utopian vision.

11. For Prairie, the 1960s are initially just a set of clichés. She watches her mother's films of demonstrations and remarks on the " 'dude ... with the long hair and love beads, and the joint in his mouth ...' 'You mean in the flowered bell-bottoms and the paisley shirt?' 'Right on, sister!' " (115). Or, as Hector Zuniga, the former DEA officer and aspiring film producer tells Zoyd, "*Caray,* you sixties people, it's amazing. Ah love ya! Go anywhere, it don't matter—hey, Mongolia! Go way out into smalltown Outer Mongolia, *ese,* there's gonna be some local person about your age come runnin up, two fingers in a V, hollering, 'What's yer sign, man?' or singin 'In-A-Gadda-Da-Vida' note for note" (28). And we should note in Hector's ridicule of 1960s nostalgia the repeated presence of Pynchon's favorite recurring consonant, perhaps a parodic nostalgia for his own productions from the 1960s.

12. Morrison's novel is unusual, though not unique, among representations of American slavery in its emphasis on a slave or former slave woman killing her child. Historians agree that actual cases of slave infanticide were extremely rare (see Deborah Gray White, Eugene Genovese, and Randall M. Miller and John David Smith). Furthermore, Miller and Smith note that cases like that of Margaret Garner, in which the mother killed her child in order to save the child from slavery, were rarer still. More common were instances in which a mother killed her child in order to conceal the very fact of its birth, or because the father was a slave owner (Miller and Smith, 365). The latter is the case in Elizabeth Barrett Browning's poem, "The Runaway Slave at Pilgrim's Point." White cites evidence suggesting that a significant portion of alleged infanticides were actually cases of Sudden Infant Death Syndrome (89). Accounts of slave infanticides were also rare in the contemporary writings of abolitionists. There are no references at all, for instance, in Theodore Dwight Weld's *American Slavery As It Is*. Harriet Beecher Stowe, in *The Key to Uncle Tom's Cabin,* does refer at one point to "a case of this kind" in which a slave mother kills a child who is about to be sold (86), and the story of Cassy in *Uncle Tom's Cabin* provides the closest parallel in literature to Sethe's story in *Beloved*. Cassy, however, is a minor character in Stowe's novel, while Sethe, of course, is central. In her analysis of the rhetoric of suffering and cruelty in abolitionist writing, Elizabeth Clark shows that graphic accounts of slave owners' cruelty toward their slaves and the slaves' passive suffering were "riveting ... and proved to be among

the most effective and dramatic weapons in the reform arsenal" (467). Given Clark's analysis and the limited presence of slave infanticide in the documentary and literary record, we should see Morrison's focus on infanticide as both unusual and significant. Sethe's own suffering is foregrounded, but so is her own act of cruelty. The focus on infanticide, then, allows Morrison to represent the damages done to African American families both by racist institutions directly and by some families themselves, acting under pressure from these institutions.

13. For other treatments of the apocalyptic, or post-apocalyptic, imagery in *Beloved,* see Susan Bowers, "*Beloved* and the New Apocalypse"; and Josef Pesch, "*Beloved:* Toni Morrison's Post-Apocalyptic Novel."

14. For a history of American debates regarding the moral status of poverty that culminated in the "underclass" debates of the 1980s, see Michael Katz, *The Undeserving Poor: From the War on Poverty to the War on Welfare.* Two influential accounts of the underclass and its origins are Ken Auletta's *The Underclass* and Nicholas Lemann's *The Promised Land: The Great Black Migration and How It Changed America.* Auletta's book is largely an anecdotal report on poor families in New York City. Lemann traces urban poverty in Chicago to a "culture of poverty" that he locates in the rural South. Lemann's book has aroused significant controversy and has been attacked in many of the same terms as those used to attack the Moynihan Report. Jacqueline Jones, in particular, regards *The Promised Land* as another instance of blaming the victim. We should note, however, that Lemann does not discuss the black rural southern culture of poverty in isolation from the racist environment in which it developed. His emphasis, that is, is as much structural as behavioral. For important reviews of and contributions to the literature on the underclass, see *The Underclass Debate: Views from History,* ed. Michael Katz, in which appears Jones's discussion of Lemann ("Southern Diaspora: Origins of the Northern 'Underclass' ").

15. George Gilder, for example, disputes what he regards as "false theories of discrimination and spurious claims of racism and sexism as the dominant forces in the lives of the poor," and claims that "it would seem genuinely difficult to sustain the idea that America is still oppressive and discriminatory" (153, 155). Lawrence Mead argues that for the poor, including the urban black poor, "the main barrier to acceptance is no longer unfair social structures, but their own difficulties in coping" (7). Charles Murray, who achieved renewed notoriety for his opinions on poverty, race, and genetics in *The Bell Curve,* argued in *Losing Ground: American Social Policy, 1950–1980* that poverty in the late 1960s and 1970s was, in fact, created, not alleviated, by Great Society antipoverty programs.

16. Lee Rainwater and William L. Yancey thoroughly describe the controversies that arose after the Moynihan Report was released as well as presenting the text of the report, of Lyndon Johnson's 1965 commencement speech at Howard University, and

of a variety of critical responses to the report. Rainwater and Yancey stress the effects of the early press coverage of the report, particularly as details were leaked before its release, and discuss how conservatives immediately used Moynihan's conclusions to "explain" the Watts riots. According to Rainwater and Yancey, many critics of the report based their analyses primarily on newspaper accounts and proceeded to advance arguments regarding unemployment and structural problems in the economy not fundamentally different from Moynihan's own (154). At the same time, these critics' fears that the report's emphasis on African American "pathology" would be appropriated by racists and conservatives were quickly borne out. Writing in 1967, Rainwater and Yancey manifest an obvious blind spot regarding the sexual politics of the report, noting women's objections to Moynihan's criticisms of "matriarchy," but failing to see the persistent misogyny that appears so glaring on reading the report today.

17. See Katz, *The Undeserving Poor*; Lemann, *The Promised Land*; and Allen Matusow, *The Unraveling of America: A History of Liberalism in the 1960s*.

18. As Rainwater and Yancey point out, this reception of the report was partly shaped through its early dissemination via press leaks. At the same time, the report does reveal a blindness toward African American cultural traditions and toward the role of women that, as I will show, was characteristic of the liberal sociology on which the Moynihan Report relied.

19. Walter A. Jackson notes the wide range of contributors, especially African American social scientists, whom Myrdal recruited—and funded—for his project, quoting St. Clair Drake that "when Myrdal comes in he puts them all on the payroll. Anybody who was willing to get on that payroll is on there" (111). Myrdal's own funding came from the Carnegie Corporation. Jackson attributes the widespread acceptance of Myrdal's work, as opposed to the widespread rejection of Moynihan's similar work, to Myrdal's openness and inclusiveness, as opposed to Moynihan's secrecy.

20. The extreme instance of this emphasis on the cultural trauma induced by slavery is Stanley Elkins's (1959) description of slavery as a "closed system" analogous to Nazi concentration camps. Coming in the wake of the Holocaust, Elkins's theorizing takes to another level Frazier's fascination with locating a limit case of brutality in which both personality and culture are erased and replaced with degraded forms. It should not be surprising that the Moynihan Report invoked Elkins, whose work constitutes a logical end point for a line of thinking whose premise is a traumatic eradication of African American culture.

21. Likewise, the liberal consensus was shattered by the emergence of the New Left, which split from liberals on the basis both of racial policies and, more crucially, over disagreements concerning the war in Vietnam. See work by Todd Gitlin, Maurice Isserman and Michael Kazin, and Sara Evans on the development of the New Left and its relations with liberalism, the civil rights movement, and feminism.

22. A 1964 discussion published in *Commentary* ("Liberalism and the Negro: A Round Table Discussion") shows the extent to which not only militants but also black intellectuals rejected the liberal consensus. "The liberal record," says James Baldwin, "is a shameful record. And the reason it is so shameful is that white liberals — with some exceptions — have been unable to divest themselves of the whole concept of white supremacy" (41). For Kenneth Clark, the liberal is "much more insidious than the out-and-out bigot." Liberalism "as it is practiced — I am not talking of it as it is verbalized — *is* an affliction. It is an insidious type of affliction because it attempts to impose guilt upon the Negro when he has to face the hypocrisy of the liberal" (39).

23. As Morrison said in an interview in 1989, *Beloved* confronts a "national amnesia." "I thought this has got to be the least read of all the books I'd written because it is about something that the characters don't want to remember, I don't want to remember, black people don't want to remember, white people don't want to remember" ("The Pain of Being Black," 257). That Morrison was wrong about *Beloved*'s popularity indicates the complexity of the response to this novel. On one hand, we might infer that a large audience is indeed ready to remember American racial trauma in all its aspects. On the other hand, the enormous popularity of a novel that confronts "national amnesia" suggests that *Beloved* may have inspired new forms of amnesia in its readers.

24. See Deborah Horvitz, "Nameless Ghosts: Possession and Dispossession in *Beloved*"; and David Lawrence, "Fleshly Ghosts and Ghostly Flesh: The Word and the Body in *Beloved*," on the symptomatic function of the embodied ghost.

25. Based largely on a reading of Beloved's disjunctive monologue that places it in part on a slave ship during the Middle Passage, Horvitz argues for "a fluidity of identity among Sethe's mother, Sethe's grandmother, and the murdered two-year-old, so that Beloved is both an individual and a collective entity" (163).

26. In *How Societies Remember,* Paul Connerton describes how social memory is created performatively, as forms of ritual commemoration inform a "recollection of bodies" (4). The written text, then, becomes less important than the actions people perform in memory of those histories they periodically enact. What is missing from Connerton's account, however, is a sense of compelled repetition, that is, repetition of traumatic events. I agree with Connerton that, in some sense, the body remembers, but his bodies seem to remember only the official versions of events, with no traumatic residue. If I read Connerton correctly, a somatic memory of Beloved would perhaps be the act of annually placing flowers on her grave. For Morrison, this would be an instance of how historical memory is buried, not of how it returns.

27. *Beyond the Pleasure Principle* is the principal text in which Freud discusses traumatic repetition. Such repetition's resistance to therapy is what moves Freud's thinking in the direction of a biological "death drive." If, however, we move away from biology and back toward history, these repetitions may appear as symptoms of historical

events that have not been adequately addressed, remembered, and retold. I have attempted such a social and historical reinterpretation of Freud's discussion of trauma and repetition in chapter 2. In the critical literature on *Beloved,* Emily Miller Budick's "Absence, Loss, and the Space of History in Toni Morrison's *Beloved*" provides an excellent treatment of the novel's presentation of memory and repetition. As Budick writes, "The problem that Beloved poses to the family at 124 is how the family, which has suffered so much loss and devastation, might remember the past without literally re-membering it" (120).

28. The question of the location and origin of the "inner jungle" returns us to the conservative-liberal-leftist debate, the Moynihan controversy, and Morrison's efforts to reveal the traumatic moments buried by these debates. Stamp Paid does not deny a violent presence in African American culture, but he places it in a structural context of white psychic and institutional violence. In this way Morrison replaces the structural and behavioral violence omitted by conservatives and leftists, respectively. At the same time, portraying Stamp Paid explicitly as an *agent* — an agent of the abolitionist movement as well as an individual moral agent — Morrison critiques the traditional liberal emphasis on an absolutely incapacitating traumatization of African Americans.

29. David Lawrence, in an excellent account of Beloved's antagonistic relation with the symbolic and social order, writes, "Beloved has not yet learned the codes that give shape to and control desire. . . . Beloved recognizes no social bounds, showing a resistance to conventional form that is registered in the disturbing 'cadence' of her own words. While she craves adult language, particularly those stories that 'construct out of the strings' of Denver and Sethe's experience 'a net' to hold her, she is incapable of such construction herself" (196).

30. We might refer also at this point to Orlando Patterson's enormously suggestive notion of slavery as "social death." "Perhaps the most distinctive attribute of the slave's powerlessness," he writes, "was that it always originated (or was conceived as having originated) as a substitute for death, usually violent death." The slave was therefore "a socially dead person. Alienated from all 'rights' or claims of birth, he ceased to belong in his own right to any legitimate social order" (5).

31. Deborah McDowell also discusses the importance of scars in a post-slavery novel in "Negotiating between Tenses: Witnessing Slavery after Freedom — *Dessa Rose.*" McDowell refers to the description of the scars on Dessa's thighs as "history writ about her privates," and writes that for Dessa to speak of these scars would be "baring a past too painful to bear" (154).

32. Sethe's chokecherry tree also marks a literary return, as Morrison uses this tree to revisit and critique Zora Neale Hurston's vision in *Their Eyes Were Watching God* of Janie's pear tree, an emblem of unbounded individual and erotic potentials. The flaw of Janie's tree is its lack of relation to history, its implication (shared, in large part, by

the novel as a whole) that slavery definitively had ended. The repressed traumas of American racial and sexual histories explode at the end of the novel in the hurricane and, more specifically, in the figure of the mad dog riding the cow and in Teacake's subsequent infection. This violent climax to Janie's promising bildungsroman adds force to Morrison's implicit suggestion that the personal tree is inseparable from the historical.

33. For Ernesto Laclau and Chantal Mouffe, the place of "antagonism" marks not simply a physical or political opposition, nor a logical contradiction. It is the point, rather, where a society, in trying to construct itself, reaches its conceptual limit: a point of impossibility. "Antagonism," they write, "as a witness of the impossibility of a final suture [i.e., a final coherence or connection], is the 'experience' of the limit of the so-cial. Strictly speaking, antagonisms are not *internal* but *external* to society; or rather, they constitute the limits of society, the latter's impossibility of fully constituting it-self" (125). Zizek uses Laclau and Mouffe's term in his psychoanalytic theorizing of ideology as "a fantasy-construction which serves as a support for our 'reality' itself: an 'illusion' which structures our effective, real social relations and thereby masks some insupportable, real, impossible kernel (conceptualized by Ernesto Laclau and Chantal Mouffe as 'antagonism': a traumatic social division which cannot be symbolized)" (*Sub-lime Object,* 45). The traumatic (non-) place of race in 1980s political discourse would be the site of antagonism Morrison seeks to unsuture.

34. The critical debate concerning the ending of *Beloved* constitutes, I believe, an-other chapter in the larger controversies within African Americanist literary criticism regarding the appropriate forms of representation of African American men and women and the uses of literary theory in readings of African American texts. See, for instance, the essays in Houston Baker and Patricia Redmond, eds., *Afro-American Literary Study in the 1990s,* especially the exchange of views in the essays by Deborah McDowell and Michael Awkward concerning the values attributed to "wholeness" in African Amer-ican writing. See also the controversy centering around Joyce Joyce's attack on theory in *New Literary History* 18 (1987).

35. I agree entirely with Deborah Horvitz on this point, that "the paradox of how to live in the present without canceling out an excruciatingly painful past remains un-resolved at the end of the novel. At the same time, something healing has happened" (166). See also Caroline Rody, who describes how *Beloved* brings "history to an un-closed closure and the haunt to our own houses" (113).

36. Morrison explicitly referred to the abandoned liberal agenda in a 1989 inter-view, saying, "of course, a new President can make a difference — he can reassemble the legislation of the past twenty years that has been taken apart and put it back. They said it didn't work. It's like building a bridge a quarter of the way across the river and saying, 'You can't get there from here.' Twenty years! It never had a generation to complete the work" ("The Pain of Being Black," 259).

1. From Yeats's "Nineteen Hundred and Nineteen." "Many ingenious lovely things are gone / That seemed sheer miracle to the multitude" (*Collected Poems,* 204).

2. From William Carlos Williams, *Spring and All.*

3. "If the doors of perception were cleansed every thing would appear to man as it is, infinite" (William Blake, *The Marriage of Heaven and Hell,* in *Complete Writings,* 154).

4. "I will call them my people, which were not my people; and her beloved, which was not beloved"; epigraph at the beginning of Toni Morrison's *Beloved.*

Abraham, Nicolas, and Maria Torok. *The Shell and the Kernel: Renewals of Psycho-analysis.* Ed. and trans. Nicholas T. Rand. Chicago: University of Chicago Press, 1994.

Adorno, Theodor W. *Negative Dialectics.* Trans. E. B. Ashton. New York: Continuum, 1992.

———. "What Does Coming to Terms with the Past Mean?" In *Bitburg in Moral and Political Perspective,* ed. Geoffrey H. Hartman, 114–29. Bloomington: Indiana University Press, 1986.

Adorno, Theodor W., and Max Horkheimer. *Dialectic of Enlightenment.* Trans. John Cumming. New York: Continuum, 1982.

Amis, Martin. *Time's Arrow.* New York: Vintage, 1991.

Andersen, Robin. *Consumer Culture and TV Programming.* Boulder: Westview Press, 1995.

Auletta, Ken. *The Underclass.* New York: Vintage, 1983.

Baker, Houston. "Handling 'Crisis': Great Books, Rap Music, and the End of Western Homogeneity." In *Wild Orchids and Trotsky: Messages from American Universities,* ed. Mark Edmundson. New York: Penguin, 1993.

Baker, Houston Jr., and Patricia Redmond, eds. *Afro-American Literary Study in the 1990s.* Chicago: University of Chicago Press, 1989.

Barthelme, Donald. *The Dead Father.* New York: Farrar, Straus and Giroux, 1975.

Barthes, Roland. *Mythologies.* Trans. Annette Lavers. New York: Noonday Press, 1972 [1957].

———. *The Pleasure of the Text.* Trans. Richard Miller. New York: Hill and Wang, 1975.

Bataille, Georges. *Visions of Excess: Selected Writings, 1927–1939.* Ed. Allan Stoekl. Trans. Allan Stoekl, Carl R. Lovitt, and Donald M. Leslie Jr. Minneapolis: University of Minnesota Press, 1985.

Batman. Dir. Tim Burton. Warner Brothers, 1989.

Baudrillard, Jean. *America.* Trans. Chris Turner. London: Verso, 1988.

———. "The Anorexic Ruins." In *Looking Back on the End of the World,* ed. Dietmar Kamper and Christoph Wulf, trans. David Antal, 29–45. New York: Semiotext(e), 1989.

———. "The Ecstasy of Communication." In *The Anti-Aesthetic: Essays on Postmodern Culture,* ed. Hal Foster, 126–34. Port Townsend, Wash.: Bay Press, 1983.

———. *Simulations.* Trans. Paul Foss, Paul Patton, and Philip Beitchman. New York: Semiotext(e), 1983.

Bauman, Zygmunt. *Modernity and the Holocaust.* Ithaca: Cornell University Press, 1991.

Bayles, Martha. "Special Effects, Special Pleading." *The New Criterion* 12 (Jan. 1988): 34–40.

Bell, Bernard W. "*Beloved:* A Womanist Neo-Slave Narrative; or Multivocal Remembrances of Things Past." *African American Review* 26 (1992): 7–16.

Benjamin, Walter. *Illuminations.* Trans. Harry Zohn. New York: Schocken, 1969.

Bercovitch, Sacvan. *The American Jeremiad.* Madison: University of Wisconsin Press, 1978.

Berman, Marshall. *All That Is Solid Melts into Air: The Experience of Modernity.* New York: Simon and Schuster, 1982.

Bernstein, Michael André. *Foregone Conclusions: Against Apocalyptic History.* Berkeley: University of California Press, 1994.

Berressem, Hanjo. *Pynchon's Poetics: Interfacing Theory and Text.* Urbana: University of Illinois Press, 1993.

Bersani, Leo. *The Freudian Body: Psychoanalysis and Art.* New York: Columbia University Press, 1986.

———. "Is the Rectum a Grave?" In *AIDS: Cultural Analysis/Cultural Activism,* ed. Douglas Crimp. Cambridge: MIT Press, 1988.

Berube, Michael. *Marginal Forces/Cultural Centers: Tolson, Pynchon, and the Politics of the Canon.* Ithaca: Cornell University Press, 1992.

Bettelheim, Bruno. *The Informed Heart: Autonomy in a Mass Age.* Glencoe, Ill.: Free Press, 1960.

Blade Runner. Dir. Ridley Scott. Warner Brothers, 1982.

Blake, William. *Complete Writings.* Ed. Geoffrey Keynes. Oxford: Oxford University Press, 1972.

Bloch, Ernst. *The Utopian Function of Art and Literature: Selected Essays.* Trans. Jack Zipes and Frank Mecklenburg. Cambridge: MIT Press, 1988.

Bloom, Harold. *Omens of Millennium: The Gnosis of Angels, Dreams, and Resurrection.* New York: Riverhead Books, 1996.

Blumenthal, Sidney. *Our Long National Daydream: A Political Pageant of the Reagan Era.* New York: Harper and Row, 1988.

Bowers, Susan. "*Beloved* and the New Apocalypse." *Journal of Ethnic Studies* 18 (1990): 59–77.

A Boy and His Dog. Dir. L. Q. Jones. LQ/JAF, 1975.

Boyarin, Jonathan. *Storm from Paradise: The Politics of Jewish Memory.* Minneapolis: University of Minnesota Press, 1992.

Boyer, Paul. *When Time Shall Be No More: Prophecy Belief in Modern American Culture.* Cambridge: Harvard University Press, 1992.

Brinkley, Robert, and Steven Youra. "Tracing *Shoah.*" *PMLA* 111 (1996): 108–27.

Brockman, Stephen. "Bitburg Deconstruction." *The Philosophical Forum* 17 (1986): 159–74.

Brown, Bernard E. *Protest in Paris: Anatomy of a Revolt.* Morristown, N.J.: General Learning Press, 1974.

Brown, Norman O. *Life against Death: The Psychoanalytic Meaning of History.* Middletown, Conn.: Wesleyan University Press, 1959.

Budick, Emily Miller. "Absence, Loss, and the Space of History in Toni Morrison's *Beloved.*" *Arizona Quarterly* 48 (1992): 117–38.

Bull, Malcolm, ed. *Apocalypse Theory and the Ends of the World.* Oxford: Blackwell, 1995.

Butler, Judith. *Bodies That Matter: On the Discursive Limits of "Sex."* New York: Routledge, 1993.

Calinescu, Matei. "The End of Man in Twentieth-Century Philosophy: Reflections on a Philosophical Metaphor." In *Visions of Apocalypse: End or Rebirth?* ed. Saul Friedlander et al., 171–95. New York: Holmes and Meier, 1985.

Cannon, Lou. *President Reagan: The Role of a Lifetime.* New York: Simon and Schuster, 1991.

————. *Reagan.* New York: G. P. Putnam, 1982.

Carmichael, Stokely, and Charles V. Hamilton. *Black Power: The Politics of Liberation in America.* New York: Random House, 1967.

Carter, Angela. *The Passion of New Eve.* London: V. Gollancz, 1977.

Carter, Dan T. *From George Wallace to Newt Gingrich: Race in the Conservative Counterrevolution, 1963–1994.* Baton Rouge: Louisiana State University Press, 1996.

Caruth, Cathy. *Unclaimed Experience. Trauma, Narrative, and History.* Baltimore: Johns Hopkins University Press, 1996.

————, ed. *Trauma: Explorations in Memory.* Baltimore: Johns Hopkins University Press, 1995.

Cassara, Ernest. "The Development of America's Sense of Mission." In *The Apocalyptic Vision in America: Interdisciplinary Essays on Myth and Culture,* ed. Lois Parkinson Zamora, 64–96. Bowling Green, Ohio: Bowling Green University Popular Press, 1982.

Citizen Kane. Dir. Orson Welles. Mercury Theater Productions for RKO, 1941.

Clark, Elizabeth B. "'The Sacred Rights of the Weak': Pain, Sympathy, and the Culture of Individual Rights in Antebellum America." *Journal of American History* 82 (1995): 463–93.

Cleaver, Eldridge. *Soul on Ice.* New York: Dell, 1968.

Cohen, Arthur A. *The Tremendum: A Theological Interpretation of the Holocaust.* New York: Crossroad, 1981.

Cohn, Norman. "Medieval Millenarism: Its Bearing on the Comparative Study of Millenarian Movements." In *Millennial Dreams in Action: Studies in Revolutionary Religious Movements,* ed. Sylvia L. Thrupp. New York: Schocken, 1970.

———. *The Pursuit of the Millennium: Revolutionary Millenarians and Mystical Anarchists of the Middle Ages.* Rev. ed. New York: Oxford University Press, 1970.

Collier, Peter, and David Horowitz, eds. *Second Thoughts: Former Radicals Look Back at the Sixties.* Lanham, Md.: Madison Books, 1989.

Collins, Adela Yarbro. *Crisis and Catharsis: The Power of the Apocalypse.* Philadelphia: Westminster Press, 1984.

Collins, John J. *The Apocalyptic Imagination: An Introduction to the Jewish Matrix of Christianity.* New York: Crossroad, 1984.

Connerton, Paul. *How Societies Remember.* Cambridge: Cambridge University Press, 1989.

Coontz, Stephanie. *The Way We Never Were: American Families and the Nostalgia Trap.* New York: Basic Books, 1992.

Crouch, Stanley. "Aunt Medea." *The New Republic,* Oct. 19, 1987, 38–43.

Dallek, Robert. *Ronald Reagan: The Politics of Symbolism.* Cambridge: Harvard University Press, 1982.

Daniel, Alma. *Ask Your Angels!* New York: Ballantine, 1992.

Davidson, Donald. "On the Very Idea of a Conceptual Scheme." In *Inquiries into Truth and Interpretation,* 183–98. Oxford: Clarendon Press, 1985.

Davis, Mike. *Prisoners of the American Dream: Politics and Economy in the History of the U.S. Working Class.* London: Verso, 1986.

Deleuze, Gilles, and Félix Guattari. *Anti-Oedipus: Capitalism and Schizophrenia.* Trans. Robert Hurley, Mark Seem, and Helen R. Lane. Minneapolis: University of Minnesota Press, 1983 [1972].

DeLillo, Don. *White Noise.* New York: Penguin, 1985.

Dellamora, Richard. *Apocalyptic Overtures: Sexual Politics and the Sense of an Ending.* New Brunswick, N.J.: Rutgers University Press, 1994.

———, ed. *Postmodern Apocalypse: Theory and Cultural Practice at the End.* Philadelphia: University of Pennsylvania Press, 1995.

Derrida, Jacques. *Cinders.* Trans. Ned Lukacher. Lincoln: University of Nebraska Press, 1991.

———. "Force of Law: The 'Mystical Foundation of Authority.'" In *Deconstruction and the Possibility of Justice,* ed. Drucilla Cornell, Michel Rosenfeld, and David Gray Carlson. New York: Routledge, 1992.

———. "Differance." In *Margins of Philosophy,* trans. Alan Bass, 1–27. Chicago: University of Chicago Press, 1982.

———. "Of an Apocalyptic Tone Recently Adopted in Philosophy." *Semeia* 14 (1982): 62–97.

———. *Of Grammatology.* Trans. Gayatri Chakravorty Spivak. Baltimore: Johns Hopkins University Press, 1976.

———. *Of Spirit: Heidegger and the Question.* Trans. Geoffrey Bennington and Rachel Bowlby. Chicago: University of Chicago Press, 1989.

———. *Points: Interviews, 1974–1994.* Ed. Elisabeth Weber. Trans. Peggy Kamuf. Stanford: Stanford University Press, 1995.

———. *Positions.* Ed. and trans. Alan Bass. Chicago: University of Chicago Press, 1981.

———. "Shibboleth." Trans. Joshua Wilner. In *Midrash and Literature,* ed. Geoffrey H. Hartman and Sanford Budick, 307–47. New Haven: Yale University Press, 1986.

———. "Structure, Sign, and Play." In *Writing and Difference,* trans. Alan Bass, 278–93. Chicago: University of Chicago Press, 1978.

———. "Violence and Metaphysics: An Essay on the Thought of Emmanuel Levinas." In *Writing and Difference,* trans. Alan Bass, 79–153. Chicago: University of Chicago Press, 1978.

Des Pres, Terrence. *The Survivor: An Anatomy of Life in the Death Camps.* New York: Oxford University Press, 1976.

Dews, Peter. *The Limits of Disenchantment: Essays of Contemporary European Philosophy.* London: Verso, 1995.

Doane, Janice, and Devon Hodges. *Nostalgia and Sexual Difference: The Resistance to Contemporary Feminism.* New York: Methuen, 1987.

Doctorow, E. L. "False Documents." In *E. L. Doctorow: Essays and Conversations,* ed. Richard Trenner, 16–27. Princeton, N.J.: Ontario Review Press, 1983.

Doneson, Judith E. *The Holocaust in American Film.* Philadelphia: Jewish Publication Society, 1987.

Donner, Frank J. *The Age of Surveillance: The Aims and Methods of America's Political Intelligence System.* New York: Knopf, 1980.

Du Bois, W. E. B. *The Souls of Black Folk.* 1903. Millwood, N.Y.: Kraus-Thomsom, 1973.

Dugger, Ronnie. "Does Reagan Expect a Nuclear War?" *Washington Post,* Apr. 8, 1984, C1, 4.

Dworkin, Andrea. *Pornography: Men Possessing Women.* New York: Dutton, 1989.

Echols, Alice. "We Gotta Get Out of This Place: Notes toward a Remapping of the Sixties." *Socialist Review* 22 (1992): 9–33.

Edsall, Thomas Byrne. "The Changing Shape of Power: A Realignment in Public Policy." In *The Rise and Fall of the New Deal Order: 1930–1980,* ed. Steve Fraser and Gary Gerstle, 269–93. Princeton: Princeton University Press, 1989.

Ehrenreich, Barbara. *The Hearts of Men: American Dreams and the Flight from Commitment.* Garden City, N.Y.: Anchor, 1983.

Elkins, Stanley M. *Slavery: A Problem in American Institutional Life.* 3d ed. Chicago: University of Chicago Press, 1976.

Engelhardt, Tom. *The End of Victory Culture: Cold War America and the Disillusioning of a Generation.* New York: Basic Books, 1995.

Epstein, Barbara. "Family Politics and the New Left: Learning from Our Own Experience." *Socialist Review* 12 (1982): 141–61.

Erickson, Paul D. *Reagan Speaks: The Making of an American Myth.* New York: NYU Press, 1985.

Escape from New York. Dir. John Carpenter. Avco Embassy, 1981.

Evans, Sara. *Personal Politics: The Roots of Women's Liberation in the Civil Rights Movement and the New Left.* New York: Vintage, 1979.

Ewen, Stewart, and Elizabeth Ewen. *Channels of Desire: Mass Images and the Shaping of American Consciousness.* New York: McGraw-Hill, 1982.

Farias, Victor. *Heidegger and Nazism.* Ed. Joseph Margolis and Tom Rockmore. Trans. Paul Burrell, Dominic Di Bernardi, and Gabriel R. Ricci. Philadelphia: Temple University Press, 1989.

Felman, Shoshana, and Dori Laub. *Testimony: Crises of Witnessing in Literature, Psychoanalysis, and History.* New York: Routledge, 1992.

Ferry, Luc, and Alain Renaut. *French Philosophy of the Sixties: An Essay on Antihumanism.* Trans. Mary Schnackenberg. Amherst: University of Massachusetts Press, 1990.

Finkielkraut, Alain. *The Imaginary Jew.* Lincoln: University of Nebraska Press, 1994.

———. *Remembering in Vain: The Klaus Barbie Trial and Crimes against Humanity.* Trans. Roxanne Lapidus with Sima Godfrey. New York: Columbia University Press, 1992.

Foner, Philip S. *The Industrial Workers of the World: 1905–1917.* New York: International Publishers, 1965.

Foucault, Michel. *Discipline and Punish.* Trans. Alan Sheridan. New York: Pantheon, 1977.

———. *The Order of Things: An Archaeology of the Human Sciences.* New York: Vintage, 1973.

Frazier, E. Franklin. *The Negro Family in the United States.* Chicago: University of Chicago Press, 1969 [1939].

Freud, Sigmund. *Analysis Terminable and Interminable. The Standard Edition of the Complete Psychological Works of Sigmund Freud.* Trans. James Strachey, 23: 209–53. London: Hogarth Press, 1955.
———. *Beyond the Pleasure Principle. S.E.* 18: 7–64.
———. *Civilization and Its Discontents. S.E.* 21: 57–145.
———. "Fetishism." *S.E.* 21: 149–57.
———. "Fragment of an Analysis of a Case of Hysteria." *S.E.* 7: 1–122.
———. *The Interpretation of Dreams. S.E.* 4: xi–338, 5: 339–627.
———. *Moses and Monotheism. S.E.* 23: 3–137.
———. "Mourning and Melancholia." *S.E.* 14: 237–58.
———. "Negation." *S.E.* 19: 235–40.
———. "Remembering, Repeating, and Working-Through." *S.E.* 12: 145–56.
———. "The Splitting of the Ego in the Process of Defense." *S.E.* 23: 271–78.
———, with Josef Breuer. *Studies on Hysteria. S.E.* 2.
———. "The Uncanny." *S.E.* 17: 217–56.
Friedlander, Judith. *Vilna on the Seine: Jewish Intellectuals in France since 1968.* New Haven: Yale University Press, 1990.
Friedlander, Saul. *Reflections of Nazism: An Essay on Kitsch and Death.* Trans. Thomas Weyr. Bloomington: Indiana University Press, 1993.
Friedlander, Saul, Gerald Holton, Leo Marx, and Eugene Skolnikoff, eds. *Visions of Apocalypse: End or Rebirth?* New York: Holmes and Meier, 1985.
Friedman, Ellen G. "Where Are the Missing Contents?: (Post)modernism, Gender, and the Canon." *PMLA* 108 (1993): 240–52.
Fukuyama, Francis. "The End of History?" *The National Interest* 17 (summer 1989): 3–18.
Genovese, Eugene D. *Roll, Jordan, Roll: The World the Slaves Made.* New York: Vintage, 1976.
Gibson, William. *Neuromancer.* New York: Ace, 1984.
Gilder, George. *Wealth and Poverty.* New York: Basic Books, 1981.
Gilman, Sander L. *Jewish Self-Hatred: Anti-Semitism and the Hidden Language of the Jews.* Baltimore: Johns Hopkins University Press, 1986.
Gitlin, Todd. "Car Commercials and *Miami Vice:* We Build Excitement." In *Watching Television: A Pantheon Guide to Popular Culture,* ed. Todd Gitlin, 136–61. New York: Pantheon, 1987.
———. *The Sixties: Years of Hope, Days of Rage.* New York: Bantam, 1987.
Goldenberg, Myrna. "Different Horrors, Same Hell: Women Remembering the Holocaust." In *Thinking the Unthinkable: Meanings of the Holocaust,* ed. Roger S. Gottlieb, 150–66. New York: Paulist Press, 1991.
Goldman, Richard. *Reading Ads Socially.* London: Routledge, 1992.

Goldsmith, Steven. *Unbuilding Jerusalem: Apocalypse and Romantic Representation.* Ithaca: Cornell University Press, 1993.

Grossman, David. *See Under: Love.* Trans. Betsy Rosenberg. New York: Farrar, Straus, and Giroux, 1989.

Gutman, Herbert G. *The Black Family in Slavery and Freedom, 1750–1925.* New York: Pantheon, 1976.

Habermas, Jürgen. *The Structural Transformation of the Public Sphere: An Inquiry into a Category of Bourgeois Society.* Trans. Thomas Burger. Cambridge: MIT Press, 1989.

———. *The Theory of Communicative Action.* Trans. Thomas McCarthy. 2 vols. Boston: Beacon Press, 1983.

Hall, Stuart. "The Toad in the Garden: Thatcherism among the Theorists." In *Marxism and the Interpretation of Culture,* ed. Cary Nelson and Lawrence Grossberg, 35–73. Urbana: University of Illinois Press, 1988.

Hanson, Paul D. "Old Testament Apocalyptic Reexamined." In *Visionaries and Their Apocalypses,* ed. Paul D. Hanson, 37–60. Philadelphia: Fortress, 1983.

Haraway, Donna. *Simians, Cyborgs, and Women: The Reinvention of Nature.* New York: Routledge, 1991.

Harris, Middleton, comp. *The Black Book.* New York: Random House, 1974.

Hartman, Geoffrey H., ed. *Bitburg in Moral and Political Perspective.* Bloomington: Indiana University Press, 1986.

———. *The Longest Shadow: In the Aftermath of the Holocaust.* Bloomington: Indiana University Press, 1996.

———. "On Traumatic Knowledge and Literary Studies." *New Literary History* 26 (1995): 537–63.

———. "Words and Wounds." In *Saving the Text: Literature/Derrida/Philosophy,* 118–57. Baltimore: Johns Hopkins University Press, 1981.

Hayden, Tom. *Reunion: A Memoir.* New York: Random House, 1988.

Hayles, N. Katherine. "'Who Was Saved?': Families, Snitches, and Recuperation in Pynchon's *Vineland.*" *Critique* 32 (1990): 77–91.

Heidegger, Martin. "The Age of the World Picture." In *The Question Concerning Technology, and Other Essays,* trans. William Lovitt, 115–54. New York: Harper and Row, 1977.

———. "Letter on Humanism." In *Basic Writings,* ed. David Farrell Krell, 189–242. New York: Harper and Row, 1977.

———. "The Question Concerning Technology." In *The Question Concerning Technology, and Other Essays,* trans. William Lovitt. New York: Harper and Row, 1977.

———. "Time and Being." In *On Time and Being,* trans. Joan Stambaugh, 1–24. New York: Harper and Row, 1972.

Hellholm, David, ed. *Apocalypticism in the Mediterranean World and the Near East.* Tubingen: J. C. B. Mohr (Paul Siebeck), 1983.

Henderson, Mae G. "Toni Morrison's *Beloved:* Re-Membering the Body as Historical Text." In *Comparative American Identities: Race, Sex, and Nationality in the Modern Text,* ed. Hortense J. Spillers, 62–86. New York: Routledge, 1991.

Hertz, Neil. *The End of the Line: Essays on Psychoanalysis and the Sublime.* New York: Columbia University Press, 1989.

Hertz, Robert. *Death and the Right Hand.* Trans. Rodney and Claudia Needham. Glencoe, Ill.: Free Press, 1960 [1907].

Hilberg, Raul. *The Politics of Memory: The Journey of a Holocaust Historian.* Chicago: Ivan R. Dee, 1996.

Hirsch, Marianne. "Family Pictures: *Maus,* Mourning, and Post-Memory." *Discourse* 15 (1992): 3–29.

Holst, Spencer. "The Santa Claus Murderer." In *The Zebra Storyteller: Collected Stories of Spencer Holst,* 91–94. Barrytown, N.Y.: Station Hill, 1993.

Horvitz, Deborah. "Nameless Ghosts: Possession and Dispossession in *Beloved.*" *Studies in American Fiction* 17 (fall 1989): 157–67.

Hurston, Zora Neale. *Their Eyes Were Watching God.* Urbana: University of Illinois Press, 1978.

Hutcheon, Linda. *A Poetics of Postmodernism: History, Theory, Fiction.* London: Routledge, 1988.

Isserman, Maurice. "Democracy Is in the Streets." *American Historical Review* 94 (1989): 990.

Isserman, Maurice, and Michael Kazin. "The Failure and Success of the New Radicalism." In *The Rise and Fall of the New Deal Order: 1930–1980,* ed. Steve Fraser and Gary Gerstle, 212–42. Princeton: Princeton University Press, 1989.

Jackson, Walter A. *Gunnar Myrdal and America's Conscience: Social Engineering and Racial Liberalism, 1938–1987.* Chapel Hill: University of North Carolina Press, 1990.

Jameson, Fredric. *Postmodernism, or, The Cultural Logic of Late Capitalism.* Durham: Duke University Press, 1991.

———. "Reification and Utopia in Mass Culture." *Social Text* 1 (1979): 130–48.

Jardine, Alice A. *Gynesis: Configurations of Woman and Modernity.* Ithaca: Cornell University Press, 1985.

Jay, Martin. "The Apocalyptic Imagination and the Inability to Mourn." In *Force Fields: Between Intellectual History and Cultural Critique,* 84–98. New York: Routledge, 1993.

Jones, Jacqueline. "Southern Diaspora: Origins of the Northern 'Underclass.'" In *The Underclass Debate: Views from History,* ed. Michael B. Katz, 27–54. Princeton: Princeton University Press, 1993.

Joyce, Joyce A. "The Black Canon: Reconstructing Black American Literary Criticism." *New Literary History* 18 (1987): 335–44.

Judis, John B. *Grand Illusion: Critics and Champions of the American Century.* New York: Farrar, Straus and Giroux, 1992.

Kant, Immanuel. *The Critique of Judgement.* Trans. J. H. Bernard. London: Macmillan, 1914.

Katz, Michael B. *The Undeserving Poor: From the War on Poverty to the War on Welfare.* New York: Pantheon, 1989.

———, ed. *The "Underclass" Debate: Views from History.* Princeton: Princeton University Press, 1993.

Kaye, Harvey J. *The Powers of the Past: Reflections on the Crisis and the Promise of History.* Minneapolis: University of Minnesota Press, 1991.

Kermode, Frank. *The Sense of an Ending: Studies in the Theory of Fiction.* London: Oxford University Press, 1968.

Kierkegaard, Søren. *Either/Or: A Fragment of Life.* Trans. David F. Swenson and Lillian Marvin Swenson. 2 vols. Princeton: Princeton University Press, 1946.

———. *Fear and Trembling.* Trans. Alastair Hannay. New York: Penguin, 1987.

———. *Repetition: An Essay in Experimental Psychology.* Trans. Walter Lowrie. Princeton: Princeton University Press, 1941.

King, Stephen. *The Stand.* Complete and uncut ed. New York: Doubleday, 1978, 1990.

Krieger, Joel. *Reagan, Thatcher and the Politics of Decline.* New York: Oxford University Press, 1986.

Kritzman, Lawrence D., ed. *Auschwitz and After: Race, Culture, and "the Jewish Question" in France.* New York: Routledge, 1995.

Kroker, Arthur and Marilouise, and David Cook, eds. *Panic Encyclopedia: The Definitive Guide to the Postmodern Scene.* New York: St. Martin's, 1989.

Kundera, Milan. *The Unbearable Lightness of Being.* Trans. Michael Henry Heim. New York: Harper and Row, 1984.

Kushner, Tony. *Angels in America. Part One: Millennium Approaches* (1993). *Part Two: Perestroika* (1994). New York: Theater Communications Group, 1992, 1993, 1994.

Kushner, Tony. *The Holocaust and the Liberal Imagination: A Social and Cultural History.* Oxford: Blackwell, 1994.

Kuznetzov, Anatoly. *Babi Yar: A Documentary Novel.* Trans. Jacob Guralsky. New York: Dial Press, 1967.

LaCapra, Dominick. *Representing the Holocaust: History, Theory, Trauma.* Ithaca: Cornell University Press, 1994.

Laclau, Ernesto, and Chantal Mouffe. *Hegemony and Socialist Strategy: Towards a Radical Democratic Politics.* London: Verso, 1985.

Lang, Berel. *Act and Idea in the Nazi Genocide.* Chicago: University of Chicago Press, 1990.

Langer, Lawrence. *The Holocaust and the Literary Imagination.* New Haven: Yale University Press, 1975.

———. *Holocaust Testimonies: The Ruins of Memory.* New Haven: Yale University Press, 1991.

Lawrence, David. "Fleshly Ghosts and Ghostly Flesh: The Word and the Body in *Beloved.*" *Studies in American Fiction* 19 (fall 1991): 189–201.

Lears, T. J. Jackson. "From Salvation to Self-Realization: Advertising and the Therapeutic Roots of the Consumer Culture." In *The Culture of Consumption: Critical Essays in American History, 1880–1930,* ed. Richard Wightman Fox and T. J. Jackson Lears, 1–38. New York: Pantheon, 1983.

Leithauser, Brad. "Anyplace You Want." *New York Review of Books* 15 (Mar. 15, 1990): 7–10.

Lem, Stanislaw. *His Master's Voice.* Trans. Michael Kandel. San Diego: Harvest/HBJ, 1983 [1968].

Lemann, Nicholas. *The Promised Land: The Great Black Migration and How It Changed America.* New York: Knopf, 1991.

Levi, Primo. *The Drowned and the Saved.* Trans. Raymond Rosenthal. New York: Vintage, 1989.

Lévinas, Emmanuel. *Otherwise Than Being or Beyond Essence.* Trans. Alphonso Lingis. The Hague: Martinus Nijhoff, 1981.

"Liberalism and the Negro: A Round Table Discussion." *Commentary* 37 (Mar. 1964): 25–42.

Lifton, Robert Jay. *The Broken Connection: On Death and the Continuity of Life.* New York: Simon and Schuster, 1979.

———. *The Future of Immortality, and Other Essays for a Nuclear Age.* New York: Basic Books, 1987.

Linenthal, Edward T. *Preserving Memory: The Struggle to Create America's Holocaust Museum.* New York: Viking, 1995.

Livingstone, Sonia, and Peter Lunt. *Talk on Television: Audience Participation and Public Debate.* London: Routledge, 1994.

Lowenthal, David. "Nostalgia Tells It Like It Wasn't." In *The Imagined Past: History and Nostalgia,* ed. Malcolm Chase and Christopher Shaw, 18–32. Manchester: Manchester University Press, 1989.

Luke, Timothy W. *Screens of Power: Ideology, Domination and Resistance in Informational Society.* Urbana: University of Illinois Press, 1989.

Lyotard, Jean-François. *The Differend: Phrases in Dispute.* Trans. G. Van Den Abbeele. Minneapolis: University of Minnesota Press, 1988.

———. *The Postmodern Condition: A Report on Knowledge.* Trans. Geoff Bennington and Brian Massumi. Minneapolis: University of Minnesota Press, 1984.

Mad Max. Dir. George Miller. Crossroads International. 1979.

Maier, Charles S. *The Unmasterable Past: History, Holocaust, and German National Identity.* Harvard University Press, 1988.

Manuel, Frank E., ed. *Utopias and Utopian Thought.* Boston: Houghton Mifflin, 1965.

Marchand, Roland. *Advertising the American Dream: Making Way for Modernity, 1920–1940.* Berkeley: University of California Press, 1986.

Marcus, Greil. *Lipstick Traces: A Secret History of the Twentieth Century.* Cambridge: Harvard University Press, 1989.

Marks, Elaine. "*Cendres Juives:* Jews Writing in French after Auschwitz." In *Auschwitz and After: Race, Culture, and "the Jewish Question" in France,* ed. Lawrence D. Kritzman, 35–46. New York: Routledge, 1995.

Marks, Herbert. "On Prophetic Stammering." *Yale Journal of Criticism* 1 (1987): 1–20.

Marx, Karl. *Capital: A Critique of Political Economy.* Ed. Frederick Engels. Trans. Samuel Moore and Edward Aveling. New York: Modern Library, 1936.

Masson, Jeffrey Moussaieff. *The Assault on Truth: Freud's Suppression of the Seduction Theory.* New York: Farrar, Straus and Giroux, 1984.

Massumi, Brian, ed. *The Politics of Everyday Fear.* Minneapolis: University of Minnesota Press, 1993.

Matusow, Allen J. *The Unraveling of America: A History of Liberalism in the 1960s.* New York: Harper and Row, 1984.

McCoy, Drew R. *The Elusive Republic: Political Economy in Jeffersonian America.* New York: W. W. Norton, 1980.

McDowell, Deborah E. "Negotiating between Tenses: Witnessing Slavery after Freedom—*Dessa Rose.*" In *Slavery and the Literary Imagination,* ed. Deborah E. McDowell and Arnold Rampersad. Baltimore: Johns Hopkins University Press, 1989.

McHoul, Alex. "TEENAGE MUTANT NINJA FICTION (Or, St. Ruggles' Struggles, Chapter 4)." *Pynchon Notes* 26–27 (1990): 97–106.

McMillan, James F. *Twentieth-Century France: Politics and Society, 1898–1991.* London: Edward Arnold, 1992.

Mead, Lawrence. *Beyond Entitlement: The Social Obligations of Citizenship.* New York: Free Press, 1986.

Medved, Michael. "Ironies of a Political Decade." In *Second Thoughts: Former Radicals Look Back at the Sixties,* ed. Peter Collier and David Horowitz. Lanham, Md.: Madison Books, 1989.

Miller, Henry. *Tropic of Cancer.* New York: Grove, 1961.

Miller, Mark Crispin. *Boxed In: The Culture of TV.* Evanston, Ill.: Northwestern University Press, 1988.

Miller, Randall M., and John David Smith, eds. "Infanticide." *Dictionary of Afro-American Slavery.* New York: Greenwood, 1988.

Miller, Walter M., Jr. *A Canticle for Leibowitz.* New York: Bantam, 1988 [1959].

Mintz, Alan. *Hurban: Responses to Catastrophe in Hebrew Literature.* New York: Columbia University Press, 1984.

Minuchin, Salvador. *Families and Family Therapy.* Cambridge: Harvard University Press, 1974.

Morreale, Joanne. *A New Beginning: A Textual Frame Analysis of the Political Campaign Film.* Albany: SUNY Press, 1991.

Morrison, Toni. *Beloved.* New York: Knopf, 1987.

———. "The Pain of Being Black: An Interview with Toni Morrison." With Bonnie Angelo. In *Conversations with Toni Morrison,* ed. Danille Taylor-Guthrie, 255–61. Jackson: University Press of Mississippi, 1994.

Moynihan, Daniel Patrick. *The Negro Family: The Case for National Action.* In *The Moynihan Report and the Politics of Controversy,* Lee Rainwater and William L. Yancey, 39–124. Cambridge: MIT Press, 1967.

Munson, Wayne. *All Talk: The Talkshow in Media Culture.* Philadelphia: Temple University Press, 1993.

Murray, Charles. *Losing Ground: American Social Policy, 1950–1980.* New York: Basic Books, 1984.

Myrdal, Gunnar. *An American Dilemma: The Negro Problem and Modern Democracy.* New York: Harper & Brothers, 1944.

Niethammer, Lutz. *Posthistoire: Has History Come to an End?* Trans. Patrick Camiller. London: Verso, 1992.

Night of the Living Dead. Dir. George Romero. Image Ten/Continental, 1968.

Niven, Larry, and Jerry Pournelle. *Lucifer's Hammer.* New York: Fawcett Crest, 1977.

Norris, Christopher. "Versions of Apocalypse: Kant, Derrida, Foucault." In *Apocalypse Theory and the Ends of the Earth,* ed. Malcolm Bull, 227–49. Oxford: Blackwell, 1995.

O'Leary, Stephen D. *Arguing the Apocalypse: A Theory of Millennial Rhetoric.* New York: Oxford University Press, 1994.

Ozick, Cynthia. *Art and Ardor: Essays.* New York: Knopf, 1983.

———. "An Interview with Cynthia Ozick." Conducted by Elaine M. Kauvar. *Contemporary Literature* 34 (1993): 359–94.

———. *The Messiah of Stockholm.* New York: Vintage, 1987.

Paine, Thomas. *Common Sense.* Ed. Isaac Kramnick. New York: Penguin, 1976.

Parfrey, Adam. *Apocalypse Culture.* Rev. and expanded ed. Los Angeles: Feral House, 1990.

Patterson, Orlando. *Slavery and Social Death: A Comparative Study.* Cambridge: Harvard University Press, 1982.

Peirce, Charles S. *Selected Writings: Values in a Universe of Chance.* Ed. Philip P. Wiener. New York: Dover, 1958.

Perrin, Norman. "Apocalyptic Christianity." In *Visionaries and Their Apocalypses,* ed. Paul D. Hanson. Philadelphia: Fortress, 1983.

Pesch, Josef. "*Beloved:* Toni Morrison's Post-Apocalyptic Novel." *Canadian Review of Comparative Literature* 20 (1993): 395–408.

———. "Beyond Dystopia: Post-Apocalyptic Writing." In *Proceedings of the Workshop on Teaching Utopian Fiction,* ed. Jurgen Klein and Dirk Venderbeke, 447–51. Tubingen: Niemeyer, 1996.

———. "End in Ruin—Ruined Ends? Some Remarks on Conspicuous Absences in Recent Publications on Ends and Ruins." *Krieg & Literatur* (forthcoming).

———. "Frank Gehry's 'Ginger and Fred' in Prague: Playfully Postmodern or Seriously Post-Apocalyptic?" *Lava* (Lab Voor Architectuur) Sept. 1997, http://www.tue.nl/lava/data/praha/tgehryen.htm.

———. "Post-Apocalyptic War Histories: Michael Ondaatje's *The English Patient.*" *Ariel* 28 (1997): 117–39.

Petchesky, Rosalind Pollack. "Antiabortion and Antifeminism." In *Major Problems in American Women's History,* ed. Mary Beth Norton, 438–52. Lexington, Mass.: D. C. Heath, 1989.

Phillips, Kevin P. *Post-Conservative America: People, Politics and Ideology in a Time of Crisis.* New York: Random House, 1982.

Phillipson, Michael. *Painting, Language, and Modernity.* London: Routledge and Kegan Paul, 1985.

Prager, Emily. *Eve's Tattoo.* New York: Vintage, 1991.

Price, John Randolph. *Angel Energy: How to Harness the Power of Angels in Your Everyday Life.* New York: Fawcett, 1995.

Pynchon, Thomas. *Gravity's Rainbow.* New York: Viking, 1973.

———. *Vineland.* New York: Penguin, 1990.

Quinby, Lee. *Anti-Apocalypse: Exercises in Genealogical Criticism.* Minneapolis: University of Minnesota Press, 1994.

Rainwater, Lee, and William L. Yancey. *The Moynihan Report and the Politics of Controversy.* Cambridge: MIT Press, 1967.

Rambo: First Blood Part II. Dir. George P. Cosmatos. With Sylvestor Stallone. Anabasis/Tristar, 1985.

Reagan, Ronald. *Speaking My Mind: Selected Speeches.* New York: Simon and Schuster, 1989.

Reed, Lou. *New York.* Sire Records, 1988.

Rice, Anne. *The Queen of the Damned.* New York: Ballantine, 1988.

Rieder, Jonathan. "The Rise of the 'Silent Majority.'" In *The Rise and Fall of the New Deal Order: 1930–1980,* ed. Steve Fraser and Gary Gerstle, 243–68. Princeton: Princeton University Press, 1989.

Ringelheim, Joan. "Thoughts about Women and the Holocaust." In *Thinking the Unthinkable: Meanings of the Holocaust,* ed. Roger S. Gottlieb, 141–49. New York: Paulist Press, 1990.

Road Warrior. Dir. George Miller. Warner Brothers. 1981.

Robertson, Mary F. "Hystery, Herstory, History: 'Imagining the Real' in Thomas's *The White Hotel.*" *Contemporary Literature* 25 (1984): 452–77.

Rody, Caroline. "Toni Morrison's *Beloved:* History, 'Rememory,' and the 'Clamor for a Kiss.'" *American Literary History* 7 (1995): 92–119.

Rogin, Michael. "Make My Day!: Spectacle as Amnesia in Imperial Politics." *Representations* 29 (1990): 99–123.

———. *"Ronald Reagan," the Movie: and Other Episodes in Political Demonology.* Berkeley: University of California Press, 1987.

Rose, Elizabeth. "Cynthia Ozick's Liturgical Postmodernism: *The Messiah of Stockholm.*" *Studies in American Jewish Literature* 9 (1990): 93–107.

Rosen, Norma. "The Second Life of Holocaust Imagery." *Midstream* 33 (Apr. 1987): 56–59.

Rosenfeld, Alvin. "Another Revisionism: Popular Culture and the Changing Image of the Holocaust." In *Bitburg in Moral and Political Perspective,* ed. Geoffrey H. Hartman, 90–102. Bloomington: Indiana University Press, 1986.

———. *Imagining Hitler.* Bloomington: Indiana University Press, 1985.

———. "Popularization and Memory: The Case of Anne Frank." In *Lessons and Legacies: The Meaning of the Holocaust in a Changing World,* ed. Peter Hayes, 243–78. Evanston: Northwestern University Press, 1991.

Roskies, David G. *Against the Apocalypse: Responses to Catastrophe in Modern Jewish Culture.* Cambridge: Harvard University Press, 1984.

Roth, Philip. *The Ghost Writer.* New York: Vintage, 1995.

Roudiez, Leon S. "Lyrical Illusions and Their Succession." *Contemporary French Civilization* 6 (1981–82): 1–21.

Rousso, Henry. *The Vichy Syndrome: History and Memory in France since 1944.* Trans. Arthur Goldhammer. Cambridge: Harvard University Press, 1991.

Rubenstein, Diane. "The Mirror of Reproduction: Baudrillard and Reagan's America." *Political Theory* 17 (1989): 582–606.

Rushdy, Ashraf H. A. "Daughters Signifyin(g) History: The Example of Toni Morrison's *Beloved.*" *American Literature* 64 (1992): 567–97.

Santner, Eric. "History beyond the Pleasure Principle: Some Thoughts on the Representation of Trauma." In *Probing the Limits of Representation: Nazism and the "Final Solution,"* ed. Saul Friedlander, 143–54. Cambridge: Harvard University Press, 1992.

Scarry, Elaine. *The Body in Pain: The Making and Unmaking of the World.* New York: Oxford University Press, 1985.

Schickel, Richard. "No Method to His Madness." *Film Comment* 23 (June 1987): 11–19.

Schwartz, Hillel. *Century's End: A Cultural History of the Fin de Siècle from the 990s through the 1990s.* New York: Doubleday, 1990.

Scott, Gini Graham. *Can We Talk? The Power and Influence of Talk Shows.* New York: Plenum Press, 1996.

Shippey, Tom. "Semiotic Ghosts and Ghostliness in the Work of Bruce Sterling." In *Fiction 2000: Cyberpunk and the Future of Narrative,* ed. George Slusser and Tom Shippey. Athens: University of Georgia Press, 1992.

Sidney, Sir Philip. "An Apology for Poetry." In *Selected Poetry and Prose.* ed. David Kalstone, 213–70. New York: Signet, 1970.

Silko, Leslie Marmon. *Ceremony.* New York: Penguin, 1977.

Silverman, Kaja. *Male Subjectivity at the Margins.* New York: Routledge, 1992.

Slotkin, Richard. *Gunfighter Nation: The Myth of the Frontier in Twentieth-Century America.* New York: Atheneum, 1992.

Sontag, Susan. *Styles of Radical Will.* New York: Farrar, Straus and Giroux, 1969.

Spiegelman, Art. *Maus: A Survivor's Tale.* 2 vols. New York: Pantheon, 1986 and 1991.

Stack, Carole. *All Our Kin: Strategies for Survival in a Black Community.* New York: Harper and Row, 1974.

Steiner, George. *The Portage to San Cristobal of A.H.* New York: Washington Square Press, 1981.

Stern, Barbara B., and Katherine Gallagher. "Advertising Form, Content, and Values: Lyric, Ballad, and Epic." *Current Issues and Research in Advertising* 13 (1991): 79–103.

Stern, Fritz. *The Politics of Cultural Despair: A Study in the Rise of the Germanic Ideology.* Berkeley: University of California Press, 1961.

Stoekl, Allan. *Agonies of the Intellectual: Commitment, Subjectivity, and the Performative in the Twentieth-Century French Tradition.* Lincoln: University of Nebraska Press, 1992.

Stowe, Harriet Beecher. *The Key to Uncle Tom's Cabin.* New York: Arno; New York Times, 1969.

———. *Uncle Tom's Cabin.* New York: Signet, 1981.

Strozier, Charles B. *Apocalypse: On the Psychology of Fundamentalism in America.* Boston: Beacon Press, 1994.

Styron, William. *Sophie's Choice.* New York: Vintage, 1992.

Tal, Kalí. *Worlds of Hurt: Reading the Literatures of Trauma.* Cambridge: Cambridge University Press, 1996.

Tanner, Laura E. "Sweet Pain and Charred Bodies: Figuring Violence in *The White Hotel.*" *Boundary* 2 18 (1991): 130–49.

Terminator II: Judgment Day. Dir. James Cameron. Tristar, 1992.

Tetel, Marcel. "Whither the Holocaust?" *Contemporary French Civilization* 6 (1981–82): 219–35.

Theweleit, Klaus. *Male Fantasies.* Trans. Stephen Conway, Erica Carter, and Chris Turner. 2 vols. Minneapolis: University of Minnesota Press, 1987, 1989.

Thomas, D. M. *The White Hotel.* New York: Viking, 1981.

Thrupp, Sylvia L., ed. *Millennial Dreams in Action: Studies in Revolutionary Religious Movements.* New York: Schocken, 1970.

Tom, Gail, Stephen Calvert, Rita Gookatsian, and Arlene Zumsteg. "An Analysis of Informational Content in Television Advertising: An Update." *Current Issues and Research in Advertising: Original Research and Theoretical Contributions* 1984: 161.

Tuveson, Ernest Lee. *Redeemer Nation: The Idea of America's Millennial Role.* Chicago: University of Chicago Press, 1968.

12 Monkeys. Dir. Terry Gilliam. Polygram/Universal, 1996.

Until the End of the World. Dir. Wim Wenders. Australian Film Finance Corp., Road Movies Filmproduction, Argos Films SA, and Warner Brothers, 1991.

Weber, Timothy P. *Living in the Shadow of the Second Coming: American Premillennialism, 1875–1925.* Chicago: University of Chicago Press, 1983.

Weld, Theodore Dwight. *American Slavery as It Is: Testimony of a Thousand Voices.* New York: Arno; New York Times, 1968.

Werckmeister, O. K. *Citadel Culture.* Trans. Carl Hanser Verlag. Chicago: University of Chicago Press, 1991.

"What's Happening to America?" *Partisan Review* 34 (1967): 13–63.

White, Deborah Gray. *Ar'n't I a Woman? Female Slaves in the Plantation South.* New York: W. W. Norton, 1985.

White, Hayden. *The Content of the Form: Narrative Discourse and Historical Representation.* Baltimore: Johns Hopkins University Press, 1987.

———. "Historical Emplotment and the Problem of Truth." In *Probing the Limits of Representation: Nazism and the "Final Solution,"* ed. Saul Friedlander, 37–53. Cambridge: Harvard University Press, 1992.

Whitman, Walt. *Leaves of Grass.* Facsimile ed. of the 1860 text. Ithaca: Cornell University Press, 1961.

Wiesel, Elie. "Art and Culture after the Holocaust." In *Auschwitz: Beginning of a New Era? Reflections on the Holocaust,* ed. Eva Fleishner. New York: KTAV Publishing House, 1974.

———. *Night. The Night Trilogy.* Trans. Stella Rodway. New York: Noonday Press, 1985 [1960].

Wilde, Alan. "Love and Death in and around Vineland, U.S.A." *Boundary 2* 18 (1991): 166–80.

Williams, Raymond. *Problems in Materialism and Culture: Selected Essays.* London: Verso, 1980.

Williams, William Carlos. *Spring and All. Imaginations,* ed. Webster Scott, 85–151. New York: New Directions, 1970.

Williamson, Judith. *Decoding Advertisements: Ideology and Meaning in Advertising.* London: Marion Boyars, 1978.

Willis, Susan. "Earthquake Kits: The Politics of the Trivial." *South Atlantic Quarterly* 89 (1990): 761–85.

Wills, Gary. *Reagan's America: Innocents at Home.* New York: Doubleday, 1987.

Wilson, William Julius. *The Truly Disadvantaged: The Inner City, the Underclass, and Public Policy.* Chicago: University of Chicago Press, 1987.

Wittgenstein, Ludwig. *Tractatus Logico-Philosophicus.* Trans. C. K. Ogden. London: Routledge and Kegan Paul, 1981.

Wolfson, Elliot R. "Circumcision and the Divine Name: A Study in the Transmission of Esoteric Doctrine." *Jewish Quarterly Review* 78 (1987): 77–112.

Wyschogrod, Edith. *Spirit in Ashes: Hegel, Heidegger, and Man-Made Mass Death.* New Haven: Yale University Press, 1985.

Yack, Bernard. *The Longing for Total Revolution: Philosophic Sources of Social Discontent from Rousseau to Marx and Nietzsche.* Princeton: Princeton University Press, 1986.

Yeats, William Butler. *The Collected Poems of W. B. Yeats.* New York: Macmillan, 1956.

Young, James E. *The Texture of Memory: Holocaust Memorials and Meaning in Europe, Israel and America.* New Haven: Yale University Press, 1993.

———. *Writing and Rewriting the Holocaust: Narrative and the Consequences of Interpretation.* Bloomington: Indiana University Press, 1988.

Zizek, Slavoj. *Looking Awry: An Introduction to Lacan through Popular Culture.* Cambridge: MIT Press, 1991.

———. *The Sublime Object of Ideology.* London: Verso, 1989.

James Berger is assistant professor of English at Hofstra University. Before becoming a literary and cultural scholar, Berger enjoyed a dual career teaching creative writing and theater in elementary schools and performing and directing theater in New York City. He also taught in Tanzania for three years.

Printed and bound by CPI Group (UK) Ltd, Croydon, CR0 4YY

25/03/2025

14647327-0001